SYSTEMATIC PSYCHOLOGY:
PROLEGOMENA

Edward Bradford Titchener.

Systematic Psychology

PROLEGOMENA

By Edward Bradford Titchener

With a Foreword by Rand B. Evans
and Robert B. MacLeod

Cornell University Press

ITHACA AND LONDON

International Standard Book Number 0-8014-0707-9
Library of Congress Catalog Card Number 72-38117

PRINTED IN THE UNITED STATES OF AMERICA BY VAIL-BALLOU PRESS, INC.

*Librarians: Library of Congress cataloging information
appears on the last page of the book.*

FOREWORD

It is quite appropriate that Edward Bradford Titchener (1867–1927) should have made as his last contribution to scientific psychology this *Prolegomena* to a systematic psychology. The long systematic work it was to have prefaced was to be the culmination of Titchener's intensive study and research, spanning almost forty years. In some ways the work was the focal point of Titchener's entire career. That Titchener's death found the 'big' *System* not yet begun and even the *Prolegomena* lacking its last chapter must be accounted as one of the great losses to students of the systems and logic of psychology and, for that matter, of science as a whole. The *Prolegomena* remains his final summation.

During his professional life, Titchener pursued several goals, but there were three that could be considered of paramount importance: (1) to describe the facts of experience, (2) to develop a logical scaffolding on which to hang those facts, and (3) to have psychology recognized as a formal science and to find a place for this scientific psychology in the structure of institutional science. This book represents some aspect of each of these goals.

The first of these, the description of experience, represents Titchener's scientific side and was undoubtedly his primary goal. An understanding of Titchener's stance on the description of experience and the nature of observation is the key to understanding his psychology and his view of science as a whole. The products of this scientific observation were the many experimental theses and minor studies generated in the Cornell laboratory during Titchener's tenure there, as well as the factual detail found in his *Textbook of Psychology*.[1]

The second of these goals, the search for a logical scaffolding for the facts of experience derived from observation and experiment, represents Titchener's systematic side—the side seen most often in his articles, notes, and published lectures, and which was to have culminated in the body of his *Systematic Psychology*. Although the greater part of Titchener's published work was systematic rather than observational, he always considered systemization as secondary to observation. The role of system, as Titchener saw it, was to provide a logical array so that an understanding of the nature of experience could be gained. It is here that the 'acquaintance-with' of observation becomes the 'knowledge-about' of systematic understanding.

A *Systematic Psychology* had been in Titchener's plans from his earliest days at Cornell. At first he seems to have planned a massive systematic catalogue on the lines of Wundt's *Grundzüge der physiologischen Psychologie,* or so he told one student in the 1890's.[2]

---

[1] W. S. Foster, "A bibliography of the published writings of Edward Bradford Titchener 1889–1917," in *Studies in Psychology: Titchener Commemorative Volume* (Louis N. Wilson: Worcester, Mass., 1917), pp. 323–337; Karl M. Dallenbach, "Bibliography of the writings of Edward Bradford Titchener," *Amer. Journ. Psych.,* xl, 1928, 121–125; E. B. Titchener, *A Textbook of Psychology* (Macmillan: New York, 1910.)

[2] W. B. Pillsbury, "The psychology of Edward Bradford Titchener," *Philos. Rev.,* xxxvii, 1928, 105. The place of publication indicates the anomalous position of psychology at the time.

The *Grundzüge* in its many editions was Wundt's great achievement, and it was only natural for Titchener, just out of the Leipzig atmosphere, to want to pattern his own 'great work' after his master's. By 1909, however, the plan for a massive system in the Wundtian style seems to have been abandoned. "A system of psychology, fully rounded out and complete, could hardly nowadays be more than philosophical," he told a visitor to Cornell at the time.[3]

It was about this time that Titchener's *Textbook of Psychology* was published. It was the updating of his *Outline of Psychology* and has been taken generally as Titchener's system.[4] It was intended as a textbook for the student, however, and not as a formal systematic exposition. In fact, Titchener specifically complained of its use to characterize his systematic views.[5] It *is* fair to say that the *Textbook* was as close to a system as Titchener ever got into print. But even to the degree that the *Textbook* represented his views in 1909, it was out of date by 1915 and did not adequately represent his views in the last years of his life.

In 1917 Titchener again approached the *Systematic Psychology*, although apparently on a much less grand scale than in his plan of twenty years before. He still believed that a completely rounded scientific system of psychology was not feasible, at least in his generation, but he also believed that one could talk about psychol-

---

[3] Letter to G. Tschelpanow, Oct. 25, 1924, Cornell University Archives.

[4] *An Outline of Psychology* (Macmillan: New York, 1897).

[5] Titchener, "Sensation and system," *Amer. Journ. Psych.*, xxvi, 1915, 258.

ogy systematically: "I think we have a large enough
body of data to be able to present the subject in a
systematic schema, so that future generations may see
that we had not been altogether dependent upon philosophy for our conceptual scaffolding." [6]

H. P. Weld, Titchener's second-in-command for so
long at Cornell, tells us in his Preface to the *Prolegomena* of the delays that prevented the completion of
Titchener's work. Students and colleagues waited for a
decade—and not particularly patiently—for the system
to appear in print. They referred to it already as *the*
system, an indication of the feeling they had for the un-
seen volume and its author. They would never see it.
The disappointment these students and colleagues experienced on receiving this slim work when they were
expecting something on the order of Wundt's 2357-
page monster may have caused them to miss the importance of what they were given. What they expected of
the work was the very part they did not get—Titchener's specific psychological systemization of observational facts. They expected at very least a great ex-
pansion of Titchener's *Psychology of Feeling and Attention* and of his *Experimental Psychology of the
Thought-Processes* to cover the entire subject-matter of
psychology.[7] What they did get, however, was probably more important in the long-range history of psychology as science. Titchener chose to introduce his

---

[6] Letter to Tschelpanow, Oct. 25, 1924.

[7] Titchener, *Lectures on the Elementary Psychology of Feeling and
Attention* (Macmillan: New York, 1908); *Lectures on the Experimental Psychology of the Thought-Processes* (Macmillan: New York,
1909).

System with a logic of system-making and, even more important, a statement in the context of the history of science about just what it is to be scientific—not only in psychology but in any discipline. In carrying out this logical construction, Titchener fulfilled the third of his goals—to define psychology as a formal science and to find a place for it in the structure of the other formal sciences. As such this book is a remarkable document in the history of science.

For this task of writing a logic of psychology as science, and of science itself from the point of view of a scientist, one could hardly ask for a more appropriate author than E. B. Titchener. By training, inclination, and sheer erudition only Wundt in psychology's past could have come near to matching Titchener, and certainly few, if any, of his calibre have been in the field since.[8]

Titchener summarized his intentions for the *Prolegomena* as follows:

---

[8] Titchener's time at Oxford was spent studying the classics, philosophy, and then finally physiology. He came into close contact with men like Walter Pater, John Scott Burdon-Sanderson, George John Romanes, Thomas Henry Huxley, Francis Darwin, and many others. He spent an entire year in Burdon-Sanderson's physiology laboratory. He was with Wundt during the most productive period of the Leipzig laboratory. In short, his exposure to the sciences was great for a psychologist in his day. As to his erudition, Howard C. Warren wrote: "His acquaintance with the older writers extended to medieval and ancient times. He would frequently refer quite incidentally to contributions or hints in some classic source bearing upon a topic on which he or another was working. At the same time he kept fully abreast with literature. One could not mention in his presence any recent periodical article, however trivial, that he did not show himself perfectly familiar with its contents" ("Edward Bradford Titchener," *Science,* lxvi, 1927, 208).

What I have set myself to do is to study the history of what is called 'science' and to see if, under all the ramifications and vagaries of this title, I could get at something essential, constant, uniform, persistent,—something that all scientific men approximate, though some blindly and blunderingly, some explicitly and clearly. I hope that now I have it. I have no idea of reform: people will still go on calling all sorts of mixed things 'science,' and I do not mind—it would be useless if I did, but in point of fact I don't. What I hope to do is to trace the lines of this essential core of science clearly, so that those who are interested as I am myself can use me as a preliminary guide in their own work and be saved the trouble that I have had in getting to a clear-cut view.[9]

Titchener honed his concepts razor-sharp for this work. The terms he used have specific and technical meanings, often quite different from their commonly used definitions. We have added as an appendix a few explanatory notes on Titchener's terminology, where present-day readers might have in mind other meanings for the terms used.

In his introductory chapter, Titchener poses the problem that is the dominant theme of the entire work —What is scientific psychology? Both Wundt and Brentano claimed to represent it, yet one is hard put to find any common ground between their two positions. What is it, then, that separates psychology as science from the applied and speculative disciplines that wave the banner of psychology and make the pretense of being scientific?

The answer to this question first necessitates some general agreement on the definition and criteria of

---

[9] Letter to Adolf Meyer, May 13, 1918, Cornell University Archives.

science in general—the common attributes shared by formal scientists, no matter what their specific subject-matter, but not shared with groups outside. After finding a definition of science in the abstract, the next task is to describe the structure of formal or institutional science. Science is both a concept and an organization. As organization, it has constituent 'special sciences,' which must be defined on some basis. A basis of classification of the sciences, if it is possible, suggests some logical pattern of interaction. Within this pattern, psychology, if it is a formal science, must fit. If all this can be worked out, the original question may be considered answered—in general. But there are many schools and movements in psychology. For a detailed answer to the question "What is scientific psychology?" each major movement or representative of a class of movements must be subjected to the criteria of psychology as science to ascertain whether it is, indeed, scientific, or whether it belongs in the classifications of technology, axiology, or common-sense—terms that must also be defined and supplied with criteria. These are the problems and questions to which Titchener addresses himself in this 'slim' volume.

For Titchener, only one source of data was available for science—the existential universe. An understanding of the term 'existence' and its various adjectival forms is important for an understanding of Titchener's view. He uses these terms in a way that bears little relation to the work of such recent Existentialist writers as Heidegger, Sartre, Merleau-Ponty, Binswanger, and others in the Existentialist movement in philosophy, psychology, and psychiatry. What Titchener meant by existence was "the mode of being of observable facts." [10] It is what the naïve epistemologist calls the 'real world,' things as they 'really are.' As such the existential universe comprises the primordial subject-matter of all the sciences. The objects of this universe simply exist; they have no meanings or values in themselves. They are simply available for description. It is the observer who appends to these existences the meanings and values which permeate casual, common-sense description. All experience is necessarily mediate, because of the structure of our nervous system. Besides this, the observer, once he comes to observe, has developed a wide variety of common-sense values which color and alter what he sees. What is 'given,' then, is not existential experience, but common-sense experience.

It is the task of the observer in science to strip away all of these common-sense values and meanings, as best he can. The resultant scientific description is what Titchener terms 'fact.' Fact is the basic building-block of all science. Titchener tells us: "The Fact, a matter of direct-acquaintance-with, I regard as scientifically ultimate. The System of Science I take to be built of nothing more than facts and logic." [11] The fact derived from observation is not the same as the existential object since, even if meanings have been stripped away, observation is always from a given determinate point of view. Each science has its point of view, taking a different stance toward the existential world.

Other men, those of an applied bent or who are interested in a system of values, also describe this same

---

[10] *Ibid.,* May 4.   [11] *Ibid.,* Nov. 7.

existential universe, but they do not separate facts from value. The resulting value-systems and applications Titchener terms technology, axiology, or common-sense.

Titchener's main focus is on science and the facts that make up science. Since Titchener holds that facts of experience are mediate things, there are for him no immediate channels to the 'real world,' the existential universe. Even within science, there are many different stances that cause descriptions of the same existential object to differ. These 'objects' are all viewed by human observers, from particular points of view and under logical control of different methods. As Titchener puts it: "For me nothing is literally given and nothing therefore is nakedly found; but in every case the *object* dealt with is a function of the *method* which deals with it. I think that Science deals with existential experience from the three methodologically different points of view of physics, biology, psychology." [12]

Physics, which Titchener lumps together with chemistry and physical chemistry, is "the science of existential experience regarded as functionally or logically interdependent." Biology is "the science of existential experience regarded as functionally or logically dependent upon the physical environment." Psychology is "the science of existential experience regarded as functionally or logically dependent upon the nervous system (or its biological equivalent)." [13]

The sciences in their early stages of development may be classified by their particular points of view—

---

[12] *Ibid.*   [13] *Prolegomena*, p. 142.

from their different stances, which influence the form of the facts gleaned from observation. Scientists from different points of view may describe the same existential 'object' but will give different descriptions, different facts. The Müller-Lyer illusion is an example of this. How does one describe it? Someone holding the point of view of physics might describe it as "two linear distances which, as measured in centimeters, are equal within the margin of error of the measuring rod." Someone holding a psychological point of view might describe it as "two visual space-perceptions which are unequal." The common-sense observer, who makes no distinction between observational fact and meaning, might describe it as "two black lines on white paper which *look* different but are *really* equal." [14] Titchener compares the different scientific points of view in the description of the existential universe to a handbook on a certain city or area written by a group of experts. The first chapter might describe the geological structure of the area, the second the distribution and variety of plant and animal life, the third the climatic conditions, and so forth. Each expert describes the same location, but from different points of view. So it is with scientific description in general.

It is in this manner of classification of the formal sciences by means of point of view that Titchener finds the place for scientific psychology. Psychology represents one of the three basic points of view in the description of the existential world. But it is also pos-

---

[14] Letter to Adolf Meyer, May 4, 1918.

sible to differentiate sciences by their special subject-matter.

The sciences are differentiated by point of view. It is obvious, however, that when a science has described from its point of view, for any length of time, what is visible from that point of view,—when it has done this, it will have amassed a special subject-matter—this subject-matter being, evidently, the transcript of existential experience as made from the determined point of view, and therefore being strictly correlative with (and indicative of) the point of view. Definition by subject-matter is possible, as logically posterior to point of view, not otherwise.[15]

The basic differentiation among the formal sciences grouped under the three basic headings of physics, biology, and psychology remains, however, point of view.

In the latter portion of the book Titchener returns to his original problem of defining scientific psychology. Taking as his rule the criteria of science, he interrogates the major lines of orthodox psychology, seeking how closely each conforms to the rule. The orthodox dichotomy of act versus content is examined again, as it was in the introductory chapter, but this time within the context of definite criteria.

This last section still stands as the best presentation of the orthodox psychological systems available and has served as such for forty years. Were the book serviceable only in that respect, it would still be worth reading.

Titchener's *Prolegomena* was not understood in his time, but he expected that. His hope was that students

---

[15] *Ibid.*, May 13.

of the future would be better grounded in science, history, and logic and so be in a better position to understand: "Sad experience has taught me that my own training and that of many of my contemporaries did not insist on clear thinking. So I am trying to be so far clear as that those who read me later on will be able to accept or reject with full understanding of what it is they are accepting or rejecting." [16] This reissue of Titchener's *Systematic Psychology: Prolegomena* offers a new generation that chance to accept or reject.

The text of the 1929 edition has been photographically reproduced with typographical errors in the original corrected. Weld's Preface has been retained; his index has been expanded.

We wish to thank the Titchener family for permission to reprint this book and to include in this Foreword excerpts from Titchener's letters. We are grateful to the late Karl M. Dallenbach for permission to reproduce the portrait of Titchener and to reprint the sections in Chapter III that first appeared in the *American Journal of Psychology*.

RAND B. EVANS
Wright State University
ROBERT B. MACLEOD
Cornell University

February 1972

---

[16] *Ibid.,* Nov. 7.

PREFACE

In the early summer of 1917, Professor Titchener began writing his Systematic Psychology —a book long projected. There was to be a first volume of Prolegomena, and as many subsequent volumes as the systematic setting-forth of the facts of psychology required. The book was to be his final word on the establishment of scientific psychology, coördinate with biology and physics; in a very concrete sense, it was to be a summing up of the reading, thinking, and experimental investigation in psychology which had occupied him during his entire professional life.

Characteristically, he faced the problem afresh. He put behind him his previous judgments, dropped the polemic attitude which had shaped much of his earlier writing, and, as best he could, assumed an open mind. For two years he worked indefatigably. The Introduction was ready for the printer, and the original draft of Chapter I written, by November. The first chapter, however, did not reach its final form until the early spring of the next year and was typewritten for the last time in 1923. In the meantime, he was at work on Chapter II, which he finished in May, 1918. Chapter III engrossed his attention thenceforth, and was not put aside as complete until December, 1919. Of the projected first volume there remained only a chapter on Method in Psychology. But work on the book was stopped by the influx of graduate students who returned to continue the studies interrupted by the World War.

In 1921, Professor Titchener became editor of the *American Journal of Psychology*. He then decided to print the Introduction, and the greater part of Chapter III, in the *Journal*. Earlier, when the third chapter had just been finished, I suggested to him that he publish in some journal the critical part of the chapter, which was especially detailed and technical, and that, with the criticism thus placed on record, he then re-write the chapter. At the time my suggestion was not accepted. He believed that the chapter as it stood was of a piece with the book as a whole, and that, with the critical analysis omitted, it would be difficult to escape the appearance of dogmatism. He later decided, however, to make the venture, and part of the chapter was published with the following footnote:

"In writing a chapter on the Definition of Psychology: Subject-Matter, for the introductory volume of a systematic psychology, I have been obliged to take critical account of functional psychology and the psychology of act. Since it seems fruitless to publish conclusions without giving the evidence on which they rest, and since at the same time a book such as I have planned is not the place for these criticisms of detail, I print my comments in the Journal."

The chapter was, however, never re-written and the proposed chapter on Method was not even begun. He was unable to give the book the long-continued and laborious effort which his standard of scholarship de-

manded. Nevertheless, he definitely planned to complete the first volume during the summer of 1928. His
untimely death in August, 1927, thus found it un-
finished.

Fortunately, in preparing the manuscript for publication, I find that, although Chapter III remains as it
was originally conceived, the re-publication in their
original context of the parts already printed places
them in a new and truer perspective. Furthermore,
while the unwritten chapter on Method is an inestima-
ble loss to psychology, the main argument is complete.
As the book stands, it is without a parallel in the history of psychology, or, for that matter, in the history
of science. No other writer in systematic science has
taken such pains in the laying of foundations or
brought to it so happy a combination of an ability of
seeing science from within, a broad historical background, sympathetic critical insight, and exceptional
literary skill.

The reader will note that, in formulating a definition of psychology, the author could not escape the
similar task of defining biology and physics, and that
this threefold task required an envisagement of the
essential character of science. His conception of psychology, therefore, stands or falls with his conception
of science. If his reading of science is true, his conception of psychology must follow. By the term "conception" one should understand not the verbal formulas
which he selected to clothe his thought, but rather the
meaning which he tried to express. The author himself
had no doubt of the essential correctness of his ideas;
but he had no less doubt that a later generation would

succeed better than he in finding their adequate formulation.

My editorial task has been relatively simple. There was no question as to which draft the author regarded as final; and the earlier drafts contained nothing which was not already incorporated in the final draft. I have found it necessary to re-number the footnotes, and to add an occasional note of my own. I am also responsible for the table of contents and the index.* Thanks are due to the *American Journal of Psychology* for permission to reprint the sections hereinafter specified, and to my colleagues Professor K. M. Dallenbach and Dr. S. Feldman for their valuable advice and assistance.

H. P. WELD

CORNELL UNIVERSITY
May, 1929

---

* [Professor Weld's titles in the original table of contents have been retained. His index has been expanded. R. B. E.]

CONTENTS

CHAPTER II

THE DEFINITION OF PSYCHOLOGY:
POINT OF VIEW

CHAPTER III

THE DEFINITION OF PSYCHOLOGY:
SUBJECT-MATTER

INTRODUCTION

BRENTANO AND WUNDT: EMPIRICAL AND EXPERIMENTAL PSYCHOLOGY

INTRODUCTION

BRENTANO AND WUNDT: EMPIRICAL AND EXPERIMENTAL PSYCHOLOGY *

§ 1. The year 1874 saw the publication of two books which, as the event has shown, were of first-rate importance for the development of modern psychology. Their authors, already in the full maturity of life, were men of settled reputation, fired as investigators with the zeal of research, endowed as teachers with a quite exceptional power to influence younger minds, ready as polemists to cross swords with a Zeller or a Helmholtz. Yet one would look in vain for any sign of closer intellectual kinship between them; hardly, indeed, could one find a greater divergence either of tendency or of training. Psychology, seeing how much their work and example have done to assure her place among the sciences, may gladly confess her debt to both. The student of psychology, though his personal indebtedness be also twofold, must still make his choice

---

* [Published under this title, but without the word "Introduction," in the *Amer. Journ. Psych.*, xxxii, 1921, 108 ff. with the following note: "The following paragraphs form the introduction to the first volume of my long-projected and long-delayed work upon Systematic Psychology. When I wrote them, Brentano and Wundt were still living. Brentano died at Zurich, March 17, 1917; Wundt died at Leipsic, Aug. 31, 1920." H. P. W.]

for the one or the other. There is no middle way between Brentano and Wundt.[1]

Franz Brentano began his career as a catholic theologian. In 1867 he published an outline of the history of philosophy within the mediaeval church which sets forth, as clearly and sharply as the essay of thirty years later, his famous doctrine of the four phases.[2] Early and late, however, his intellectual interest has centred in the philosophy of Aristotle. He came to psychology by way of an intensive study of the *De Anima,* and he has made the Aristotelian method his pattern of scientific procedure. We possess, unfortunately, only the first volume of his *Psychologie*: Brentano seems always to have preferred the spoken to the written word: but this volume, like everything else that he has given to the press, is complete in itself, the finished expression of his mature thought.

Wilhelm Wundt started out as a physiologist, interested in the special phenomena of nerve and muscle. In 1862 he had sought to lay the foundations of an 'experimental psychology' (the phrase now appears in

---

[1] F. Brentano, *Psychologie vom empirischen Standpunkte* (henceforth cited as *PES*), i, 1874. Cf. the Biographical Note in F. Brentano, *The Origin of the Knowledge of Right and Wrong,* trs. C. Hague, 1902, 119 ff.; M. Heinze, *F. Ueberwegs Grundriss der Geschichte der Philosophie,* iv, 1906, 332 ff.; W. Wundt, *Grundzüge der physiologischen Psychologie* (henceforth cited as *PP*), 1874. The first ten chapters of Wundt's work were issued in 1873 and are utilised by Brentano. For a bibliography of Wundt's scientific writings, see *Amer. Journ. Psych.,* xix (1908) ff.; cf. Heinze, *op. cit.,* 322 ff.

[2] J. A. Möhler, *Kirchengeschichte,* ii, 1867, 539 f.; F. Brentano, *Die vier Phasen der Philosophie und ihr augenblicklicher Stand,* 1895. The four phases, repeated in the three great philosophical periods, are those of scientific construction, failure or perversion of the scientific interest, scepticism and mysticism.

print for the first time) [3] in a theory of sense-perception. Here he fell into the mistake to which every student of natural science is liable who turns, without due preparation, to the things of mind: the mistake, namely, of supposing that psychology is nothing more than an applied logic; and the mistake was repeated in a popular work upon human and animal psychology which followed on the heels of the technical volume. By 1874 he had definitely discarded this earlier view for the conception of psychology as an independent science. He still maintained, however, that the path to it leads through the anatomy and physiology of the nervous system.

Such, in briefest outline, were the conditions under which the two psychologies acquired their form and substance. We see, on the one hand, a man who has devoted his 'hours of solitary reflection' to ancient and mediaeval philosophy; we see, on the other hand, a man who has wrought out in the laboratory his contributions to the latest-born of the experimental sciences. They are both professors of philosophy, and they are both to range widely, in the future, over the varied fields of philosophical enquiry. Yet it would be wrong to suppose that the psychology to which they have now attained, and which, by a happy chance, they give to the world in the same year, represents merely an incident, even if it were the central incident, of their philosophical history. Psychology, on the contrary, has laid strong hands upon them, and is to dominate all their further thinking. Wundt, a gen-

---

[3] W. Wundt, *Beiträge zur Theorie der Sinneswahrnehmung*, 1862, vi.

eration later, will round off the manifold list of his books with the encyclopaedic folk-psychology, and Brentano never gives up the hope of a descriptive—to be followed, perhaps, at long last by a genetic—psychology as the ripe fruit of his studious old age.

§ 2. We shall better understand the nature of this choice which lies before us if we first note the points of resemblance between the two systems. For even in 1874 psychology was not in such bad case that Brentano and Wundt are always at variance. They agree that psychology holds a place of high importance in the fellowship of the sciences, and that it is logically prior to natural science.[4] They agree that it may dispense with the concept of substance and confine itself to an account of phenomena.[5] They reject the unconscious as a principle of psychological explanation.[6] They define the unity of consciousness in substantially the same terms.[7] So far there is agreement: and though the agreement is largely of a formal kind, and though a good deal of it has a negative ground in the reaction against Herbart, it serves nevertheless to mark out a common universe of discourse.

On the material side there is also agreement, with such difference of emphasis as the difference of authorship would lead us to expect. We find, for instance, that Brentano deals at length with the general method of psychology, and is at pains to distinguish inner per-

---

[4] *PES,* 24 ff., 119; *PP,* 4, 863.
[5] *PES,* 10 ff.; *PP,* 9, 12, 20.
[6] *PES,* 133 ff.; *PP,* 644 f., 664, 708 f., 712, 790 ff.
[7] *PES,* 204 ff.; *PP,* 715 ff., 860 ff.

ccption from inner observation, while Wundt takes
inner observation for granted and describes in detail
only those special procedures which raise it to the rank
of experiment.[8] We find that Wundt devotes much
space to Fechnerian psychophysics, and interprets the
psychophysical law as a general psychological law of
relativity, while Brentano makes only incidental and
critical mention of Fechner's work.[9] The differences
are striking enough, but behind them lies agreement
regarding the subject-matter of psychology. Even in
the extreme case, where the one book emphasises what
the other omits, difference does not of necessity mean
disagreement. We find, again, that Wundt says nothing
of a question which for Brentano is the essential problem of psychology as it was the first problem of psychophysics, the question of 'immortality,' of the continu-
ance of our mental life after death, and conversely that
Brentano fails to discuss Wundt's cardinal problem of
attention. Yet Wundt had touched upon the question
of immortality in his earlier writing, and Brentano
plainly recognises that there is a problem of attention,
although (as we may suppose) he has put off its discussion to his second volume.[10]

So the student of psychology who read these two
books in their year of issue might, if he had made due
allowance for the training and natural tendencies of

---

[8] *PES*, 34 ff., 184; *PP*, 1 ff.

[9] *PP*, 421; *PES*, 9 f., 87 ff.

[10] *PES*, 17 ff., 32 f., 95 f.; Wundt takes up the question of immortality (indirectly, it is true) in *Vorlesungen*, etc., ii, 1863, 436, 442;
cf. the direct treatment in the later edition, 1892, 476 ff. Brentano
recognises the problem of attention in *PES*, 91, 155; cf. 263, and
C. Stumpf, *Tonpsychologie*, i, 1883, 68; ii, 1890, 279 f.

the authors, have entertained a reasonable hope for the future of his science; and we ourselves, who see their differences far more plainly than was possible for him, may still hope that the main issue can be taken on common ground and fought out at close quarters.

§ 3. Brentano entitles his book 'psychology from the empirical standpoint,' and Wundt writes 'physiological psychology' on his title-page and suggests 'experimental psychology' in his text.[11] The adjectives do not greatly help us. For all experimental psychology is in the broad sense empirical, and a psychology which is in the narrow sense empirical may still have recourse to experiment. To show the real difference between the books, the difference that runs through their whole texture and composition, we need at this stage terms that are both familiar and clear; the time has not yet come for technicalities and definitions. We may say, as a first approximation, that Brentano's psychology is essentially a matter of argument, and that Wundt's is essentially a matter of description.

At the end of his discussion of method Brentano refers with approval to Aristotle's use of *aporiae,* of difficulties and objections, wherein a subject is viewed from various sides, and opinion is weighed against opinion and argument against argument, until by comparison of pros and cons a reasonable conclusion is reached.[12] This is, in the large, his own way of work-

---

[11] *PP,* 3.

[12] *PES,* 96 f.; cf. J. S. Mill, Grote's Aristotle, *Fortnightly Rev.,* N. S. xiii, 1873, 48 ff. Brentano had earlier noted, with the same approval, the use of *aporiae* by Thomas Aquinas: see J. A. Möhler, *Kirchengeschichte,* ii, 1867, 555.

ing. He appeals but rarely, and then only in general terms, to facts of observation. His rule is to find out what other psychologists have said, to submit their statements to a close logical scrutiny, and so by a process of sifting to prepare the reader's mind for a positive determination. When the ground has thus been cleared Brentano's doctrine, novel though it may be, has the appearance (so to say) of a necessary truth; we feel that we have duly considered the possibilities in the case and have come to the one rational decision; and if for conscience's sake we go on to deduce and to verify, we still are assured beforehand that everything will fit together within the system. Minor points may need to be expanded; even, perhaps, in the light of further *aporiae,* to be corrected; but the whole exposition gives the impression of finality.[13] It is no wonder,

---

[13] I know of only three corrections that Brentano has made to his psychology. (1) In *PES,* 292, degree of conviction, as intensity of judgment, is declared analogous to degree of intensity of love and hate (cf. 203); in the notes to *The Origin of the Knowledge of Right and Wrong* (1889), 1902, 52 f., this analogy is denied. (2) In *PES,* 202 f., feeling is said to be always present along with ideation; the belief to the contrary is due to the mistaken preference of memory over inner perception (44); but in *Untersuchungen zur Sinnespsychologie,* 1907, 119, 124, the acts of the two higher senses are not intrinsically emotive. (3) In *PES,* 115, the object upon which a psychical phenomenon is directed is not to be understood as *eine Realität*; but the notes appended to the reprinted section *Von der Klassifikation der psychischen Phänomene* (1911, 149) lay it down that "nie etwas anderes als Dinge, welche sämtlich unter denselben Begriff des Realen fallen, für psychische Beziehungen ein Objekt abgibt."—There would, no doubt, if the book were rewritten, be many other modifications of detail, and yet others if the second volume were undertaken; the discussion of the modi of ideation in the *Klassifikation* shows that Brentano had not in 1874 thought out the doctrine of his Bk. iii. In the main, nevertheless, the doctrine of 1874 has

then, that many students have judged the author successful in his aim of writing, not Brentano's psychology, nor yet a national psychology, but—psychology.[14]

Wundt's book, on the contrary, abounds in facts of
observation: anatomical facts, physiological facts, results of psychophysical and psychological experiment.
Its introductory chapter is brief to the point of perfunctoriness, and criticism of psychological theories is
packed away into fine-print paragraphs that, to all in-
tents and purposes, are a series of appendices. There
is, to be sure, a great deal of argument. Where the
facts are scanty, they must not only be generously interpreted but must also be eked out by hypothesis; if a
leading physiologist has mistaken the problem of sense-
perception, he must be argued into a better way of
thinking; in any case, the new science of experimental
psychology must offer a bold front to her elder sisters.[15]
The argument, none the less, is always secondary and
oftentimes plainly tentative; so that the book as a
whole gives the impression of incompleteness, of a first
essay which can be improved when more work (and a

---

stood the test of Brentano's own continued reflection and of the
attacks of critics.

Such an achievement is worthy of all admiration. Only we must
add—those of us who challenge Brentano's premises—that even isolated changes are disconcerting. The first statement is so serenely
confident, and the changes are again so confidently made!

[Still other corrections that Brentano made to his psychology have
been noted by O. Kraus, editor of a new edition of *PES*, published in
two volumes in 1924 and 1925. See the author's review of the first of
these volumes in *Amer. Journ. Psych.*, xxxvi, 1925, 303. H. P. W.]

[14] *PES*, vi.

[15] *PP*, Vorwort.

great many suggestions of further work are thrown out [16]) has been accomplished. Hence it is no accident, but rather a direct reflex of the spirit in which the authors approached their task, that Brentano's volume still bears the date 1874 while Wundt's book, grown to nearly triple its original size, has come to a sixth edition.[17]

This thorough-going difference of argument and description means, of course, a radical difference of attitude toward psychology itself. It means that Brentano and Wundt, in spite of formal and material agreement, psychologise in different ways. Our next step, therefore, is to place ourselves inside the systems and to realise, so far as we may without too much detail, what manner of discipline they intend psychology to be. We have to choose: and the illustrations that follow will show the alternatives of choice in concrete and tangible form.

§ 4. Brentano defines psychology as the science of psychical phenomena. The term may easily be misleading: for the phenomena in question are very far from being static appearances. Generically they are activities; in the individual case they are acts. Hence they can properly be named only by an active verb. They fall into three fundamental classes: those, namely, of Ideating (I see, I hear, I imagine), of Judging (I

---

[16] *PP*, 284, 293, 314, 317, 373, 394, 399, etc., etc.

[17] See the prefaces to the successive editions of the *PP*. Even the sixth edition, as I have shown elsewhere (*Psych. Rev.*, xxiv, 1917, 52 f.), has not attained to systematic completion, and only in the fifth (*PP*, i, 1902, ix) did Wundt set himself definitely to the task of system-making.

acknowledge, I reject, I perceive, I recall), and of Loving-Hating (I feel, I wish, I resolve, I intend, I desire). We may use substantives if we will, and may speak of sensation and idea, memory and imagination, opinion, doubt, judgment, joy and sorrow, desire and aversion, intention and resolution; but we must always bear in mind that the psychical phenomenon is active, is a sensing or a doubting or a recalling or a willing.

It is true that we never have act without content. When we ideate, we sense or imagine something; when we judge, we perceive something, acknowledge the truth of something, recall something; when we love or hate, we take interest in something, desire or repudiate something. This, however, is precisely the difference between psychical and physical phenomena. The latter are blank and inert: the color or figure or landscape that I see, the chord that I hear, the warmth or cold or odor that I sense, the like objects that I imagine, all these things are described when their given appearance is described; their appearance sums them up and exhausts them; they have no reference, and do not carry us beyond themselves. Psychical phenomena, on the other hand, are precisely characterised by relation to a content, by reference to an object; they contain an object intentionally within them; and this character of immanent objectivity, in virtue of which they are active, marks them off uniquely from the physical phenomena upon which they are directed or toward which they point. Even in cases where the content of a psychical phenomenon is not physical, but is another psychical phenomenon, the distinction holds good. For the act which becomes content or object of another act is not thereby deprived of its essential character; it is still active in its own right; and it is therefore by no means confusable with bare physical appearance.[18]

These are Brentano's views of the subject-matter of psychology. He begins by considering the alleged differences between physical and psychical, finds an adequate *differentia* of the psychical, and is therefore able to define psychology in terms of the matter with which it deals. He then reviews the principal classifications hitherto made of psychical phenomena, and arrives at a classification of his own, in which judgment is accorded independent rank, and feeling and will are bracketed under a single heading. Throughout the discussion his chief reliance is upon argument. To be sure, he takes the testimony of inner perception; but inner perception is not observation; it is rather a self-evident cognition or judgment; and as such it is, if we may use the phrase, of the same stuff as argument.[19] Psychological observation is possible for Brentano only when past acts are recalled in memory; then indeed, as he admits, even a sort of experimentation becomes possible. Not only, however, is memory subject to gross illusion, but the act of memory, once more, falls under the category of judgment, so that experiment itself takes place in the world of argument.[20] The empirical psychology thus employs the same psy-

---

[18] *PES*, 23 f., 35, 101 ff., 161, 167, 256 ff. On the problem of natural science as an explanatory discipline, see 127 ff.

[19] *PES*, 35 ff., 181 ff. (summary 202 f.), 262. Cf. *Klassifikation*, 1911, 129.

[20] *PES*, 42 ff., 162, 169, 262; *Klassifikation*, 130.

chical activities to establish the nature of its subject-matter and to discuss the variety of psychological opinion.

§ 5. For Wundt, psychology is a part of the science of life. Vital processes may be viewed from the outside, and then we have the subject-matter of physiology, or they may be viewed from within, and then we have the subject-matter of psychology.[21] The data, the items of this subject-matter, are always complex, and the task of experimental psychology is to analyse them into 'the elementary psychical processes.' If we know the elements, and can compare them with the resulting complexes, we may hope to understand the nature of integration, which according to Wundt is the distinguishing character of consciousness.[22]

Analysis of the processes of the inner life brings us, in the last resort, to pure sensations, constituted originally of intensity and quality. Sensations carry no reference; they look neither before nor after; they tell us nothing of their stimuli, whether external or organic, and nothing of their point of excitation, whether peripheral or central, nor do they forecast the ideas in which we find them synthetised. They simply run their course, qualitatively and intensively, and may be observed and described as they proceed.[23] Ideas, in their turn, are originally constituted of these sensations;

---

[21] PP, 1 ff.

[22] PP, 5, 20, 717.

[23] PP, 273 ff., 484 f. When sensations enter into connection with one another, the third attribute of affective tone or sensory feeling is added. Intensity and quality are, however, the 'more original' constituents.

there is nothing within or upon them to show whether they are ideas of imagination or perceptions.[24] Individual ideas differ psychologically from general ideas solely in the nature of their sensory constituents: in the former the complex of sensations is constant, in the latter it is variable.[25] Concepts are not 'psychical formations' at all; if we psychologise them, we discover only their substitutes in consciousness, spoken or written words, accompanied by a vague and indeterminate feeling.[26] Judgments, in the same way, belong to logic, and not primarily to psychology; logic and psychology approximate only as a result of the parallel growth, long-continued, of conceptual thinking and its expression in language; our "conscious psychological processes" consist originally of nothing more than ideas and their connections.[27]

The trend of all this analysis is clear: Wundt is trying to describe mind, to show the stuff of which it is made, to reduce it to its lowest terms. When, however, he turns from analysis to synthesis, the exposition is less easy to follow. Sensations are integrated into ideas by a 'psychical synthesis' which Wundt himself compares to a chemical synthesis and which critics have assimilated to Mill's 'mental chemistry.' [28] Ideas gain their objective reference by a 'secondary act' which seems to consist, psychologically, in the simple addition

---

[24] PP, 464 f.   [26] PP, 672.

[25] PP, 468.   [27] PP, 709 ff.

[28] PP, 484 f.; J. S. Mill, A System of Logic, 1843, bk. vi, ch. iv (ii, 1856, 429); An Examination of Sir William Hamilton's Philosophy, 1865, 286 f.; note in J. Mill, Analysis of the Phenomena of the Human Mind, i, 1869, 106 ff. The original source is D. Hartley, Observations on Man, 1749, pt. i, ch. i, sect. 2, prop. 12, cor. 1 (i, 1810, 77 f.).

of further ideas,[29] yet the objective reference is itself put, later on, to psychological purposes. Concepts and forms of intuition are made 'postulates' of advancing thought,[30] as if the logical and practical aspects of mind were necessarily implied in its given or phenomenal aspect, and as if the psychologist might shift from one aspect to another without breach of scientific continuity. But though we may puzzle over details, there is nothing obscure in the general situation. Wundt, like many others of his generation, is dazzled by the vast promise of the evolutionary principle; [31] 'original' is for him more or less what 'nascent' is for Spencer; the later must derive from the earlier, because that is the way of things, and the later has no other basis. Let us remember, all the same, that Wundt's primary effort is to describe, and that he falls back upon 'genetic explanation' only when some phase of the traditional subject-matter of psychology proves to be indescribable.

That, then, is one of the threads of Wundt's system. Even a descriptive psychology cannot, however, be written simply in terms of sensations and their modes and levels of psychological integration. For the field of consciousness, Wundt reminds us, is not uniformly illuminated; it shows a small bright area at its centre and a darker region round about; the ideas which occupy it differ in their conscious status. So arises the problem of attention. Descriptively—Wundt takes up the task of description piecemeal, in different contexts,

---

[29] *PP*, 465.
[30] *PP*, 672, 680.
[31] *PP*, vi.

as if it were 'on his conscience'—attention reduces to
clearness of ideas and characteristic feelings of effort
or strain.[32] It has two concrete manifestations, apperception and voluntary action; we speak of apperception when we are considering the internal course of
ideas, and of voluntary action when we are considering
the issue of an emotion in external movement.[33] Both
forms of the attentional process are subject to conditions, and both are strictly correlated with physiological
processes in the cerebral cortex; they therefore fall
within the limits of a scientific psychology.[34] Yet psychologists have neglected them, and have paid the
penalty of this neglect in inadequate psychology and
untenable philosophy.[35]

We need not here trace the doctrine of attention
further; we need not either debate whether the problem of attention is included in Wundt's formal statement of the task of experimental psychology. We may,
however, as an illustration of the interweaving of the
two systematic threads, glance at his treatment of the
association of ideas. He begins, as we might expect,
with mode of integration; and under this heading declares that the recognised laws, of similarity and of
frequency of connection in space and time, are imperfect even as empirical generalisations. We find, it is
true, two forms of association, distinguishable in the
free play of fancy and in reflective thought. But the one
is wider than association by similarity, in that the effec-

---

[32] *PP*, 717 ff., esp. 724.
[33] *PP*, 831, 835.
[34] *PP*, 720 f., 723 f., 834 f.
[35] *PP*, 792 f., 831 ff.

tive resemblance may reside in any and every sensory
constituent of the ideas concerned, and especially in
their affective tone, while the other reveals itself simply
as an affair of habit. Wundt therefore proposes to term
them, respectively, 'association by relationship' and
'association by habituation.' The new names, he main-
tains, are not indifferent; for they do fuller justice than
the old to the facts of self-observation, and they also
point us to the conditions of association in the central
nervous substance.[36]

Here then is an improvement on the side of analysis
and synthesis; but that is not enough. For ideas do not
associate automatically, as it were of their own mo-
tion; the laws of association are, on the contrary, under
the universal dominance of attention. And now there
opens up for experimental attack a whole series of
special problems which an empirical psychology, following only the single line of enquiry, must naturally
miss. In their light we pass beyond associationism to a
more faithful transcript of the 'course and connection
of ideas';[37] and in like manner we avoid, in our psychology of will, the philosophical *impasse* of indeter-
minism.[38]

These paragraphs express, in rough summary, the
teaching of the Wundt of 1874. He does not give psychology a distinct and peculiar subject-matter; the difference between physiology and psychology lies simply

---

[36] *PP*, 788 ff.

[37] *PP*, 793; cf. the earlier sections of ch. xix.

[38] *PP*, 837 f.

in our point of view. Wundt had already published a comprehensive work upon physiology, and now that he has turned to psychology he carries his knowledge and method with him; he is convinced that the processes of the inner life are best set forth in close connection with those of the outer life, and that the results of inner observation are surest when the appliances of external observation, the procedures of physiology, are pressed into psychological service. He spends little time upon preliminaries, but gets as quickly as may be to the exposition of facts. Where facts are few or lacking, he seeks to supplement or to supply them by observations of his own. His primary aim in all cases is to describe the phenomena of mind as the physiologist describes the phenomena of the living body, to write down what is there, going on observably before him: witness his treatment of idea, of concept, of attention, of association. There is still great space for argument, and the argument, we must admit, is often influenced by previous habits of thought, by psychological tradition, by a certain tendency to round things off to a logical completeness, by a somewhat naïve trust in the principle of evolution. The argument, however, does not impress the reader as anything but secondary: Wundt is at once too dogmatic and too ready to change his views. The recurring need of further facts and the patchwork character of the argument suggest, both alike, that psychology, under his guidance, has still a long systematic road to travel.

§ 6. We have now viewed our two psychologies from within. Brentano, we have found, looks back

over the past, weeds out its errors with a sympathetic
hand, accepts from it whatever will stand the test of his
criticism, and organises old truth and new into a system
meant, in all essentials, to last as long as psychology
shall be studied; Wundt, after he has acknowledged his
debt to the past, turns away from it and plunges into
the multifarious and detailed work of the laboratories,
producing a psychology that is as much encyclopaedia
as system, and that bears on its face the need for continual revision. Which of the two books holds the key
to a science of psychology?

Brentano has all the advantage that comes with historical continuity. His doctrine of immanent objectivity
goes back to Aristotle and the Schoolmen, and the
classification of psychical acts into ideas, judgments,
and phenomena. of love and hate goes back to Des-
cartes.[39] More than this: he can claim kinship with
every psychologist, of whatever school, who has approached his subject from the technically 'empirical'
standpoint. For the 'empirical' psychologist means to
take mind as he finds it; and like the rest of the world,
who are not psychologists, he finds it in use; he finds it
actively at work in man's intercourse with nature and
with his fellow-man, as well as in his discourse with
himself. Terms may change and classifications may
vary, but the items of classification are always activities, and the terms employed—faculties, capacities,
powers, operations, functions, acts, states—all belong
to the same logical universe. Brentano, innovator

---

[39] *PES*, 115 f.; *The Origin of the Knowledge of Right and Wrong*, 47.

though he is, takes his place as of right in a great psychological community.[40]

To offset this advantage, and to justify his own break with tradition, Wundt holds out the promise of an experimental method. He should have been more explicit: for technology as well as science—medicine as well as physiology, engineering as well as physics—makes use of experiment. His actual purpose, as we trace it in the chapters of his book, is to transform psychology into an experimental science of the strict type, a science that shall run parallel with experimental

---

[40] In spite of the remarks in §3 and in §6 below it may seem unjust to Brentano if, even in this preliminary sketch of the psychological issue, his interest in experiment is left without record. We note, then, that as early as 1874 he urged the establishment at Vienna of a psychological laboratory (*Ueber die Zukunft der Philosophie*, 1893, 47 f.); that he has published *Untersuchungen zur Sinnespsychologie* (1907) and in particular that he brought the Müller-Lyer illusion to the attention of psychologists (*Zeits. f. Psych. u. Phys. d. Sinnesorgane*, iii, 1892, 349); and that Stumpf, who was his pupil (Ueberweg-Heinze, iv, 1906, 334 f.), has given us the experimental *Tonpsychologie*. All this, however, does not prevent his being, in the narrow sense, an 'empirical' psychologist. Stumpf tells us that his own work is to "describe the psychical functions that are set in action by tones" (*Tonpsych.*, i, 1883, v) and declares later that "there cannot be a psychology of tones; only a psychology of tonal perceptions, tonal judgments, tonal feelings" (*Zur Einteilung der Wissenschaften*, 1907, 30). Brentano, even with a laboratory, would not have been, in Wundt's sense, an 'experimental' psychologist. We know, besides, something of Brentano's systematic programme. The empirical psychology is not to be concluded; it is to be supplemented and replaced by a 'descriptive' psychology. (*The Origin*, etc., vii, 51 f.), fragments of which have appeared in *The Origin of the Knowledge of Right and Wrong* (dealing with the phenomena of love and hate and, in the Notes, with judgment) and in the *Untersuchungen* (sense-perception). This in turn is to be followed by an 'explanatory' or 'genetic' psychology, a sample of which is given in *Das Genie*, 1892 (see *The Origin*, etc., 123).

physiology.[41] He failed, no doubt, to see all that this purpose implied, and his earlier readers may be excused if they looked upon his work as an empirical psychology prefaced by anatomy and physiology and interspersed with psychophysical experiments. There is plenty of empirical psychology in the volume. If, however, we go behind the letter to the informing spirit; if we search out the common motive in Wundt's treatment of the familiar topics; if we carry ourselves back in thought to the scientific atmosphere of the seventies, and try in that atmosphere to formulate the purpose that stands out sharp and clear to our modern vision; then the real significance of the *Physiological Psychology* cannot be mistaken. It speaks the language of science, in the rigorous sense of the word, and it promises us in this sense a science of psychology.

But Brentano also speaks of a 'science' of psychology. Which of the two authors is in the right?

---

[41] The substitution of folk-psychology for experiment in the study of the more complicated mental processes appears in the fourth edition (*PP*, i, 1893, 5); the reservation in regard to psychophysical parallelism in the fifth edition (*PP*, iii, 1903, 775 ff.).

CHAPTER I

SCIENCE

CHAPTER I

SCIENCE

§ 1. Those who write about science at second hand, for the enlightenment of the general public, are likely to dwell upon its material achievements, the mastery of nature and the annihilation of time and space, and to set these things in high relief against the simple, modest, unselfish lives of the men who compassed them; and those who tell us of scientific work as seen from within are likely to lay stress upon the need of unremitting toil and the scanty prospect of its successful outcome.[1] We get, by comparison, but little information as to what science really is. The popular writer, who has never been inside the ring, simply does not know. The man of science is busy about some special task, and lacks leisure and inclination, as he may also lack the training, to set his intellectual world in order. The philosopher, who might be expected to know, has been brought up in another school, and can

---

[1] "The world little knows how many of the thoughts and theories which have passed through the mind of a scientific investigator have been crushed in silence and secrecy by his own severe criticism and adverse examination; that in the most successful instances not a tenth of the suggestions, the hopes, the wishes, the preliminary conclusions have been realised": M. Faraday, *Experimental Researches in Chemistry and Physics*, 1859, 486; *The Culture Demanded by Modern Life*, ed. E. L. Youmans, 1867, 216.

rarely overcome his prepossession that the sciences are local and imperfect philosophies. So the curious visitor from a distant planet who should ask us, in Maxwell's phrase, what is the 'particular go' of the scientific man, what it is that he does when he is behaving as scientific man, and how the books in which he sets forth the results of that behaviour differ from the books that are not scientific, would hardly find us ready with an answer. We could give him a personal impression, with a few illustrations and a few references; but we should be obliged, most of us, to add that we had not thought the question through, and that he must settle it for himself.

It is not, of course, that there is any lack of sources. We have the whole vast range of scientific documents; we have histories of special sciences; we have biographies of the leaders in science. We have a certain number of secondary sources: grammars of science, introductions to science. We have also, and they are often illuminating, the utterances of scientific men who, led to reflection by the occasion of some commemorative ceremony or public address, show how an insistent problem has dominated the various endeavours of a lifetime.[2] All these sources are valuable, if only we can bring them into some relation and perspective, and make due allowance for temperament and specialisation; all are valuable, though the prevailing confusion of thought and laxity of usage prove that they are not unequivocal. Taken together, even within the narrow

---

[2] Cf. Kelvin's confession of failure and his biographer's remarks thereon: S. P. Thompson, *The Life of William Thomson*, ii, 1910, 984, 1012 ff. (esp. 1084 f.).

limits of individual enquiry, they should also be sufficient. It would be strange indeed if, in an age which is
proud to call itself scientific, we could not by definitely
directed effort find out what science essentially is.

Our own interest is psychological; and our present
effort to frame a conception of science at large, and to
test by that conception the mixed medley that passes
current today as scientific psychology, is warranted by
the fact that works upon general science break down,
hopelessly and completely, when they leave the sciences
of 'matter' and 'life' for the science of 'mind.' Yet
if there is unity in this world of intellectual diversity,
psychology must take its equal place beside physics and
biology. No mere authority can set it there, though it
were the authority of Aristotle, and no urgency of
man's desire, though it were the desire for life after
death. Only science can give title to science: and if
psychology is to fill a chapter in the history of science,
it must be because the facts and laws of psychology are
strictly coordinate, formally interchangeable, with facts
and laws of the established sciences. But if we are
rightly to understand this requirement, if we are to go
behind casual acknowledgment to living realisation,
then we must know what the established sciences have
in common, and must carry over our conception of
science to the domain of mind.

We need not strive for a logical definition. It may
be that science, viewed from its own level, is too complicated an affair to be pressed into a single formula.
Conception is the more modest word; and we may
hope that a working conception of science will be
enough.

§ 2. A familiar rule of method lays it down that we proceed, wherever possible, from the simple to the complex; we can thus be sure that every step taken is a step in advance, based upon clear thinking, and that there is no neglect of fact or obscurity of argument in what lies behind. We shall follow this rule in our present search. We therefore put aside, for a while, all thought of science as one of the great institutional factors of modern civilisation, and fix our attention upon the individual man of science. In other words, we choose as our starting-point the scientific temper or attitude or frame of mind, as it is shown by those who do their business in science. We seek, first of all, to realise the scientific temper, to place ourselves in the scientific attitude; and in so doing we mark off the scientific from the non-scientific.

This negative side of our task is, indeed, easier than the positive. It seems to be pretty generally agreed that the adjectives which best serve to differentiate the scientific attitude are 'disinterested' and 'impersonal.' If witness be necessary, a psychologist will naturally wish to quote the well-known passage in James' *Will to Believe*: "When one turns to the magnificent edifice of the physical sciences, and sees how it was reared; what thousands of disinterested moral lives of men lie buried in its mere foundations; what patience and postponement, what choking down of preference, what submission to the icy laws of outer fact are wrought into its very stones and mortar; how absolutely impersonal it stands in its vast augustness, —then how besotted and contemptible seems every little sentimentalist who comes blowing his voluntary

smoke-wreaths, and pretending to decide things from
out of his private dream!"[3] But there is no need to
multiply witnesses; we read everywhere of a 'disinterested curiosity' and of an 'impersonal love of truth.'

It is less generally recognised that the negative form
of these adjectives is really significant. If, however, we
try to replace the negative terms by positive, we soon
discover that the task is impossible; there are no precise equivalents; and if we run through a list of the
positive traits that are ascribed to the typical man of
science—truthfulness, alertness of mind, courage,
humility, patience, assiduity, caution, accuracy, clearness of vision—we find that neither singly nor in combination do they suffice to differentiate the scientific
temper. We can, indeed, force them into that service
only in a specific sense and by way of their negative
implication. When Faraday enjoins us to caution, he
remarks that "it may be very distasteful, and great
fatigue, to suspend a conclusion"; the majority of mankind jump to their beliefs.[4] When Huxley bids us be
humble he bids us also "be prepared to give up every
preconceived notion."[5] When the same Huxley declares that "in strictness all accurate knowledge is
science," he promptly adds: "there is not one person in
a hundred who can describe the commonest occurrence
with even an approach to accuracy."[6] The positive
trait characterises the scientific attitude only in so far

[3] W. James, *The Will to Believe*, 1897, 7.

[4] M. Faraday, *Experimental Researches*, etc., 465, 483; *The Culture Demanded by Modern Life*, 189, 213.

[5] L. Huxley, *Life and Letters of Thomas Henry Huxley*, i, 1900, 235.

[6] T. H. Huxley, *Science Primers: Introductory*, 1880, 16 f.

as it contrasts that attitude with a more familiar opposite.

It is clear gain thus to realise at the outset that the scientific habit of mind is something unusual, something that (if we are willing to risk the charge of exaggeration) we may even term unnatural or abnormal. We are thereby saved from many errors: among them —to take a single example—from the common mistake of supposing that science evolves from practice, that "the sciences sprang out of the lore of occupations." [7] It is true, by every indication we can find, that science had its origin in a predominantly practical environment just as it is true that the man of science lives in such an environment today. But we do not know that the scientific attitude of dissent, however rare it may have been, is not as old as the orthodoxy of practical occupation; and if it be fact that organised practice is older than theory, then we may be sure that science arose only when some member of the guild turned in intellectual revolt, and reacted directly against the occupational restriction of his knowledge. For there can be no science until and unless man's activities become disinterested and impersonal; the negatives are of its very nature.

§ 3. The man of science, then, is out of accord with the majority of his fellow-men. He does not chiefly value the things that men ordinarily care for. If he is a

---

[7] J. A. Thomson, *Introduction to Science*, 1911, 229 f. A serious attempt to trace the genesis of science has been made by E. Mach, *Die Principien der Wärmelehre*, 1896, 365 ff. If it is not altogether satisfactory, it is at any rate far removed from the customary easygoing evolutionism.

Copernicus, he puts away reverence for antiquity, pleasure in the esteem of colleagues, regard for the countenance of the church. If he is a Newton, he lacks all desire for fame; he holds back his discoveries, and shrinks from any sort of personal discussion. If he is a Huxley, he prays to be indifferent "whether the work is recognised as mine or not, so long as it is done." [8] The negatives, however —who can doubt it, with these names before him?—tell only a part of the story. There is, without question, something positive in the scientific temper, something that compensates and replaces what has been put away. We must try to make this something explicit.

The attitude which our two adjectives qualify is usually spoken of as an emotive disposition, a 'curiosity,' a 'love of truth,' a 'passion for facts.' At first sight such phrases look contradictory: disinterestedness is paired off with a particular interest, and impersonality with a personal predilection. In fact, however, there is no contradiction, since 'disinterested' does not necessarily mean 'uninterested,' and 'impersonal' does not mean 'unfeeling.' The man of science feels as strongly as anyone else. We must, nevertheless, if we are rightly to understand the scientific temper, go behind feeling to organic tendency.

For what characterises the man of science, on this positive side, is an instinctive determination to identify himself with his subject-matter, to lose himself in it, to become one with it. We know how some men, devoted to the study of savage life, will throw off the habits

[8] L. Huxley, *op. cit.*, i, 162.

of civilisation and themselves live for years as savages, blood-brothers of their chosen tribe. Just so does the man of science, untouched by the interests of everyday life, merge himself by instinctive tendency with the special objects of his study. Copernicus, turning his back upon the earth and all the human interest of the earth, became the sun, and scanned the heavens from the sun's point of view. Newton, in like manner, became the moon and, as the moon, fell toward the earth; became, indeed, every physical mass, and identified himself with the general law of gravitation. Or, if such language sounds extravagant, let us say, more moderately, that the man of science reads out all prior meaning, all interpretation, from the objects of his enquiry, and considers them for their sake, in their right, as they are. The data of science are in this sense meaningless; they are stripped of meaning, bare existences. It is true that they at once acquire a new meaning, a meaning for science; but this new meaning is, precisely, that they shall henceforth remain without meaning in the old sense, that their meaning shall be their mode of natural existence, their constitutional manner of being. If science is curiosity, therefore, it is the curiosity which pierces the overlay of interpretation to arrive at sheer existence; if it is love of truth, then truth is the face its objects wear to themselves and their kind and the man who identifies himself with them, and science seeks to know that face; if it is a passion for facts, then facts are the materials of a world scoured clean of belief and inference and all such evaluative accretion, and science aims to explore this world. The instinctive tendency of the scientific man is toward the existential substrate that appears when use and purpose—cosmic significance, artistic value, social utility, personal reference—have been removed. He responds positively to the bare 'what' of things; he responds negatively to any further demand for interest or appreciation.

All this has been said many times before, and every statement might be documented, in the spirit if not in the letter, by manifold quotation. But just as men may fail to recognise the pregnant negatives in 'disinterested' and 'impersonal,' so may they fail of the insight that the data of science, regarded positively, are and in the nature of the case must be what we have called existential. In the instance of psychology, more particularly, such dullness of vision is lamentably common. Huxley, for example, remarks, quite rightly, that the first business of the student of psychology is to rid himself of various prepossessions and to "form conceptions of mental phenomena as they are given us by observation"; but he neither says nor sees that mental phenomena, if they can thus be given, must share the nature of scientific data in general, and that psychology, if it is thus to become a science, must deal with an existential subject-matter.[9] Practice, we are told, is

---

[9] T. H. Huxley, *Hume*, 1881, 62. Compare the statement (51), "on whatever ground we term physiology science, psychology is entitled to the same appellation," with the list of the "elementary states of consciousness" (71 f.).

A. Hill (*Introduction to Science*, 1900, 14, 28 ff.) remarks, and in its context the remark is again correct, that "science cannot penetrate into the world of consciousness"; while yet he proceeds to discuss the senses as "agents of the mind," tells us that "the mind has come to ignore the faults of the retinal image," and asks what "information"

better than precept: and one reason is that a precept, adopted in all good faith and sincerity, does not always bring clearly to mind the kind of practice that its adoption logically implies.

If now we attempt, on our own behalf, to sum up in a single word this positive aspect of the scientific temper, we shall hardly find a better term than observance. Inadequate as the word is, it still suggests something of the reverence for fact, sympathy with fact, loss of self in fact, that we have seen to be characteristic of the man of science. It shows us, too, that the contradiction of which we spoke above lies in words only and not in things: for observance may be utterly disinterested and yet absorb all our interest, and may be altogether impersonal, and yet maintain a whole-souled personal devotion. So the 'particular go' of the scientific man is a disinterested and impersonal observance of the world of human experience. He is the servant of nature; interpretation he leaves to those of different bent.

§ 4. We must now turn from the individual man of science to the world of fact in which he works, and must examine a little more closely into the nature of that subject-matter with whose constitutional manner of being, as we put it, he seeks to identify himself. Many attempts have been made, from the time of Bacon down to the present day, to classify the sciences, to parcel out the world of fact into its natural divisions.

---

the various senses give us "as to the properties of the things which belong to the external world." Here is downright muddle, though we must add in all fairness that muddles just as bad are made by professional psychologists.

We are ourselves concerned not with the results of classification, but with the principle upon which classification is to be based. It is, for our ultimate psychological purpose, a real question whether the special sciences are differentiated by the objects with which they deal or by the point of view which they take up; whether, that is, certain shifts of scientific attitude are forced upon us by given differences in the existential universe, or whether we ourselves create new sciences by change of attitude toward that universe. In the former case, the sciences would be like countries on a map, each one covering a certain field or territory to the exclusion of all the rest. In the latter case, they would rather resemble the successive chapters of a hand-book written by a number of experts, and dealing with one and the same general subject-matter considered under various aspects.

We get little help from current speech or the titles of books. Crystallography is still accounted a science, as if crystals and crystallisation occupied a compartment of their own, definitely set off from the remaining phenomena of physics and chemistry; and physical chemistry, again, is accounted a science, as if the mere adoption of a novel point of view, without change of phenomena, were enough to give it independent rank. There can, however, be no doubt that the tendency of the time is away from classification by objects and toward classification by point of view; the binomial sciences, as we may call them, sciences like physical chemistry and physiological psychology and social anthropology, are growing both in number and in relative importance. Bain, writing in 1870, could mark off certain fundamental sciences, in every one of which "there is a distinct department of phenomena; taken together they comprehend all known phenomena." [10] Such a view will hardly find representatives today. Pearson, for example, warns us that, however ingeniously we may map out the territory of knowledge, "every branch of science passes, at one or more points, not only into the domain of adjacent, but even of distant branches"; [11] which is practically an admission that a compartmental classification of the sciences cannot be carried through. Thomson declares outright that a science "is defined not by its subject-matter, but by the categories under which it thinks of that subject-matter"; "what defines a science is not its subject-matter, but its point of view—the particular kind of question it asks." [12]

This tendency to substitute point of view for object leads in the right direction, but it may also lead us too far. For if the facts of a particular science are functions of its special point of view, they are still facts,

---

[10] A. Bain, *Logic: i. Deduction*, 1879, 25 ff.

[11] K. Pearson, *The Grammar of Science*, 1900, 514. So St.-G. Mivart observes (*The Groundwork of Science*, 1898, 26): "all the sciences are connected by such a labyrinth of interrelations that the construction of a really satisfactory classification of them appears to be an insuperable task"; he evidently has in mind a compartmental classification. R. Flint remarks (*Philosophy as* Scientia Scientiarum *and a History of the Classification of the Sciences*, 1904, 183) that "the fundamental sciences are not classed according to individual objects. Every object is complex, and can only be fully explained by the concurrent application of various sciences."

[12] J. A. Thomson, *op. cit.*, 54 f., 116 f., 130. So A. Hill (*op. cit.*, 44): "the students of science can be classified with more success than the subdivisions of knowledge which they severally endeavour to make their own."

stubborn and upstanding things. All that the point of view does is to reveal, to discover, particular facts, and to hold us consistently to facts of the one particular kind.[13] Differentiation of scientific attitude and definition of scientific object thus go hand in hand. At first, as it emerges from the undifferentiated matrix of common-sense, science naturally follows the gross lines of cleavage in the world of experience, and tries to deal with certain kinds or classes of things in their concrete totality. A classification of the sciences, in this era, would necessarily be compartmental, a classification by mutually exclusive objects. Later, when it becomes evident that one and the same concrete object forms part, under its various aspects, of the subject-matter of many sciences, the emphasis tends to fall upon specific attitude or point of view; and tends to fall all the more strongly, because the breaking up of the object means also the breaking down of the older compartmental lines of classification. We can no longer define botany as the science of plants, partly because plants figure in many sciences beside botany, but partly also because nobody can say exactly what a plant is.

So far, then, the tendency to classify by point of view seems justified: but that is not the end of the argument. For since the maintenance of a special attitude or point of view means a growing subject-matter, an increasing store of kindred facts, the science may presently be differentiated in terms of this subject-matter and classified by reference to the objects with

---

[13] Cf. H. Poincaré, *The Foundations of Science*, 1913, 325 ff.

which it deals. There is danger, certainly, of a relapse into compartmentalism; but on the other hand there is danger of a one-sided exaggeration of point of view and a consequent underestimation of the stubbornness and independence of fact. We must be clear that the new objects are not the concrete objects of common-sense and of early science, but only factual aspects of those objects, and that they gain their objective status through correlation with the specific and long-continued attitude.

We conclude, therefore, that a science may be characterised, at a moderately advanced stage of its development, either by point of view, the kind of question it asks of the existential world, or by subject-matter, the objective answer to its questioning. A full and precise characterisation will include both terms of the correlation.

§ 5. With this point settled, it is not difficult to answer the next question that confronts us, the question of the special method of science. The man of science takes up a certain point of view, and from this standpoint looks out over his world, scans it, watches it, scrutinises it; in technical terms, observes it. Observation is, in fact, the universal and peculiar method of scientific work. It is the unique way in which the scientific attitude bears upon an existential subject-matter. Sometimes the fact will make its own appeal, present itself 'for' observation, obtrude itself 'upon' observation; sometimes, and the more often as the science advances, the observer sets himself to observe, seeks to acquire his facts 'by' observation. In either case, observation is the elementary way of gaining scientific knowledge, and its result is a direct 'acquaintance with' the object observed.

Science is not concerned to go behind this statement; it is concerned only that nothing shall pass muster as fact which has not, in the strict sense, been observed. It therefore prefers illustration to definition: indeed, the beginner in science is often required to 'observe' under circumstances which permit the influence of some interpretative bias, and is then sharply corrected; have we not all been tricked by the air-bubble seen under the microscope? Malobservation is thus brought into positive contrast with observation proper, and the student's scientific education has begun. If we ourselves wish to get beyond illustration and to attempt a paraphrase, we may perhaps say that observation is a clear and sympathetic awareness, an intensive living-through, of some item of the existential universe. Always there is upon it this touch of sympathy, of felt realisation: observation, we may remember, has an older meaning of observance, and observance is the term we chose to express the positive side of the scientific attitude. The scientific enquirer wants to know how the facts, if they could see, would look to one another; he is not the indifferent detective, but the sympathetic witness; observation, like every first-hand acquaintance, is a sort of participation. So much we may say, though all such forms of speech are open to misunderstanding if one has not observed for oneself.

Observation is sometimes treated, too lightly, as "the mere sensory recognition of any phenomenon"; "when we merely note and record the phenomena which occur around us in the ordinary course of nature,

we are said to observe." [14] Yet if that were all, observation would not be as rare and as difficult as it is:
we have taken Huxley's testimony to its rarity, and we
shall presently find Darwin testifying to its difficulty.
It is direct, to be sure; it is a method of personal contact, of intimacy, of unmediated acquaintance; but the
short way is not always the easy way. Its proper conduct requires, indeed, both the scientific temper and a
scientific training. And as it is only the man of science
who can employ this method, so also is everyone who
employs it, in so far, a scientific man. The professional
man of science employs it habitually, the amateur, as
we call him, only occasionally. But the amateur, in its
employment, is truly and completely scientific, and
science, in whatever sense the word is understood, is
nothing else than "the elaborated product of observation." [15]

Every method, however, has its limitations. We said
above that observation is an awareness of some 'item'
of the existential universe, and the word was used for
a reason. For our range of clear awareness, at any
moment, is limited, so that we are not adequate to
more than a minute area of the prospect that spreads

---

[14] F. Gotch, in *Lectures on the Method of Science,* ed. T. B. Strong,
1906, 28, 42; W. S. Jevons, *The Principles of Science,* 1900, 400.
There are many good things in this chapter of Jevons', as there are
also in the corresponding chapter of J. S. Mill's *Logic.* The *Dict.
Philos. Psych.* defines observation as "attentive experience," defines
attention as "the mind at work or beginning to work upon its
object," and defines experience, in the ordinary application of the
term, as "a phase of conscious life which some individual 'passes
through.' " The resultant of these definitions, even if it escape the
charge of tautology, is too vague and general to suit the case.
[15] A. Hill, *op. cit.,* 25.

before us. Even so, the straightforward fixation of the object of observation is, in most cases, the last and not the first term of scientific procedure. Phenomena are complicated and facts are elusive; we must peer and pry, and must call in our fingers to assist our eyes. In technical phrase, again, observation passes over into experiment. There is here no real change in scientific method; an experiment is always set up with a view to observation; and as a whole, as method, experiment is just observation itself, with helps to offset the observer's natural helplessness. All the arrangements of our laboratories are, in one regard, so many confessions of observational weakness, though in another regard they are the means whereby that weakness is overcome. Let us see what it is that the laboratory accomplishes.

§ 6. Experiment is observation made in accordance with a pre-arranged plan. The details of the plan, and its immediate intention, will naturally differ in different instances. Speaking generally, however, we may say that the intention is threefold: an experiment is an observation which may be repeated, which may be isolated, and whose circumstances may be varied.[16] In the most favourable case all of these results are attained.

---

[16] The outline of experiment here given may be filled in from various sources: see, *e.g.,* the chapter on observation and experiment in Mill's *Logic*; the chapter on experiment in Jevons' *Principles of Science*; the chapter on experience in W. Thomson and P. G. Tait, *Treatise on Natural Philosophy,* i, pt. i, 1879; various passages in Wundt's *Methodenlehre: Logik der exakten Wissenschaften,* 1907, and *Logik der Geisteswissenschaften,* 1908; the works already cited of A. Hill and J. A. Thomson. It is curious that the leading encyclopaedias (such as the *Britannica* and the *New International*) have no article on the subject.

There is no need to dwell at length upon the advantage of repetition. Whether we are observing the spectrum of a luminous body, or the avoiding reaction of paramecium, or the course of the negative after-image, we evidently do well to observe over and over again. Facts, we said, are elusive; there is always the risk that, in the particular observation, we fail to see something that is actually present or think we see something that is not present; and repetition enables us to build up our acquaintance with fact little by little, adding, eliminating, correcting as the observations recur. There is no need, either, to emphasise the advantage of isolation. Phenomena are complicated; and if we are to observe at all, it is plainly to our purpose to rule out irrelevant and disturbing factors from the setting of our observation. A great many scientific instruments are, in essential design, devices for the isolation of the phenomena to be observed.

Sometimes, however, we cannot isolate the particular object of investigation, and sometimes we are not sure whether certain factors in the setting of the observation are relevant or irrelevant. In such cases we vary the circumstances of observation. Thus we cannot set up a rhythm except at a certain rate; and so, if we are studying rhythm, we have to vary the rate. Or again, it is an historical problem in psychology whether and how far muscular sensations are involved in the perception of distance; and so, if we are studying that perception, we have to vary the problematical factor of muscular sensation. Variation is not only, however, an aid to isolation; it is also of direct value on its own account, as the means whereby we group or connect our observations, and pass beyond the isolated fact to law or uniformity. We are interested to know, for example, whether and in what way a spectrum changes with change of the physical condition (density, pressure, temperature) of the body that emits it; whether and in what way the avoiding reaction of paramecium changes with change of the stimuli (mechanical, chemical, thermal) presented to the organism; whether and in what way the course of the after-image changes with change of the background (black, grey, white) upon which it is projected. All information of this sort we gain by varying the circumstances of our original observation.

When we remember the manifold advance in scientific knowledge that the threefold control of observation has made possible—Mach avers that experiment lays the very foundations of science [17]—we shall not wonder that observation receives less than its due share of attention in general treatises, and we can even make allowance for its dismissal as a 'mere noting' of phenomena. It is true, nevertheless, that observation is the single and proprietary method of science, and that experiment, regarded as scientific method, is nothing else than observation safeguarded and assisted. No line of methodological division can be drawn between observation and experiment. The line of distinction runs rather between observation, on the one hand, and the plan and arrangement of experiment, on the other hand. It makes no difference whether the observation

---

[17] E. Mach, *Erkenntnis und Irrtum*, 1906, 186; cf. H. Poincaré, *op. cit.*, 127.

is free or controlled, taken as opportunity comes or taken as the final term of an experimental plan; it is still observation. But the plan of experiment, the setting of the observation, is another matter. To plan is to apply logic, to reason and to argue. All the prescriptions and manipulative arrangements of experiment are affairs of Why and Because; they embody and express some special purpose of the investigator; and the scientific temper, as we have seen, knows nothing of special purposes. Theoretically, then, we might arrange a division of labour, and ask the logician to plan our experimental procedures and the man of science to make the relevant observation.[18] As a matter of fact, the two rôles are ordinarily combined; the scientific man makes his observations in accordance with his own logic. It is easier for him, already acquainted with facts of the same order, to apply such logic as he has to the ascertainment of a new fact, than it is for the logician, unfamiliar with observation and accustomed to deal with facts in abstraction, to combine the scientific with his natural logical attitude. This rule, however, as well as the exceptions that illustrate it, are here in point only so far as they connect with our main thesis: the thesis that, when unaided observation passes over into experiment, the attitude of science is already complicated by the non-scientific, extra-scientific attitude of logic.

Henceforth, therefore, the typical man of science plays a double part. As man of science, in the true and

---

[18] Cf. P. Duhem, *La théorie physique*, 1906, 235, 238, 439. Duhem falls into the common error of underestimating observation.

ultimate sense, he employs the scientific method of observation: the method which confronts attitude with object, at the level of existence, merges the two into one, and brings direct acquaintance with fact. As scientific investigator, he leaves the world of existence for the world of logical meaning, the universe of sufficient reason, and thinks out experimental procedures for the controlling of his observation. In so far as this logical activity aims to safeguard and refine the single observation, it is altogether subordinate to fact; in so far as it aims to establish a scientific law or uniformity, it uses the facts which it guarantees for a further logical construction.

§ 7. Our discussion is thus brought to the point at which we must consider scientific activity in the concrete, as it actually goes on in human society; and we shall find that it is an activity in which logic, if still in a certain sense subordinate to observation, is in another sense coördinate, and may even take the lead. We began with the scientific temper, regarded *in abstracto* as the endowment of a somewhat peculiar individual; we showed that this temper is adequate to a particular kind of subject-matter; and we showed further that temper and subject-matter come into relation by way of a particular method: observance, existence and observation are interwoven in a complex particularity. The man of science, as we thus pictured him, may be credited with a wide and accurate knowledge of facts. It is clear, however, that he can give us nothing more than these facts, recorded as they were lived. He cannot at all give us a scientific memoir, a chapter of science, a connected work, a scientific system. If science is to become what we know it to be, a social institution like art and religion and philosophy, something must be done to the facts. Immediate 'acquaintance-with' must be transformed into a 'knowledge-about';[19] facts must be classified, organised, summarised, set in a perspective, made available, made fertile. And all such work is the work of applied logic.

We have just now seen that experiment opens the door to logic: opens it a little way by suggesting that observation be repeated and isolated; opens it more widely by suggesting variation of circumstances with a view to the establishment of scientific laws. That is how we were led to logic by the course of our exposition. As a matter of fact, in the actual life of science, the door has always been open; intercourse and exchange between the scientific and the logical tempers have been going on ever since science came into being; we have, indeed, only to think of the common-sense matrix from which science emerges to realise that things could not have been otherwise. We began, then, with the abstract; and now that we come to the concrete, we find ourselves involved with logic.

We note accordingly that science borrows from logic, and makes part of its own exposition, all the various procedures that logic puts at its disposal for application: induction and deduction, classification and generalisation, analogy and hypothesis, and whatever

---

[20] On this distinction, see J. Grote, *Exploratio philosophica, passim,* esp. i, (1865), 1900, 60; ii, 201 ff.; H. von Helmholtz, *The Recent Progress of the Theory of Vision* (1868), in *Popular Lectures on Scientific Subjects,* i, 1904, 269 ff.; W. James, *The Principles of Psychology,* i, 1890, 221 f., 459 ff.

others there may be. The list, it should be remarked, includes the procedures of mathematics. For mathematics, though it is accounted a science in many classifications of the sciences, is in truth not science proper but a branch of logic; Kelvin calls it "the etherealisation of common sense." [20] Science will never sublimate into mathematics, as it will never sublimate into any logical form; its laws are generalisations of fact, and its numerical formulas are observation quantified. But science uses all the procedures that logic can supply.

So intimately, indeed, are these logical matters bound up with the progress of science in its institutional form, and with the selective work of the man of science in his institutional surroundings, that they have usurped the title of 'scientific method'; the books upon logic contain a section, devoted to 'scientific methodology,' in which they set forth the procedures preferably and most profitably employed by the various sciences. The name is unfortunate, because it tends to belittle the methodical importance of observation, and ascribes a differentiating value to 'methods' which, in principle, are common to science and to other modes of intellectual construction. It may also lead into error. We are told, for example, that "scientific method is merely the way or ways of using different orders of inference in investigating any subject of science with a

---

[20] *Popular Lectures and Addresses,* i, 1889, 273, 277 .f., 285. Cf. W. K. Clifford, *Lectures and Essays,* i, 1879, 335; B. A. W. Russell, *The Principles of Mathematics,* i, 1903, 3 ff., 106, 397, 429 f., 457 f.; L. Couturat, *Les principes des mathematiques,* 1905, 3, 217 f.; W. Wundt, *Logik der exakten Wissenschaften,* 1907, 106 f.

view to its system." [21] The 'merely' is as misleading here as it was in the sentences quoted above in the case of observation; * for the subject of science is itself obtained by method, and the logical methods are scientifically secondary. We must dissent sharply from any methodology which ignores or assumes observation. We cannot, therefore, accept Huxley's famous dictum that science is "perfected common sense." [22] It is true, as Huxley says, that "scientific reasoning is simply very careful common reasoning"; logic is essentially the same, wherever it is applied. But the terms of common reasoning are worlds apart from those of scientific reasoning. 'Common knowledge' derives from tradition, from authority, from use and wont, from speculation, from success in practice, from almost anything but observation; and it is because scientific facts are got by scientific method, which in science is 'logically prior' to the methods of logic, that common sense is the very antipodes of science.[23]

We have, then, to be on guard against two possible errors. We must not let ourselves suppose that the

---

[21] T. Case, in *Lectures on the Method of Science,* ed. T. B. Strong, 1906, 4; cf. K. Pearson, *op. cit.,* 10.

* [Page 39. H. P. W.]

[22] T. H. Huxley, *Science Primers: Introductory,* 1880, 18 f.; *On the Educational Value of the Natural History Sciences* (1854), in *Lay Sermons, Addresses and Reviews,* 1887, 66 f.; *On the Method of Zadig* (1880), in *Science and Culture,* 1882, 128 ff. Cf. M. Foster, in *Nature,* lx, 1899, 468.

[23] Cf. E. Mach, *Erkenntnis und Irrtum,* 1906, 2; P. Duhem, *op. cit.,* 427 ff.; J. A. Thomson, *op. cit.,* 37 f.; A. Schuster, in *Nature,* xcvi, 1915, 38.

scientific system will ever be expressible in purely logical terms, or that a science will evaporate into a system of purely mathematical formulas; the substrate of observed fact must always be reckoned with. And we must not let ourselves think that the method of science is summed up in the rules of inference; the native method of observation lies behind. With these reservations, we may freely acknowledge the part which logic plays in scientific activity. The scientific enquirer does not observe at random; he has a question to ask, an hypothesis to verify; he calls in the aid of logic, and logic meets his need. Moreover, by the bare act of recognising or formulating a problem, by the bare act of framing or criticising an hypothesis, he transforms his knowledge-of-acquaintance into knowledge-about, and passes from the universe of fact to the universe of inference and implication. He will probably spend far more of his time in the world of applied logic—planning and preparing for observation, working up the results of observation, bringing these results into relation with the established laws and current hypotheses of his science—than he spends in the world of fact. Only, his special competency, on the score of method, is and remains his competency as observer.

§ 8. We shall hardly find a better illustration of the concrete method of science, that is, of applied logic coupled with observation, than is afforded by the work of Charles Darwin. The changes which Darwin brought about in general biology were wrought on the grand scale by the simplest means, without mathematical or instrumental complication;[24] and in Darwin himself the elements were so largely and so simply mixed that he may stand as the very pattern and exemplar of the man of science. Moreover, our information regarding the man and his work is both full and trustworthy.

As a youth, Darwin had a decided bent toward natural history. He was an indefatigable collector and a keen observer; "in my [boyish] simplicity," he tells us, "I remember wondering why every gentleman did not become an ornithologist"; and even as an amateur, working with inadequate tools, his observations resulted in minor discoveries.[25] Along with this observational interest went, on the other side, "a keen pleasure in understanding any complex subject or thing." "The logic of [Paley's 'Evidences'] and, as I

---

[24] In the case of a great physicist, like Kelvin, the continual recourse to mathematics may obscure the fundamental reliance upon facts of observation. Note, however, the remarks made by Kelvin's biographer in his chapter on the laboratory (S. P. Thompson, *The Life of William Thomson*, 1910, i): "As his investigations of physics proceeded, he [Kelvin] found himself hampered by the lack of accurate data upon which to base his theoretical investigations" (296); "Thomson set to work, with such appliances as he could lay hands upon, to supply the data of which he stood in need" (297); "When Thomson first organised a physical laboratory, it was because he found great need for physical data as to the properties of matter" (304); etc. Note also the characterisation of the Treatise (i, 472), and Helmholtz' approving comment that "consistency to physical fact was preferred to elegance of mathematical method."

[25] F. Darwin, *The Life and Letters of Charles Darwin*, i, 1888, 28, 30, 34 f., 39, 42, 50, 56. It would be a real, if modest, scientific service to provide this book with a full analytical index. [These and the following references to this work are to the London edition in three volumes; the American edition of the same date is in two volumes. H. P. W.]

may add, of his 'Natural Theology,' gave me as much delight as did Euclid. . . . Taking [the premises] on trust, I was charmed and convinced by the long line of argumentation." [26] Fact and logic, seeing and thinking, the two indispensables of the scientific system, had each its peculiar fascination.

There is scarcely a branch of natural science in which the young Darwin does not show a germinal interest; and later on, when the lines of preferred work are definitely laid out, something of this catholicity still remains.[27] In his mature life he "always had several quite distinct subjects in hand at the same time." [28] Sometimes, as in the case of his study of insectivorous plants, the scientific problem is touched off by a single, apparently casual observation; [29] sometimes, as preeminently in the case of the origin of species, it insinuates itself into his mind by many channels, bears him company for many years, and only after this term of incubation takes on its positive and final form.[30] However it may come, it serves always as the guide and fruitful source of methodical enquiry.

This enquiry is, on the one hand, a search for facts. Darwin himself lays more stress on his collection of facts, by lists of printed questions, by conversation, by extensive reading, than on his own active observing.[31] The collection, however, was very far from indiscrim-

---

[26] *Ibid.*, 33, 47, 103.

[27] *Ibid.*, 33, 126 f. In Darwin's case, the lack of mathematics here imposed its limitations.

[28] *Ibid.*, 100, 127, 150, 153.   [30] *Ibid.*, 28, 38, 68, etc., etc.

[29] *Ibid.*, 95, 130.   [31] *Ibid.*, 83.

inate: "he had the keenest of instincts as to whether a man was trustworthy or not; he seemed to form a very definite opinion as to the accuracy of the men whose books he read, and made use of this judgment in his choice of facts for use in argument or as illustrations." [32] Such instinctive or, better, empathetic judgment of the observations of others would, of course, be impossible to a man who had not schooled himself in observing, and Darwin was in fact an excellent and a persistent observer. He had the great merit of noting the negative instance, "a special instinct for arresting an exception." [33] "I think," he says, "that I am superior to the common run of men in noticing things which easily escape attention, and in observing them carefully." [34] He also observed widely. "What interested me," remarks one of his correspondents, "was to see that on this as on almost any other point of detailed observation, Mr. Darwin could always say, 'Yes; but at one time I made some observations myself on this particular point; and I think you will find, &c., &c.' " [35] The sheer pleasure of observing appears again and again in his letters. "Happy man," he once exclaims; "he has actually seen crowds of bees flying round *Catasetum*, with the pollinia sticking to their backs!" [36]

---

[32] *Ibid.,* 157; cf. 99, 102.

[33] *Ibid.,* 148.

[34] *Ibid.,* 103.

[35] *Ibid.,* iii , 279.

[36] *Ibid.,* i , 150, 349; ii , 341; iii , 264; F. Darwin and A. C. Seward, *More Letters of Charles Darwin,* ii , 1903, 116.

But Darwin did not stop short at the facts; he also, as we all know, made constant and critical search for theories that should fit the facts. He declares, indeed, that "careful observation is far harder work than generalisation." [37] "I have steadily endeavoured," he says, "to keep my mind free so as to give up any hypothesis, however much beloved (and I cannot resist forming one on every subject), as soon as facts are shown to be opposed to it." [38] On which his son comments: "it was as though he were charged with theorising power ready to flow into any channel on the slightest disturbance, so that no fact, however small, could avoid releasing a stream of theory"; "fortunately, his richness of imagination was equalled by his power of judging and condemning the thoughts that occurred to him." [39] Darwin saw clearly that "all observation must be for or against some view if it is to be of any service", yet how justly he held the balance! "*Let theory guide your observations*," he writes to a friend; and then, in the very next letter, "By no means modify even in the slightest degree any result. . . . It is a golden rule, which I try to follow, to put every fact which is opposed to one's preconceived opinion in the strongest light. Absolute accuracy is . . . the highest merit. Any deviation is ruin." [40] He had learned by experience: "with the exception of the Coral Reefs [which

---

[37] Darwin and Seward, *op. cit.*, ii, 252.

[38] F. Darwin, *op. cit.*, i, 103 f.

[39] *Ibid.*, 149.

[40] Darwin and Seward, *op. cit.*, i, 195; ii, 323 f. The balance may be held so nicely that Darwin lands himself in a formal contradiction: cf. i, 39, with i, 176.

took shape under very special circumstances], I cannot remember a single first-formed hypothesis which had not after a time to be given up or greatly modified." [41]

Toward the end of his life, Darwin summarised his mental resources in the often quoted phrase: "My mind seems to have become a sort of machine for grinding general laws out of large collections of facts." Just fifty years before, he had had it borne in upon him, by one of those natural blunders whose recoil may be more educative than many right inferences, that "science consists in grouping facts so that general laws or conclusions may be drawn from them." [42] Yet critics of his work had found it possible to say: "He is a good observer, but he has no power of reasoning!" [43] It was all, in truth, as it should have been, a matter of give and take: theory in the background guided to acquaintance-with, the facts thus gained were transformed into knowledge-about and so led to revision of theory, the revised theory called for further observation, and so on. The man of science moves freely from universe to universe, using all the tools of logic, but watching continually that logic does not colour or contaminate his essential facts.

---

[41] F. Darwin, *op. cit.*, i , 70, 104; iii , 194.

[42] *Ibid.*, i , 56 f., 101.

[43] *Ibid.*, i , 103. Those who are familiar with the immediately post-Darwinian period of biology will realise how sterile is the attempt to draw conclusions when there are no established facts to draw them from. Darwin sums up his own mental qualities as "love of science" (what we have called observance), "industry in observing and collecting facts," "unbounded patience in long reflecting over any subject" (applied logic as inference), and "a fair share of invention as well as of common sense" (applied logic as hypothesis tempered by observation): *ibid.*, i , 107.

§ 9. We set out to gain a working conception of science, and we have made some progress: we know roughly what science is when we regard it as a frame of mind, and we know what it is when we regard it as a mode of life, the activity of an individual in society. Our journey is not yet, however, at an end. The great majority of mankind know nothing of the scientific attitude, and very little of the occupation of the scientific investigator. Science, in their eyes, is something that is laid down in books, taught in schools and colleges, embodied (so to say) in the persons of a few great men and, more generally, in the membership of certain societies, expressed in discovery, and justified by invention. The word science, so far as it conveys a meaning, means to them science in its objective and institutional form. And this objective science has, plainly, a claim upon our own consideration. We must expressly raise the question of the business of institutional science; we must ask what it tries to do, what it contributes to civilisation, what is the aim of its systematic endeavour. Even if the answer to such questions is implied in our treatment of subjective science, we may still hope, by turning things about, to see our conclusions in a new perspective.

In the light of what we have already said, there can be but one task for science to perform. It must try, without distortion of the facts from which it starts, to work up observational knowledge-of-acquaintance into a body of knowledge-about that shall be manageable, compassable, available, communicable. If we turn, now, to recent discussions of the question, we find that they converge precisely upon this result. For a long time science was confused, and failed to realise its proper business; but there is general agreement at the present day that the problem of science may be summed up in the single word 'description.' When a qualification is added, the phrase runs 'the simplest possible description,' or 'description in the simplest terms.'

The word 'description,' used in this comprehensive sense, carries both positive and negative reference. On the negative side, it expresses a protest against the older confusion of thought. It denies that science has anything to do with explanation, with Why and Because; and it denies, accordingly, that science has anything to do with application, with means and end. We must first consider the main tendency of this protest; the corollary, the difference between science and technology, will occupy us later.

We have said that the scientific temper knows nothing of special purposes. Questions of Why and Because belong to the universe of sufficient reason, which is the universe of logic. We have also said, however, that observation is guided by logic. In the concrete activity of the scientific investigator logic plays a large, usually the larger, part. It is natural, then, that logic should be extended to the relations of fact within the scientific system, and that men of science should seek to 'account for' observed phenomena by appeal to attraction or affinity, cause or force, adaptation or evolution, as if these 'explanatory principles' were active in the government of the existential world. It is natural, but it is also gratuitous and misleading. Force, as Tait reminds us, is "a mere phantom suggestion of our muscular sense"; it has no physical existence; rates, accelerations, show in physics, but not forces.[44] Cause, according to Mach, "contains a strong tincture of fetichism," and attraction has an echo of the old 'search for place,' the common-sense belief that heavy bodies naturally fall and light bodies naturally rise; science must discard these ideas.[45] Purpose has been formally banished from biology, though it still runs riot in the looser expositions of the subject. "Hairs, prickles, thorns, and spiny growths upon many plants may discourage the attacks of animals, but it would be rash to assume that these protections have been developed because of the danger of such attacks": so writes the author of a recent botanical text book;[46] and he might have added that this common assumption is absolutely unscientific.

Tait and Mach do not ask that the words 'force' and 'cause' be given up. Physics could, indeed, get along very well without them; but so long as, for historical or other reasons, they are convenient in physical exposition, they will be retained. Nor would any reasonable man ask biology to dispense with the words 'adaptation' and 'evolution.' Modern science protests, not against the words, but against the mythical power of explanation which is attributed to them. Psychologists still speak of memory and imagination, while they explicitly disavow the old psychological theory of mental faculties; and it is this disavowal of common-sense

---

[44] P. G. Tait, *Lectures on Some Recent Advances of Physical Science,* 2nd ed., 1876, 338 ff.; *Properties of Matter,* 1885, 7 ff., esp. 11.

[45] E. Mach, *Popular Scientific Lectures,* 1895, *passim,* esp. 226, 254.

[46] J. M. Coulter, *Plant Relations,* 1900, 146; cf. 74, and *Plant Structures,* 1900, 324

ideas, as both superfluous and misleading, that the term 'description' in its negative sense primarily demands.

§ 10. 'Description,' however, is meant positively as well as negatively. To understand its positive significance, we must look somewhat closely at the nature of the tasks upon which science is engaged. We shall not scruple to use the ordinary logical terms, since description, if it expresses adequately the general business of science, must cover the various operations to which these terms attach.[47]

It is universally agreed, then, that the first problem of science is analysis. Logically and temporally, the first thing that a scientific man has to do, when he embarks upon a new bit of work, is to analyse. This rule, which has no exceptions in practice, follows of necessity from the limitation of the scientific method and the nature of the knowledge upon which that method is directed. We are to attain to clear awareness, to a direct acquaintance-with; and clear awareness can be gained only piecemeal, little by little, for observation, as we saw, is adequate at any one time only to a very small area of the prospect to be explored.

Analysis may be divisive, the breaking up of a given whole into its constituent parts, or it may be abstractive, the singling out by observation of some feature or property of the given whole. Chemistry performs a divisive analysis when it separates water into oxygen and hydrogen, and psychology performs an abstractive analysis when it separates colour into hue, tint and

---

[47] Cf. W. S. Jevons, *The Principles of Science,* 1900, 673 ff.; W. Wundt, *Logik der exakten Wissenschaften,* 1907, 1 ff.

chroma. These are instances of analysis at the elementary level. We go a step further when, in varying the circumstances of experiment, we take account not only of the elements to which our analysis has led but also of the functional relations of these elements within the given whole. Chemistry performs a relational analysis of this sort when it specifies the number of atoms of every kind which the molecule contains and exhibits their mode of arrangement within the molecule; psychology performs a relational analysis when it localises a given colour, by hue, by tint, and by chroma, within the colour pyramid.

All the further problems of science, now, are problems of synthesis. In what is called reproductive synthesis we put together again what analysis has disjoined, and so reproduce the given whole from which we started; we recombine the spectral colours to make white light, we recombine the simple tones to make a compound tone of a certain timbre. This reproductive synthesis, however, is nothing more than a test of analysis, useful and possible in fairly simple cases; it cannot take us far. We make better progress by variation of circumstances in the synthetic experiment: we put together portions of the spectrum, and so discover the antagonistic colours, or we put together pairs of simple tones, and so discover the degrees of tonal fusion. Experiment is thus the handmaid both of analysis and of synthesis, and one and the same experiment may subserve relational analysis or relational synthesis according as the observer turns his attention to this or that aspect of his total problem. A chemical formula may express the analysis of the molecule or the synthesis of the atoms, and the colour pyramid may be regarded as the synthesis of visual qualities or as the analysis of the world of looks.

So far, analysis and synthesis are strictly complementary. In the building up of the scientific system, however, synthesis takes a wider sweep. It appears in the three principal forms of classification, of law of facts, and of law of correlation of facts. All three forms rest upon foregone analysis, and all are logically interrelated.

Classification is arrangement of the results of analysis on the basis of relationship, a systematic association of like to like, with indication of the removes at which the various groups thus formed are connected. We may think of the classification of the chemical elements, or of the genealogical classification of biology. It is clear that the establishment of a class of similars, if it is really a natural class, may lead us to the discovery of laws of facts; for an object which has some of the characters of the class in question will very probably prove to possess the others also. It is clear, further, that the establishment of such a class may disclose unsuspected laws of correlation; phenomena and properties of phenomena, whose interdependence had not been realised, may show henceforth as connected and covariant. Classification is thus much more than a mere convenient grouping of scientific material; it is a definite problem of applied logic, and its solution contributes largely to the knowledge-about which is institutional science.

The law of facts, to which we have already referred by anticipation, is a summary statement of uniformity of constitution or uniformity of behaviour among the phenomena of the existential universe. It is an universal law of physics that gravity is proportional directly to the product of the gravitating masses and inversely to the square of their distance; and it is a local law of psychology that contrast is always in the direction of greatest qualitative opposition. Such formulas are extremely convenient; they enable us to hold in mind a great number and variety of experimental results. But they are, again, much more than convenient. In their logical status, as generalisations, they represent definite stages in the construction of the scientific system.

A law of correlation, finally, is a summary statement of uniform connection or covariation among phenomena. No hard and fast line of distinction can be drawn between the law of correlation and the law of facts. Gravitation, for instance, always goes with inertia, and inertia with gravitation; and the law may be taken either as a law of the constitution of matter or as a law of the correlation of properties of matter. We speak of correlation, more particularly, when we are examining the covariation of phenomena, both or all of which are variable functions of a common variant; when, for example, we are examining the covariation of children's height and weight, both considered as functions of age. Practically and logically, the laws of correlation stand on the same footing with the laws of facts.

The typical business of science, therefore, appears in the forms of elementary analysis, relational analysis and relational synthesis, classification, and the formulation of natural laws. Or we may say, still more briefly, that the man of science analyses with a view to some later synthesis.

§ 11. And all this complexity of operation may be summed up in the single word 'description'? Truly it may; for description is precisely what we have found the business of science to be: an analysis undertaken with the view to a later synthesis. Let us look at some simple cases.

I wish to build a house, and I ask an architect to prepare plans for the contractor. The architect lays out the house piecemeal, floor by floor, woodwork and stonework and plumbing and heating and lighting; he draughts plans and elevations and details, and draws up lists of specifications. The charts and tables that he furnishes, taken all together and in relation, are his technical description of the house. In order to describe, he has been obliged to analyse; but he has set the results of his analysis in such relation to one another that anyone who can understand them sees the house as a whole, and anyone with the right skill and materials can build it.

Or a novelist wishes to describe the scene upon which the action of his characters is projected. Let us read such a description: we find successive mention of trees, flowers, road, farmhouses, brooks, hills, sheep and cattle, fields, walls, hedges, rocks, and so forth. The description proceeds upon a basis of analysis. The items are, nevertheless, set in such relation, by various literary devices, that they produce in the reader's mind, if not a clear picture of the complex scene, at least a synthetic impression of its type; and the arousal of the picture, or the establishment of the scenic atmosphere, is of course the effect which the writer intends.[48]

These illustrations must suffice. Trivial as they are, they help us to realise that even "the grand universal laws of physics, such as apply indiscriminately to material, electrical, magnetic and other systems, are not essentially different from descriptions." [49] Science, we said, works up observational acquaintance into a manageable body of knowledge-about without distortion of the facts from which it starts. These facts are gained by analysis, and are brought by synthesis, without change of nature or relation, into groups which can be overseen and formulas which can be handled. The procedures of synthesis may be highly elaborate; the beginner in science may find them difficult to follow, and the untrained mind may find them sheerly unintelligible. Yet the outcome never transcends description, a shorthand description which, for the initiated, brackets together a multitude of related facts.

It remains to say a word about the qualification of scientific description as 'the simplest possible.' The idea which has prompted this addition is the idea of economy of thought; the simpler a description, the less effort is required (provided always that the simple description is also adequate) to comprehend it, handle

---

[48] A very good illustration is afforded by the introductory paragraphs of that once famous novel *Robert Elsmere.* All the items mentioned in the text, and more beside, will be found in these paragraphs; and yet, by such simple devices as the use of "echo" and of analogical synthesis, the author succeeds in impressing the whole complicated scene upon the reader's mind.

[49] E. Mach, *Popular Scientific Lectures,* 1895, 254; *Principien der Wärmelehre,* 1896, 436.

it, apply it in the further progress of the scientific system. In so far as simplicity does, in effect, render the facts more manageable, more available, more easily communicable, we may admit, without hesitation, that it enters by right into any statement of the business of science. We must remember, however, that science is the work of individual men, variously disposed and endowed, so that simplicity is a relative matter; and we must not seek simplicity at the expense of intelligibility. A set of mathematical formulas, intrinsically simple and clear as daylight to the advanced mathematician, may yet be far less useful to the rank and file of scientific men than the clumsier verbal equivalents. To aim at simplicity for simplicity's sake would be to follow an aesthetic, not a scientific ideal. If we conclude, then, that the business of science is to furnish as simple as possible a description of the existential world, let us add that we mean by 'simplest possible' that which does, in the given circumstances, secure the utmost economy of thought.[50]

---

[50] The view that the scientific system is essentially a matter of economical description has a long history. It finds fairly clear expression in the paper of W. J. M. Rankine, *Outlines of the Science of Energetics* (1855): see *Miscellaneous Scientific Papers,* ed. P. G. Tait and W. J. Millar, 1881, 209 ff. It was a favourite subject with E. Mach, who put it forward as early as 1871 and worked it out in an extended series of publications. See, *e.g., Popular Scientific Lectures,* 1895, esp. *The Economical Nature of Physical Enquiry* (1882), 186 ff., and *On the Principle. of Comparison in Physics* (1894), 236 ff.; *The Science of Mechanics* (1883), 1893, viii f., 4 ff., 490; *Die Analyse der Empfindungen* (1886), 1900, 37, 210 f., 219 f., 226 ff.; *Principien der Wärmelehre,* 1896, 430 ff., 459 f.; *Erkenntnis und Irrtum* (1905), 1906, 287, 314, 450.

A few references may be added; a full bibliography is out of the question. See, on the scientific side, W. K. Clifford, *On Theories of*

§ 12. Institutional science, then, is descriptive and not explanatory; it stops short of the 'why' of things. It is also—we have noted that the word 'description' enters the double protest—'pure' or theoretical and not 'applied' or practical; it stops short of the 'use' of things. Yet pure and applied science are, in fact, closely related, and the relation is every day becoming closer. What is the mark of difference, and how does difference consist with this relation?

"I often wish," said Huxley, "that the phrase 'applied science' had never been invented. For it suggests that there is a sort of scientific knowledge of direct practical use, which can be studied apart from another sort of scientific knowledge, which is of no practical utility, and which is termed 'pure science.' But there is no more complete fallacy than this." [51] The science,

---

the Physical Forces (1870) in *Lectures and Essays*, i, 1879, 109 ff.; G. R. Kirchhoff, *Vorlesungen über mathematische Physik: Mechanik* (1876), 1883, 1; H. Münsterberg, *Die Willenshandlung*, 1888, 59 ff., 162; *Psychology and Life*, 1899, 44 ff., 191 ff.; *Grundzüge der Psychologie*, i, 1900, esp. 331 ff.; K. Pearson, *The Grammar of Science* (1892), 1900, *passim*, esp. 112, 115 f., 180 f., 191; W. Ostwald, *Vorlesungen über Naturphilosophie*, 1902, 205 ff.; P. Duhem, *La théorie physique, son objet et sa structure*, 1906, 5, 26, 29, 59 ff.; J. A. Thomson, *Introduction to Science*, 1911, 35 ff.

On the philosophical side: R. Avenarius, *Philosophie als Denken der Welt gemäss dem Princip des kleinsten Kraftmasses*, 1876, 18 f., 45 ff.; *Kritik der reinen Erfahrung*, ii, 1890, 331 ff., 492 ff.; J. Royce, *The Spirit of Modern Philosophy*, 1892, 381 ff.; *The World and the Individual*, i, 1900, 29; ii, 1901, 26 ff.; J. Ward, *Naturalism and Agnosticism*, i, 1899, 62 f., 81 ff.; ii, 66 ff., 240 ff.; A. E. Taylor, *Elements of Metaphysics*, 1903, 174 ff.; J. T. Merz, *A History of European Thought in the Nineteenth Century*, i (1896) 1904, 382 f.; ii, 1903, 183 f.; iii, 1912, 282 f., 402 ff., 574 ff.; iv, 1914, 758 ff.

[51] T. H. Huxley, *Science and Culture* (1880), in *Science and Culture*, 1882, 20.

that is to say, which the technologies 'apply', technologies like medicine and agriculture, engineering and industrial chemistry and eugenics, is always and everywhere the same, the science of which we have ourselves been speaking. There is only one kind of science, whether it is applied or whether it is left without application. That is the first point to be remarked.

"What people call applied science," Huxley goes on, "is nothing but the application of pure science to particular classes of problems." Here, however, he is led by his definition of science as 'perfected common sense' into the statement of what is, at the most, only a half-truth. For the great difference between science and technology is a difference of initial attitude. The scientific man follows his method whithersoever it may take him. He seeks acquaintance with his subject-matter, and he does not at all care about what he shall find, what shall be the content of his knowledge when acquaintance-with is transformed into knowledge-about. The technologist moves in another universe; he seeks the attainment of some determinate end, which is his sole and obsessing care; and he therefore takes no heed of anything that he cannot put to use as means toward that end.[52] The special 'problems' about which the science of a given period is busy are problems set by the logic of the scientific system, and not by any consideration of utility, while scientific work of this

---

[52] E. Mach, *Principien der Wärmelehre*, 1896, 449 f.; J. T. Merz, *op. cit.,* i , 30 ff.; J. A. Thomson, *op. cit.,* 224 f., 234 ff.; E. B. Titchener, *Psychology: Science or Technology?* in *Pop. Sci. Monthly,* lxxxiv , 1914, 39 ff.

directed sort is paralleled by work undertaken, as opportunity offers, from sheer, undirected 'love of observation.' Technology, on the other hand, exists only in virtue of its special and practical problem. If we did not wish to prevent or cure disease, there would be no medicine; and if we did not wish to conserve or improve the race, there would be no eugenics.

That is the real point of difference, and it shows itself in many ways. The man of science, for example, is confined by the rules of his intellectual game to one particular point of view. The technologist, on the contrary, may change his standpoint as often as, in the interest of his aim, seems good to him. He is not bound to borrow only from a single science, but takes facts and laws, as he needs them, indiscriminately from any science. The man of science, again, surveys indifferently the whole of his subject-matter; the technologist is definitely selective, both as to what he accepts and as to what he neglects. In this sense too, therefore, there is fallacy in the phrase 'applied science.' No 'pure' science has its strict counterpart among the technologies, which rather apply many sciences, and apply these sciences in a fragmentary way, to the end in view. Medicine is both more and less than applied physiology, and engineering is both more and less than applied physics. Nor is a technology obliged to maintain an even front with the sciences which it applies. It may, by practical trial and error, anticipate the results of science; it may also, for its immediate purpose, do very well with a formula that science has already discarded. And finally, the technologist may travel out of science altogether, and may seek help from other

technologies, even as a last resort from the undifferen‑
tiated matrix of common-sense.

In such circumstances it is only natural that, to the
free-ranging man of practice, science should look nar‑
row and pedantic, and that, to the strictly methodical
man of science, technology should appear scrappy and
provisional. The difference is there, and those who
represent the extremes of temperamental divergence
will hardly be reconciled.[53] The relationship is,
nevertheless, as real as the difference.

There is, first of all, the common bond of logic.
Whenever the man of science plans an experiment,
whenever he tries to give his facts a systematic set‑
ting, he uses the same logical rules as the technologist;
nay more, when he writes a hand-book or a text-book,
for information or instruction, he becomes in so far
forth a technologist. There is, secondly, the likelihood
that any long-continued bit of work, scientific or tech‑
nological, will invite a shift of attitude. The physiol‑
ogist, anxious as professor to demonstrate a scientific
law to his classes, invents the ophthalmoscope; the
pathologist, searching for an antitoxin and finding that
the chemists cannot tell him what he wants to know,
becomes involved in a purely scientific investigation.[54]

---

[53] The extreme utilitarian temperament is, of course, common
enough; the other extreme is probably rare. It is worth while, then,
to cite an instance. At the Jubilee of the Chemical Society (1891)
Sir W. R. Grove remarked: "For my own part, I must say that
science to me generally ceases to be interesting as it becomes useful."
See *Nature*, xliii, 1891, 493.

[54] *Ansprachen und Reden gehalten bei der am 2. November 1891 zu
Ehren von Hermann von Helmholtz veranstalteten Feier,* 1892, 52 f.;
A. Hill, *op. cit.,* 7 ; Kelvin, *Popular Lectures and Addresses,* i , 1889,
232 f.; ii , 1894, 211 ff.; J. T. Merz, *op. cit.,* i , 328 ff.

And there is, thirdly, the need of technology itself. Any technology that holds steadily aloof from science must inevitably stagnate; and an instinctive submission to this law sends the technologist, however sceptical his mood may be, to talk things out with his scientific colleague.

Hence for all the difference of attitude, there may be mutual understanding, and for all the difference of aim, there is institutional relationship. If the man of science is a little insistent as regards the difference, that is because he is necessarily in the minority and usually (as that position implies) upon the defensive.[55]

§ 13. So we have come round again to our starting-point. At the end of this sketch, as at the beginning, the man of science stands apart from the great major-ity of his fellow-men. He is still the servant and not, like the generality of mankind, the interpreter of na-ture. Interpretation, indeed, we saw to be wholly for-eign to him: meanings must be stripped away before his work can begin, and meanings must be kept away while his work proceeds. Disinterested and imper-

---

[55] "The fact is that the most useful parts of science have been investigated for the sake of truth, and not for their usefulness" (W. K. Clifford, *Lectures and Essays,* i, 1879, 104); "No great law in natural philosophy has ever been discovered *for* its practical appli-cations, but the instances are innumerable of investigations ap-parently quite *useless* in this narrow sense of the word which have led to the most valuable results" (Kelvin, *Introductory Lecture,* in S. P. Thompson, *The Life of William Thomson,* i, 1910, 249). Kelvin, however, like Darwin in another connection, held the balance so nicely that elsewhere he formally contradicts his own statement: see *Popular Lectures and Addresses,* i, 1889, 79 f. In both instances the slip is instructive. Cf. H. Poincaré, *The Foundations of Science,* 1913, 279, 294, 363.

sonal, he makes himself one with the facts of nature; he moves in the domain of bare existence; and his intercourse with the facts is both observation and observance.

Turning then from the servant of nature to nature herself, we found that scientific facts are not by any means necessarily what the layman supposes them to be, natural phenomena taken in their entirety. The existential universe is, on the contrary, observed always from some particular point of view, and science is therefore always a particular science, physics or biology or psychology. Facts, in other words, are rather phases or aspects than items of natural existence.

We next considered man and nature in relation, and noted that the universal and peculiar method of science is observation. Since the phenomena to be observed are both complex and elusive, and since human capacity is variously limited, observation is difficult. Science therefore calls in the aid of experiment, which prolongs the time of observation, rules out disturbing and irrelevant phenomena, and allows variation of circumstances. Experiment, which is observation under favourable conditions, is in so far simply an extension of the universal method of science. The securing and arranging of the favourable conditions are, however, a matter of applied logic. In order to plan an experiment the man of science must return to the world of meanings which, in order to observe, he must as positively renounce. Here is a first complication of science with logic.

A second and far more radical complication follows. Observation results in the immediate awareness known as 'acquaintance-with' ; and if such knowledge is to be organised and socialised, it must be transformed into a 'knowledge-about.' We have not discussed the reasons for this transformation; it was enough for our purpose to recognise that science has, in fact, become a social institution. We showed, however, that the work of transformation falls to logic to perform, that all the modes of logical procedure are involved, and that in course of time the modes appropriate to a special science are brought together as canons of a 'scientific methodology.' In the scientific system, logic is coördinate with fact and may even, as hypothesis, run ahead of fact. Since, nevertheless, the system is a body of knowledge about the facts with which observation first made us acquainted, logic must not be permitted either to invade and colour facts or to draw conclusions that run counter to them.

So we passed from the scientific temper, taken in the abstract, to the concrete activity of the individual man of science; and this activity led us, in its turn, to institutional science, the science which is coördinate with art and religion and philosophy, and which makes its special contribution to our civilisation. We found that the business of institutional science, stated in general terms, is to set the facts of observation, transformed into knowledge-about, in their natural order of relationship and to bring them under social control. In detail, this problem divides into two part-problems, analysis and synthesis, of which analysis is both logically and temporally the prior. Synthesis, in its simpler forms complementary to analysis, broadens out into the operations of classification and the formulation of scientific laws. We found further that, in order to emphasise the prime requisite of the scientific system —that logical organisation shall not distort the facts —men of science have summed up this manifold work of arrangement and reduction in a term which carries a constant reminder of scientific origins. The business of science, they tell us, is to describe, and to describe in such wise as shall best secure economy of thought.

The name 'description,' however, suggests not only fidelity to fact but also restriction to fact; it bids us abstain from application as well as from interpretation. We followed up the suggestion, and saw that the differences between science and technology spring from a marked difference of initial attitude which, nevertheless, if it is frankly recognised, need not at all stand in the way of coöperation.

Here, then, our argument might rest. We sought for a working conception of science, not for a definition. We have tried to discover what men of science themselves say of science, as frame of mind, as a man's vocation, as a social institution; throughout our search we have kept in close touch with scientific precept and example. Now that we have got our bearings in this larger world, we might at once begin our proper work in the particular universe of scientific psychology, carrying over to the special science of mind, for our own guidance and for the test of divergent views, whatever we have learned regarding science in general. It will not be time wasted, however, if we put off this transition for a little, in order briefly to consider, first, the interrelations of the sciences and, secondly, certain corollaries to the preceding exposition.

§ 14. The business of science, as we have just now seen, is to describe its phenomena in the simplest possible way. It seems to follow that the goal of a science would be attained if it could comprehend the whole of its subject-matter in one simple and all-embracing formula, whose explication should guide us, step by step, back to the discrete facts with which our knowledge began. Let us accept this consequence; and let us further accept the postulate of the uniformity of nature. If nature really is uniform—and science seems to have earned her right to the assumption; certainly she makes it [56]—may we not go further? May we not look forward to a time, even if indefinitely distant, when all the comprehensive formulae in which the descriptions of the separate sciences have been summarised shall themselves be integrated into a single universal formula? An ideal, no doubt; but is it not also a scientific ideal?

In approaching these questions we do well to remind ourselves, at the outset, that all the uniformities of modern science are still laws, not of science at large, but of some separate and special science. Let us take, by way of illustration, the great law of the conservation of energy. This is a generalisation from physical

---

[56] The *locus classicus* is still the discussion in Mill's *Logic,* with which may be read C. S. Peirce's art. *Uniformity* in the *Dict. Philos. Psych.* It is worth pointing out in the context of our own argument that technology, in drawing simultaneously upon a number of sciences (p. 67), presupposes an interscientific uniformity. The common universe of discourse is assured, of course, by the logic which had made over acquaintance into knowledge-about. Logic, however, would be of little avail if the facts known-about did not themselves bear out the presupposition.

phenomena, accepted by physicists as valid over the whole face of their science. It is a generalisation valid, among other things, for 'living organisms.' "The conservation of energy obtains in our own frame as in the tide, the waterfall, the furnace. It is a law in the living world as well as the inanimate." [57] But it is not, on that account, a law of biology or of physiology. It is a law of physics; and the physicist, from his standpoint, can see only what is physical. The law of the conservation of energy runs throughout the physical prospect; and 'living organisms,' so far as they appear within this prospect, appear accordingly as physical aggregates, *loci* of the exchange of physical energies; they do not and they cannot show as the living organisms which make up the subject-matter of biology. If it should ever happen that the law is proved to hold of 'mind,' then the mind so characterised would, in the same way, be a physical aggregate, visible from the physical standpoint, different and distinct from the 'mind' of psychology. Science, as we know it, is made up of special sciences differentiated by point of view and correlated subject-matter; and so long as this state of things persists, so long must the laws of science submit to specific limitation. "The conceptions of science, or what are usually termed the laws of nature, such as we know them, do not refer at all to nature as a whole, but . . . are inevitably bound up with finite departments and occurrences." [58] That is the present status.

Now let us look at the single science. There can be

---

[57] C. S. Sherrington, in *Lectures on the Method of Science*, 1906, 66.
[58] J. T. Merz, *op. cit.*, iii , 610.

no doubt that every scientific vision of the existential universe appears, from its particular standpoint, to be the vision of a whole.[59] To the physicist, who can see only what is physical, the prospect is that of a physical whole, complete and self-contained, capable of organisation and system; to the biologist and psychologist it is, in like manner, the prospect of a biological and of a psychological whole. It would be interesting to trace the strands, mainly historical and logical, out of which this belief in wholeness is woven; but our immediate interest lies solely in the question whether the conception of science worked out in this chapter permits us to entertain it. The answer seems to run clearly in the affirmative: we may entertain the belief, though its justification may be indefinitely postponed. We may seek the all-embracing formula; physics, indeed, has made a valiant effort to write one for itself in terms of energy, and biology and psychology may be encouraged by the example of physics to attempt the same road; but we may find our efforts balked, for an indefinitely long future, by the obstinate variety of the facts.

Plainly, then, there is not much hope of the unification of all the sciences. It seems to be made out, with a convincingly high degree of probability, that all biological phenomena are correlated with physical,[60] and

---

[59] W. James, *The Will to Believe,* 1897, 299.

[60] The growing body of facts upon which this conclusion is based has been set in a wrong logical perspective by the fruitless controversy between mechanism and vitalism. Thomson's *Introduction to Science,* for example, shows an obsessing anxiety lest biology be swallowed up in physics and chemistry (see 48 f., 53 ff., 82, 90, 97 f., 100, 109, 117 f., 121, 145-153, 160 ff., 183 f.). But the reading of the

all psychological phenomena with phenomena of biology and thus, ultimately, of physics. Here, perhaps, is some ground of encouragement—and here the issue must be left. There will always be investigators whose special temperament and special insight lead them to search for unity, whether within the single science or among the totality of the sciences; and we may be assured by the history of science that their search, even if it prove unsuccessful, will not have been made in vain. Meanwhile the uniformity of nature stands as a methodological postulate, essential for the past and present of institutional science, and by all means to be retained unless and until the progress of science itself prove it untenable.

Let us suppose, however, that science has been unified; that we have obtained a single transcript of the existential universe, a formula that is a sort of composite photograph, in which all our local views are harmonised and all our partial uniformities fit together; still we shall not have exhausted the world of human experience. Existence does not adequately express experience; so that, indeed, if the word 'universe' is taken in all strictness, we have no right to speak of an exis-

---

existential world given by physics and chemistry must be a reading in physical and chemical terms; whatever the physicist sees, he describes as physicist. The biologist has then to show that he occupies a different standpoint, and that from this standpoint he sees new facts, discovers new aspects of existence. He may not convince the physicist. It is unfortunately true, as things are, that the physicist has little understanding of biology, as it is also true that physicist and biologist alike have little understanding of psychology. The important thing is, however, that he convince himself, and that as the result of his conviction he produce facts and inferences which are not those of the handbooks of physics.

tential universe.[61] What we have assumed as done for
the sciences must also be done for the disciplines of
value; they on their side must be integrated, each one
and all together, and then must follow the final integration of Existence and Value. All this is the task of
philosophy, and not of science; only, the scientific man
should remember that his own account of the world,
however far it may be carried, gives at best an incom-
plete and one-sided picture of human experience.

§ 15. If these general considerations have left us a
little in the air, our corollaries bring us back again to
earth. The first of them is this: that there is pressing
need, in education, of such teaching as shall give the
scholar an elementary insight into the nature of science.
Very few children, it is true, grow up to be men and
women of scientific vocation and attainment. When we
consider, however, the increasingly important part that
science plays in our modern civilisation, we shall surely
agree that every child ought to make at least a few
first-hand observations, and ought, further, to be
brought to understand, in an elementary way, what
observation is and what it implies. As things are, the
popularisation of science fails all too often of its mark.
It is, no doubt, of advantage in various ways when a
leading man of science writes for the layman; students
of science benefit by the clarity and simplicity of the

---

[61] Pearson's remark that "the material of science is coextensive with
the whole life, physical and mental, of the universe" is formally correct; but it is also misleading unless 'life' be qualified by 'existential' (*op. cit.*, 12, 15, 24 f.). Pearson is polemising against metaphysics and philosophical method; but he seems to admit (*e.g.*, 17)
that there is at any rate an aesthetic attitude which is different
from the scientific and equally legitimate.

statement, and the appeal of science may carry to some untrained mind that would else not have found itself. But the general reader rarely takes the point. He is interested only in the accessories of science: the adventure of the search, the long process of trial and error that culminates in the successful experiment, the controversial bearing of the results, the wonders and surprises of the world, the promise or outcome of practical application; and science itself, the heart and centre of the exposition, finds him unintelligent and unreceptive.[62]

There has been a tendency of recent years to lay the blame for this state of things upon the man of science. There is repeated demand that science come down from the clouds of theory, cease to be pedantic and aloof, busy itself henceforth with the useful, make closer contact with the realities of everyday life. Criticism of this sort, however, simply mistakes the situation. Science cannot choose what it shall do and what it shall leave undone; if it tries to do that, it ceases to be science. And to blunt the edge of science is nothing

---

[62] Pearson suggests (*op. cit.*, 11) that "works like Darwin's *Origin of Species* and *Descent of Man,* Lyell's *Principles of Geology,* Helmholtz's *Sensations of Tone,* or Galton's *Natural Inheritance,* can be profitably read and largely understood by those who are not specially trained in the several branches of science with which these works deal." Surely a counsel of perfection! The reading of such books means time and continuous effort; and if it is begun, it is likely to falter and stop precisely at the point where the preliminaries are ended and the writer comes face to face with his topic in overt scientific form. Writing that, to the man of science, seems not only luminously clear but also logically unitary will break apart for the untrained reader; where science proper begins, his comprehension halts.

less than suicidal. Our task is to lead the coming generation up to an elementary grasp of science, not to let science down to the level of a generation which, unfortunately, has not had the privilege of scientific training. The accessories need not be omitted, but the essentials must by all means be introduced: observation, and reverence for fact, and contempt of easy guesswork. We have evidence that the thing can be done, and scientific men should set about its doing.

Our second corollary is also educational. It is that the students of science, in colleges and universities, should be taught not only the facts and logic of their science but also its history. Hitherto the history of thought has been a subject for philosophy, and science has for the most part confined itself to experiment and to such systematisation as is afforded by a recent textbook. Aside, however, from the cultural value that attaches to the history of human endeavour, there is advantage from the scientific standpoint in knowing how thought dealt with fact at the birth of fact, and how later facts and later thoughts have modified man's first reading of the book of nature. Our conception of science would be clearer and more consistent, our use of scientific terms more precise, and our scientific thinking more cleanly cut, if we were better acquainted with the work of our predecessors and with the intellectual environment in which they lived.

Curricula are already overcrowded, and we may doubt if there is much to be gained—though, truly, it is a first step—by the addition of special courses in the history of science. Students who are by temperament interested in such matters would attend them, and the rank and file would stay away. What is required is, rather, that science become historically self-conscious. If all our scientific teaching were infused with the spirit of history, if it were a matter of course that experiments and laws and technical terms were shown in an historical perspective, then there would be no need of further argument regarding the cultural value of scientific studies, and the better educational method would react for good upon both teachers and taught.

Neither of these reforms would usher in the millennium, but both would accomplish something. The first would help to bring together the two camps into which educated society, much to its disadvantage, is still divided, the camps of science and of the humanities. It might also, since the prescribed observational exercises should be of all sorts, physical and chemical, biological and psychological, help to abolish the existing hierarchical arrangement of the sciences, and so pave the way for a true scientific democracy; it would, at any rate, help toward the insight that science, methodologically regarded, is all of one piece. The second would tend to bridge the chasm which still divides science and philosophy. Today the thoughtful man of science, finding small comfort in technical philosophy, writes a philosophy of his own; whereupon the philosopher, armed with his technical weapons, falls upon him critically and makes short work of his effort. Today the professional philosopher, untrained to observe and blind to the reverence for fact which is as a religion to the scientific man, preaches down to science, offers norms for its guidance, smiles a little pityingly at its provisional constructions; whereupon the man of science asks, in natural exasperation, what positive result has ever come out of metaphysics. We cannot, to be sure, lay down rules for philosophy; but if we see to it that our students of science are familiar with the history of human thought, we may at least from our own side help to destroy what is nothing less than an intellectual scandal.

§ 16. Now at last we are ready to discuss, in the light of science, the fundamental questions of a scientific psychology. The need of such discussion, made abundantly plain as our conception of science itself grew in definiteness and gradually became articulate, receives new emphasis when we follow the argument of this Chapter to its conclusion.

There is, indeed, no acknowledged science whose status and relations are so uncertain, so variously characterised and so vigorously debated, as those of psychology. The name of psychology figures in all the schemata of classification, but it appears in surprisingly different places. For Bain, psychology is fairly coördinate with logic and mathematics; for Spencer, it stands at the very opposite pole of the system. For Wundt, psychology heads the list of the real sciences on the side of mind as dynamics heads it on the side of nature; for Pearson, it is merely a subdivision of biology. The differences would not so much matter, though they would still be puzzling, if the sciences included in these classifications were all homogeneous, so that the laws and facts of any one were formally interchangeable with those of any other: but that, unfortunately, is not the case.

It is true that Hume, by his comparison of association with gravitation, long ago brought the laws of psychology into parallel with the laws of physics. His ground of comparison lay, however, in the common notion of 'attraction'; and while physics has fought free of that mysticism, the law of the association of ideas, as it runs in the popular mind and in many text-books of psychology, is still what it was in Hume's day, a law of application, a rule of thumb, an interpretative and not an existential formula. Hume's general attitude is, nevertheless, more nearly scientific than that of Spencer—who, while he includes psychology *sans phrase* in the table of the concrete sciences, holds in reserve a science of subjective psychology as a body of knowledge "totally unique, . . . independent of, and antithetically opposed to, all other sciences whatsoever"; even, we must suppose, to that logic 'in whose development it affords aid.' A psychology whose status and relations are thus defined is, in effect, beyond the pale of science.[63]

There is, again, no science which has suffered to the same extent as psychology from misunderstanding of its problem and method. Psychological observation is persistently confused with moral appreciation. Not only newspapers and magazines and works of fiction, but also books which profess the scientific spirit, represent 'introspection' as a means to the appraisal of self, the justification of conduct, the unravelling of motive; so that the phrase 'morbid introspection' has

---

[63] A. Bain, *op. cit.,* 25 ff.; H. Spencer, *Essays,* ii, 1891, 92 (Table), 100, 105 f.; W. Wundt, *Phil. Studien,* v, 1889, 43, 47; K. Pearson, *op. cit.,* 526.

become as familiar to us as 'maudlin sentimentality'
or 'shrewd common sense.' And though we smile at
James Mill's 'analysis' of his idea of a wall into the
ideas of brick, mortar, position and quantity, it is to
be feared that we are smiling rather at the crude simplicity of the result than at the wrongheadedness of the
undertaking.[64] Are we so clear that Mill confounds
relational analysis with logical explication? Yet every
normal child of high-school age can be taught to distinguish fact from meaning, as every child can be
taught also to observe psychologically.

There is, finally, no science which stands in greater
need than psychology of historical perspective and historical commentary. For the titular problems with
which psychology as science has to grapple have in
large measure come down to it from a pre-scientific
past. Our text-books speak of the psychology of perception and the psychology of thought, and seek to
safeguard themselves by the formal announcement that
psychology, of course, has nothing to do with a theory
of knowledge: whereas the terms of their exposition
are filled full of philosophical reference, and will be
assimilated by the ordinary reader, if not to a living
philosophy, at any rate to so much of dead philosophy
as common sense embalms. We cannot undo our past;
but we can prevent the evils which flow from the ignor-
ing of it. Historical perspective, combined with a
working conception of science at large, must guide the
steps and will assure the progress of those who would
rightly comprehend the facts and laws of mind.

---

[64] J. Mill, *Analysis of the Human Mind*, i, 1869, 115.

CHAPTER II

THE DEFINITION OF PSYCHOLOGY: POINT OF VIEW

CHAPTER II

THE DEFINITION OF PSYCHOLOGY: POINT OF VIEW

§ 1. We have decided that a science may be characterised, at a moderately advanced stage of its development, either by point of view or by correlated subject-matter, and that it is fully and precisely characterised when both terms of the correlation have been specified. If, then, psychology is a science, in the sense of the preceding Chapter, it must have its special point of view over against the existential universe, and must find its special subject-matter in some particular aspect of existence. We have now to learn whether these requirements can be satisfied.

In order thus to characterise a given science, however, we must evidently set it in relation to other sciences; the special standpoint and the special subject-matter must be marked off from coördinate standpoints and subject-matters. We made no attempt, in our general discussion of Science, to determine the number of separate sciences distinguishable at the present day, or to define the point at which a body of related knowledge attains the status of a separate science: we proceeded rather upon the tacit assumption that, if psychology is to be accounted a science, then there are three typical or representative sciences, namely, physics, biology and psychology. We may safely continue our enquiry upon this same basis. For it will hardly be argued that, on the plane of actual scientific knowledge, the three sciences can be reduced to two; and it will hardly be questioned that, if we can rightly differentiate these three within the common universe of existence, the other sciences, however many they may be, will fall into place beside them. Our immediate task, therefore, is to give adequate expression, in behalf of psychology, to three points of view and three corresponding subject-matters; or, in other words, to write a differential formula for psychology in terms of its relation to physics and biology. Where may we look for information?

It is indicative of the current indifference toward questions regarding Science, upon which we remarked at the outset, that the sources to which we should most naturally appeal give us very little assistance. It is true that writers of scientific text-books are accustomed to begin by defining, in set terms, the subject of discourse. Ordinarily, however, the deference paid to this custom is no more than perfunctory, and the definition offered is nothing more than a sort of formal password to the science, an affair of etymology or tradition, devoid both of binding force and of expository value. The histories of science, on their side, seldom rise above the level of chronicles. They tell us of great men and notable discoveries, of laws established and of hypotheses entertained; but only by exception do they speak of the relations of the sciences, whether to one another or to the general intellectual movement of the time.[1] The introductions to science, in accordance with their aim of popularisation, pass forthright from broadest statements of tendency to concrete example, and neglect the middle ground of definition. Even the classifications, when we challenge them on the score of principle, prove to be disappointingly barren. Formally, of course, their problem is akin to our own; in practice, however, their range is too wide and their data are too heterogeneous for thorough-going characterisation; they leave the impression of artificiality, of a local *tour de force*.[2] While, therefore, it would be an exaggeration to say that these various sources do not help us at all, it is the fact, nevertheless, that they help us rather by suggestion and implication than by any express recognition of our need and any explicit endeavour to meet it.

So we must extend our search; and we find what we want, as it happens, in the two quarters to which, in strictness, we have no right of direct appeal: in philosophy and in science itself. Although philosophy normally views the sciences only from the outside, yet

---

[1] See, *e.g.*, W. T. Sedgwick and H. W. Tyler, *A Short History of Science*, 1917. This book, good as it is in many ways, appears to contain no definition of science. Nor is there any section or chapter on psychology, nor any reference to psychology in bibliography or index, although psychology is said (395) to have helped to establish the 'descent of man.'

[2] C. Stumpf's *Zur Einteilung der Wissenschaften* (1907) is valuable; but its value lies rather in the reflections and critical remarks that accompany the work of classification than in the principle upon which the classifications are based and the results to which it leads.

there are philosophers who, like Avenarius, write with sympathetic understanding of science; and although science can see itself only from within, yet there are men of science who, like Mach and Wundt, rise above their specialty to a comprehensive survey of the scientific universe. We must hasten to add, however, that the spirit of logical adventure is far commoner among men of science than the spirit of scientific understanding and sympathy among philosophers. The system of science is built up, as we have seen, by the coöperation of the logical and the strictly scientific tempers; and it is therefore natural that the man of science, who has successfully applied the rules of logic in his own province, should be tempted to cross the border in the hope of applying them more widely. The philosopher, on the other hand, usually has no desire, as he also has made no special preparation, to meet the man of science upon even terms.

This distinction must, however, be supplemented by another, drawn within the universe of science. The temptation to logical adventure does not, we must acknowledge, press with equal force upon the representatives of all our three typical disciplines. The physicist feels it least: partly because the century-old growth and manifold achievement of his science give him a sense of self-sufficiency, and partly because the vast range of physical hypothesis already offers free scope to his logical ambitions. The psychologist feels it most, because the youth of his science makes him jealous of its scientific standing, and the recency of its separation from philosophy keeps him still logically

self-conscious.[3] Physical text-books thus furnish instances of perfunctoriness in definition that are astonishing to the advanced student of psychology, and psy
chological text-books may furnish instances of elaborate discussion of principles that, if he should ever read
them, would be no less astonishing to the student of
physics. In strictness, we may repeat, the physicist has
here the better of the argument. A science is not
bound to characterise its own point of view and its
own subject-matter; it is called upon only to adopt a
certain standpoint, and then from that standpoint to
describe whatever lies within its purview. While, therefore, we may congratulate ourselves that Wundt devotes a whole section of his great work on psychology
to the relations of psychology and natural science, we
cannot maintain that such a section properly belongs
to a scientific hand-book. At the same time, the physicist will be well advised not to press his point too
sharply. For since custom, as a matter of fact, enjoins
the writing of an introductory definition, it is obviously
better that the formula chosen should rest upon considered discussion than that it should be an empty
jingle of words.

An example drawn from physics will show how near
a purporting definition may come to mere abracadabra.
A further example, drawn from biology, will show how

---

[3] This difference forms part of a syndrome which has at least
three other and connected features: that the physicist, if he philos-
ophises, tends toward metaphysics, the psychologist toward theory
of knowledge; that the phy.icist has a stronger tendency than the
psychologist toward religious orthodoxy (J. H. Leuba, *The Belief in
God and Immortality*, 1916, 279 f.) ; and that the physicist is more
liable than the psychologist to the vagaries of 'psychical research.'

the logical adventurer may be diverted from his path by the allurement of controversy. The one is offered as evidence that our present task is not superfluous; the other may be of service when we are attempting that task in the interest of psychology.

§ 2. When, at an early date in his career, the future Kelvin was asked what was the object of a physical laboratory, he replied that it was "to investigate the properties of matter"; and this phrase, 'the properties of matter,' runs like a refrain throughout his lectures and addresses.[4] We might therefore expect that his definition of matter, if he ever came to formulate it, would prove to be carefully thought out and logically unimpeachable, framed according to Mill's canon by enumeration of those essential 'properties' or attributes which the term 'matter' connotes. We find nothing of the sort: the relevant paragraph in the *Treatise* of Thomson and Tait reads in full as follows:

"We cannot, of course, give a definition of *Matter* which will satisfy the metaphysician, but the naturalist may be content to know matter as *that which can be perceived by the senses,* or as *that which can be acted upon by, and can exert, force.* The latter, and indeed the former also, of these definitions involves the idea of *Force,* which, in point of fact, is a direct object of sense; probably of all our senses, and certainly of the 'muscular sense.' To our chapter on Properties of Matter we must refer for further discussion of the question, *What is matter?* And we shall then be in a position to discuss the question of the subjectivity of *Force.*"[5]

---

[4] S. P. Thompson, *The Life of William Thomson,* ii, 1910, 1016 f.

[5] W. Thomson and P. G. Tait, *Treatise on Natural Philosophy,* I, i, 1879, 219 f. The chapter on Properties of Matter was never written;

It is plain that the italicised formulas are not adequate definitions, but only what Mill calls accidental definitions, of the kind common in scientific enquiry. It is also plain, however, that they break, severally or together, practically all the cardinal rules of the logic of definition. Both alike are open to the charge of defining *ignotum per ignotius*; the first carries a denotation which is far wider than the species to be defined; and the second involves a circle. There is no need to go deeper, and to consider the terms in detail; these defects, which appear as soon as the definitions are read, are as fatal as they are obvious.[6]

Here, then, is some very poor logic; and the student of psychology will wonder how writers of the eminence of Thomson and Tait could have been content to let it pass. It may perhaps occur to him, as he casts about for an excuse, that the formulas were retained out of piety to the Newtonian tradition. Newton, in so far as he discusses matter at all, makes it the object of sensory perception; and Cotes, in his preface to the second edition of the *Principia*, virtually introduces a definition of matter in terms of force as an inference from Newton's work. Thomson and Tait might, therefore, with full knowledge of what they were about, have been pouring their own new wine into the Newtonian

---

but, regrettable as its loss is, we have no ground for supposing that it would have contained either a formal definition or a differential characterisation of matter.

[6] J. S. Mill, *Logic,* bk. i, ch. viii ; W. S. Jevons, *Elementary Lessons in Logic,* 1885, 109 f.; P. G. Tait, *Lectures on Some Recent Advances in Physical Science,* 1876, 16 f., 346 f.

bottles.[7] That is a possible explanation. Or again, the
definitions may reflect Kelvin's predilection for mechanical models, for structures seen and forces felt: "I
never satisfy myself," he said, "until I can make a
mechanical model of a thing." [8] That is another possible explanation. Or it may be yet again that the authors, desiring to emphasise the importance of observation, shoot beyond their mark, and identify the
subject-matter of physics with the everyday experiences
that common-sense takes to be directly observable.[9]
Such considerations, however, while they may perhaps
account for the terms in which the definitions are
couched, do not excuse the lack of logic. No excuse
can, in fact, be found; and none, the writers would
urge, is needed. "What we want," remarks Tait in a
like context, "is merely a definition which, while not
at least *obviously* incorrect, shall for the time serve as
a working hypothesis." [10] The definitions of the *Treatise* are, to be sure, obviously incorrect; but they serve,
nevertheless, to get the chapter started.[11] Nothing

---

[7] I. Newton, *The Mathematical Principles of Natural Philosophy,*
ii, 1819, 161; R. Cotes, *ibid.,* i, 1819, xiv ff.; Thomson and Tait,
op. cit., vi ; E. Mach, *The Science of Mechanics,* 1893, 245.

[8] S. P. Thompson, *op. cit.,* ii, 830, 835, etc.; H. Poincaré, *The
Foundations of Science,* 1913, 6, etc.

[9] P. G. Tait, *Lectures,* etc., 6. For Kelvin, see p. 50, note 24,
above.

[10] P. G. Tait, *Properties of Matter,* 1885, 14.

[11] Another illustration is afforded by Kelvin's address on "The
Six Gateways of Knowledge" (1883), published in *Popular Lectures
and Addresses,* i, 1889, 253 ff. The whole atmosphere of this address,
so to say, is physical: so much so that the author's endeavour to
relate sense to force results in sheer paralogism. Odious as comparisons between great men are, it is impossible not to contrast Kelvin's attitude with that of Darwin.

further is required by a science whose self-sufficiency makes it indifferent to external criticism.

§ 3. Our second illustration is taken from biology. In the *Introduction to Science* from which we have quoted in the preceding Chapter, the biologist J. A. Thomson expressly denies that a science may be defined by its subject-matter. "What defines a science," he declares, "is not its subject-matter, but its point of view—the particular kind of question it asks. The lark singing at heaven's gate is a fact of experience which may be studied physically, biologically, and psychologically, but a complete answer to the questions asked by Physics would not answer those asked by Biology, still less those asked by Psychology." [12] We might therefore expect that, in seeking to define his own science of biology, Thomson would lay stress rather upon point of view, the kind of question asked, than upon subject-matter, the existential reply to the questions.

We find, on the contrary, that throughout Thomson's writings the 'living organism' figures very much as does the lark in the above quotation. We may contemplate the living organism in general, as we may contemplate the lark in particular, from various points of view. If, for example, we consider it from the chemist's standpoint, we discover proteids and other highly complex substances in coöperative interaction. If we look at it from the standpoint of the physicist, we see a highly efficient engine, a machine adapted to transform matter and energy. If, finally, we regard it from

---

[12] *Op. cit.,* 54 f.

the point of view of the biologist, we note growth and cyclical development and effective response and unified behaviour.[13] So Thomson teaches; and we need not raise here any objection to his teaching;[14] only we observe that all these statements contain nothing more than answers to questions already asked by chemist, physicist and biologist. The living organism is taken for granted, as a 'fact' of everyday experience; and the various sciences are supposed to recognise it, to put questions to it, and to record the answers which it returns. What, then, are the questions? The first problem, the problem of the *Introduction to Science,* is surely to determine the 'kind' of question which, addressed to the existential universe, reveals and sets apart the living organism; in other words, to characterise the point of view from which the living organism, as the specific subject-matter of biology, may be described. This fundamental problem, urged with insistence in the elementary work, drops out of sight in the author's larger treatises.[15]

Our expectation is thus disappointed; we must be content to trace the reasons for our disappointment. The search leads us to the well-known article on Biology written by Huxley for the *Britannica.* Huxley, it will be remembered, lays it down that both the biolog-

---

[13] J. A. Thomson, *The Bible of Nature,* 1908, 97 ff.

[14] Except to remark that an 'engine' or a 'machine' belongs to a technological, not to a scientific context! This point is, indeed, virtually acknowledged by Thomson himself: *op. cit.,* 101.

[15] Thus, in *The Science of Life,* 1899, to which reference is made in *The Bible of Nature,* the questions instanced as characteristic of "the modern biological attitude" are all intra-biological questions, directed upon an already 'given' organism.

ical and the physical sciences have to do with matter, biology with living matter, physics and chemistry with not-living matter. The distinctive properties of living matter he finds to be three: chemical composition (protein), disintegration and concomitant reintegration (phenomena of growth), and a tendency to undergo cyclical changes, to which he adds, as further peculiarities, dependence upon moisture and heat, and a certain structure or organisation.[16] There can be no doubt that this list was present to Thomson's mind when he described the living organism from the different standpoints of physics, chemistry and biology; and there can be no doubt that, in redistributing the properties of the organism to the separate sciences, he meant to disclaim and to correct Huxley's mechanistic view. He is resolute to maintain the independence of biology. Instead, however, of showing that biology occupies a point of view distinct from those of physics and chemistry— the point of view, namely, from which alone the living organism can be seen—he is satisfied, when he comes to close quarters with his opponents, to argue upon their logical level, and to show simply that the organism is a different thing for the three sciences: in particular, is something which "in its essential features transcends mechanical description." The general discussion, which we had a certain right to expect, is thus lost in a phase of the controversy between vitalism and mechanism.

---

[16] *Encyclopaedia Britannica,* iii, 1875, 679 f.; iii, 1910, 954 f. "A mass of living protoplasm," says Huxley, "is simply a molecular machine of great complexity."

While, however, we lose the hoped-for characterisation of biology by point of view, we get in exchange its characterisation by subject-matter. The list of attributes, which we just now accepted without comment, is evidently offered as a definition in Mill's sense. But here too, if we look a little closely, the author's logic appears to have been adapted to his controversial purpose; the four attributes are distinguished for illustrative contrast with physics and chemistry as well as for their biological adequacy; the definition enters a plea for the independence of biology at the same time that it declares the connotation of the name 'organism.' [17] We gain, nevertheless, a respectable working formula. The author, in dealing with his subject-matter, displays a serious concern such as we miss entirely in Thomson and Tait.

§ 4. These two cases are to serve us, each in its way, as warning examples; it is beside our purpose to enquire how far they may be regarded as typical of physical and biological procedure. We have, indeed, used them only to set the stage for psychology, which naturally plays the leading part in the following discussion.

Psychology, we shall find, has a good deal to say, both on point of view and on subject-matter. The psychologist cannot at all affect the careless serenity of his colleague of physics. Nor does he, on the other hand, share the hope or fear of the biologist that his science will someday be absorbed by physics; the independent growth of modern physics has implied and guaranteed the independence of psychology. His aim and desire

---

[17] Cf. *The Bible of Nature,* 103, 106 ff.

are rather to legitimate the place of psychology among
the sciences, to prove that in its position of independence it carries itself in all respects as a science. He is,
as we have put it, self-consciously scientific, and he
shows the self-consciousness in his books. Hence it
comes about that Wundt, for instance, writes again
and again, constructively and polemically, upon the
question of definition, recognising the danger that lurks
in formulas, but deliberately preferring it to the risks
that psychology must run if exposed, without guidance,
to the manifold non-scientific influence of its own past
and of the philosophical present. Wundt has every
claim to a respectful hearing; and we may therefore
begin by setting forth the conclusions that he has
reached.[18]

Through all his changes of opinion on minor issues,
Wundt has steadily maintained that psychology is dis-

---

[18] These conclusions are set forth in various books and essays: it is
important to observe dates, and to consult the last editions. Cf., in
the first place, *Physiol. Psychologie,* iii, 1903, 677 ff., esp. 761 ff.
This section, reprinted practically without change in iii., 1911, 655
ff., is also published separately under the title *Naturwissenschaft und
Psychologie.* With it may be read E. Meumann's *Besprechung* in
Arch. f. d. g. Psych., ii, 1904, *Literaturber.,* 21 ff, and Wundt's
article *Ueber empirische und metaphysische Psychologie, ibid.,* 333 ff.
Cf., further, *System der Philosophie,* i, 1907, esp. 76 ff., 138 ff., 155
ff.; and *Logik,* i, 1906, 408 ff., 448 ff.; ii, 1907, 89 ff.; iii, 1908, 243
ff., 260 ff. Cf., lastly, the two essays *Ueber naiven und kritischen
Realismus* and *Die Definition der Psychologie,* in *Kleine Schriften,*
i, 1910, 259 ff.; ii, 1911, 113 ff. (originally published in *Philos.
Studien,* xii, 1896, 307 ff., and 1895, 1 ff.).—For a critical study of the
System (first edition), cf. J. Volkelt, *Wilhelm Wundt's "System der
Philosophie,"* in *Philos. Monatshefte,* xxvii, 1891, 257 ff., 409 ff., 527
ff. Clear statements of Wundt's views are given by H. Lachelier, *La
métaphysique de Wundt,* in *Rev. philos.,* xxix, 1890, 449 ff., 580 ff.;
E. König, *W. Wundt: seine Philosophie und Psychologie,* 1901, 50 ff.;
R. Eisler, *W. Wundts Philosophie und Psychologie,* 1902, 29 ff., 84 ff.

tinguished from natural science, not by a peculiar subject-matter, but by a determinate point of view. In
order to characterise this point of view, he takes us
back, in the history of man's intellectual development,
to a naïve, non-reflective stage of immediate experience. The primary *datum,* the original content of
knowledge he terms the *Vorstellungsobjekt.* Not only
the members of this compound word, but also the manner of their combination must be noted. The *Vorstellungsobjekt* is wholly and solely 'object'; there is in it
no trace of reference to a subject. It is, however, an
object of a certain kind: namely, an object 'of perception' or, in Wundt's generalised terminology, an object
'of idea.' It is, in other words, an object equipped with
all the attributes that belong to the idea. Our ideas,
at this primitive stage, are in fact themselves the
objects. The character of objective reality is not superadded upon an originally subjective idea, but is intrinsic, present from the very first, so that it can be sepa-
rated out only by a later process of logical abstraction.

In course of time, and at the hest of motives inher-
ent in experience, motives which Wundt traces and
evaluates in detail, naïve gives way to reflective knowledge. Subject and object are now discriminative, and
the 'object of idea' appears accordingly as a content of
experience which is at the same time both objective and
subjective. Henceforth, then, two standpoints are possible to the investigator: he may view the 'objects of
idea' as objects which stand over against the subject in
independent reality; or he may view them as ideas, as
a particular kind of subjective experience. The necessity of a division of scientific labour assigns these

standpoints to separate sciences; the one is occupied by
natural science, the other by psychology.

Natural science, in limiting itself to the study of
objects, abstracts from whatever is subjective; its
standpoint is so chosen that the subject, with all that
belongs to the subject, is eliminated from the prospect.
This position, as the history of science shows, was not
established all in a moment. It has been established,
however, by the authority of natural science itself,
through application of the 'law of sufficient reason.'
For this law, in the negative form in which it is commonly employed by science, provides that everything
may be rejected as subjective which brings inconsistency
or contradiction into the scientific rendering of the
phenomena of objective nature. Natural science has
accordingly continued its rejections until, in the last
resort, it is confined to a world of occurrences in space
and time, "a multitude of various motions and their
interrelations." Such a world, constituted as it is, not
of the whole of empirical reality, but only of reality
as it appears after the fundamental abstraction from
the subject has been made, cannot be known directly,
immediately; it must be constructed conceptually. The
'objects' of natural science are therefore conceptual,
and not immediately empirical.

It might be thought, now, that psychology, the complement of natural science, performs a like abstraction
and thus acquires the same conceptual character. That,
however, is not the case. Psychology, it is true, regards
the 'objects of idea' as ideas, as a particular kind of
subjective experience. But it must be remembered
that, in the stage of knowledge before reflection, our

ideas are the objects. The 'ideas' which the standpoint of psychology reveals are therefore not only 'intellectual processes' but are also the 'objects' to which these processes refer, given in the form in which all objects are primitively given in experience. In other words, the ideas are those particular subjective experiences in which we set objects over against us as 'contents' of the subject's 'perception.' So far, then, psychology differs from natural science in that it deals with experience whole and deals with it directly.

There is still a further difference: for the range of psychology is also wider, its outlook more extensive. Natural science is limited to the objective aspect of the 'object of idea.' But the 'object of idea' is the primary datum of knowledge, not of immediate experience at large. Feeling and emotion and desire and volition combine with the 'object of idea' to make up immediate experience: or rather, the original unity of immediate experience may be analysed, by logical abstraction, into these various components. Psychology, at any rate, deals with feeling and will as well as with ideas. Hence it not only sees experience whole but it sees also the whole of experience, and its knowledge throughout is not conceptual but immediately empirical.

We may therefore say, in brief, that natural science, considering in abstraction certain aspects of the 'object of idea,' works up 'external' experience with a view to a consistent system of objective, mediate or conceptual knowledge; and that psychology, taking up a position which embraces all the given aspects of the 'object of idea,' as well as kindred phases of immediate experience, works up the total contents of external and of internal perception with a view to a consistent system of subjective, immediate or 'perceptive' knowledge. The original subject-matter is the same: but the attitude of natural science necessitates an abstraction which the attitude of psychology avoids.

For the sake of the scientific reader, who is unaccustomed to philosophical terminology, Wundt adds a remark which we shall, perhaps, do well to repeat. He reminds us that the 'subject' which is discriminated from the 'object,' and from which abstraction is made by natural science, is the psychological subject, and not the 'knowing subject' of a theory of knowledge. The 'knower' is presupposed by psychology and natural science alike.

§ 5. Psychology, in Wundt's scheme of classification, remains in principle an unitary science. Experimental psychology passes, without break, into the psychology of the "products of the collective life of mind" (*Völkerpsychologie*); there is no shift of standpoint. Natural science, on the other hand, divides into three coördinate sciences, "whose contents are determined by the different points of view" from which the material universe is surveyed. Physics deals with the general or universal properties of matter. Chemistry deals with its special properties, the properties that constrain us to assume specific differences in the material substrate of natural phenomena. Biology applies the principles of physics and chemistry to 'organisms,' that is, to certain material aggregates, of natural origin, whose teleological constitution suggests the analogy of the 'machine.' The standpoint of biology is therefore the standpoint of finality or teleology.

This statement, however, does not at all mean that biology has recourse to what are ordinarily known as 'final causes.' The word 'purpose' (*Zweck*) bears, in Wundt's system, a peculiar meaning: it is the inversion, the antithetical correlate, of 'cause.' Causation is progressive and unequivocal; we speak of cause and effect, therefore, when we proceed from definite antecedent to definite consequent. Teleology is regressive and equivocal; and we therefore speak of means and end when we look back from a definite consequent to a number of possible antecedents. Suppose, for instance —the illustration is Wundt's own—that we set out from any one of the following sets of premises:

$$a < b \qquad a = b \qquad a < b$$
$$b < c \qquad b < c \qquad b = c$$

in which the symbol $<$ expresses complete logical subsumption: we can then argue forwards, unequivocally, to the conclusion $a < c$. Suppose, contrariwise, that we set out from a conclusion $a < c$: if we then attempt to argue backwards to the premises, we are faced by the three possibilities set forth in the table; the regressive problem can be solved only equivocally. The difference between these modes of inference is precisely that of causal and teleological procedure in natural science.

No one of the three natural sciences, Wundt tells us, is in its logical framework wholly causal or wholly teleological; the great physical law of the conservation of energy is, for example, in the sense above given, a teleological principle. The ideal of natural science is, no doubt, the establishment of unequivocal causal relations among its phenomena. Meanwhile teleology, the complement of causation, is not only theoretically justified but also practically useful; it serves us in countless cases in which our ignorance of conditions forbids a recourse to cause and effect. Since biology, for all the promise of Mendelism and of developmental mechanics, is still unable to trace the physical and chemical conditions of vital phenomena—to reduce the facts of reproduction and of evolution to causal terms —it must perforce content itself with the looser principle, and adopt the standpoint of finality.

This standpoint, we may repeat, does not mean the introduction into natural science of what are called 'final causes.' Wundt illustrates his position by the extreme case of voluntary action, where the causal series is 'psychophysical,' beginning with a motivating idea and ending with a physical mass-movement. Even here, he insists, the initial idea is not a 'final cause' in any strict sense, but merely the empirical starting-point of our analysis, recognised provisionally as a cause among other causes, and accepted provisionally as a substitute for the physiological processes that our present methods cannot reach. Within the given science, teleology is never anything more than a regressive and equivocal causation. Only when we stand outside, and ask how this teleological organisation as a whole has come into being, does the question of final causes, of the creative influence of will, legitimately arise.[19]

---

[19] See esp. *Logik,* ii, 1907, 276 f.; *System,* i, 1907, 306 ff.; *Phys. Psychol.,* iii, 1911, 662 ff., 702 ff., 721 ff.

§ 6. Wundt thus appeals to point of view for the distinction, first, of psychology from natural science and, secondly, of the three major natural sciences from one another. The main distinction, of psychology from natural science, rests upon an elaborately wrought theory of knowledge. It lays claim also to empirical validity, as justified by the history of science and as adequate to its present status. In Wundt's own thinking, the logical and empirical motives are everywhere interwoven. We, however, who occupy the middle ground between science and philosophy proper, have no direct interest in a theory of knowledge. We have to decide only whether the resulting definitions of psychology and of natural science are consistent with the general idea of science and characteristic of these two great branches of scientific activity. We may then, in the light of this decision, go on to consider Wundt's secondary distinction of the three natural sciences.

(1) It seems at first sight that with psychology, at all events, everything is in order. Psychology is an independent science, characterised by a determinate point of view, from which it looks out over the whole domain of immediate experience. The existential nature of its subject-matter frees it, on the one hand, from the bugbear of 'objective reference.' Wundt had written in 1874 that "the relating of the idea to an object is only a secondary act," [20] and he now makes it clear that the act in question belongs not to psy-

---

chology but to logic.[21] In the stage of knowledge before reflection, and in our own everyday experience, so far as this has not been contaminated by the products of reflection, our ideas are the objects. In psychology, which is the science of immediate experience, they necessarily retain this objective character; they are not 'images' or 'symbols' of objects, but are themselves "taken as objects (*Gegenstände*) with objectively given properties"; they represent the 'objective' factors in the constitution of the psychological subject.[22] The 'subjective' factors, the emotive processes (*Gemütsbewegungen*), are taken in the same existential way, so that psychology is freed, secondly, from any concern about 'judgments of value.' It is true that these judgments have their growth in psychological soil, and that feeling is the basis of value.[23] Psychology, nevertheless, considers the emotive processes precisely as it considers the ideas: it analyses them, makes out their modes of interconnection, and traces the course of their development: the judgments of value, in which our reflection upon them finds various expression, it leaves to be systematised by the 'mental sciences' (*Geisteswissenschaften*).[24] So far, then, everything seems to be in order.

(2) When, however, we examine the alleged rela-

---

[21] *Ibid.,* i, 1908, 405; ii, 1910, 385. Wundt appears to speak throughout of 'reference to object,' not in the sense of immanent objectivity, but in that of our ascription of (psychological) idea to (physical) object as its cause or condition.

[22] *Ibid.,* ii, 1910, 385.

[23] *Ibid.,* iii, 1911, 732 f.; *System,* i, 1907, 122 f.

[24] *Phys. Psychol.,* iii, 1911, 497; *Logik,* iii, 1908, 114 f.

tion of psychology to natural science, Wundt's position is less satisfactory. It shows us a psychology more naïve than psychology actually is, and a natural science more sophisticated than natural science, at all events, has actually been. Natural science, it will be remembered, abstracts from everything that belongs to the subject, and is left in the last resort with space and time. But space and time themselves, in so far as they are 'perceptive' (*anschaulich*), belong to the psychological subject; the space and time of natural science, no less than the contents of these forms, must therefore be conceptual; and it follows that the 'external' experience of which Wundt speaks is not experience at all, but wholly a construction of our understanding.[25] The difficulties of such a view are obvious. For even if we grant that natural science at the present day is through and through conceptual, we must still recognise that it has only very gradually eliminated experience, that the concepts which it employs are meant to replace experience, and that its constructions are constantly put again to the test of experience. Wundt fails to account for all this give-and-take.[26] He admits, to be sure, the empirical principle of a division of scientific labour; but what is it, then, that he supposes to be divided? Psychology takes

---

[25] This seems to be clear from *System,* i , 1907, 137, although two references to 'material and form of perception' have been deleted from *System,* 1889, 152. Cf. *Phys. Psychol.,* iii , 1911, 701, 743.

[26] Wundt would reply, of course, that our ideas are 'symbols' of external, physical occurrence; cf., *e.g., System,* i , 1907, 137. The point of the objection is, however, that the 'fundamental abstraction' from immediate experience is too radical to permit of this relation.

all of the immediate experience that there is; and
natural science, in obedience to epistemological motives, is obliged to turn directly away from experience
and to fashion a thought-world of its own.

If natural science thus appears to lose its foundation in experience, psychology, in its turn, appears from
Wundt's definition to make a far smaller demand upon
the understanding than its history proves to have
been the case. We saw that the psychologist, like the
student of natural science, must work up his subject-
matter into a consistent system of knowledge. But the
task is simple: for immediate experience, by the fact
of its immediacy, is already consistent when the psychologist comes to it, and has no need of the logical
control and logical transformation that are required
by natural science. If analysis falls short or goes astray,
and if relations and connections are imperfectly or
wrongly apprehended, psychology still supplies its own
corrective in the given coherence and persistence of its
subject-matter.[27] Hence, whatever difficulties may arise
in detail, the task which Wundt assigns to the systematic psychologist is logically simple; conceptual reconstruction has no part in it.

The reader will probably agree that Wundt asks
us, in this argument, to purchase the independence of
psychology at too high a price. Is not the doctrine of
apperception, we may ask, a conceptual construction?
Or, if the *argumentum ad hominem* is not permissible,
does not history, whose jurisdiction is expressly acknowledged by Wundt himself, bear constant witness

---

[27] *Logik*, i, 1906, 421 f.; *System*, i, 1907, 127 ff., 138 ff.

to the conceptual elaboration of psychology? We have spoken of the 'psychological subject': and we all know that the meaning of this term has changed again and again in the history of psychology; that the 'substantial' subject, driven from one place of refuge to another, has now disappeared entirely from scientific exposition; and that the modern psychologist, if he uses the term 'subject' at all, uses it as a shorthand name for a group of phenomena which, in point of fact, are just as objective as the phenomena of natural science. The 'psychological subject,' then, is by all indications a conceptual construction.[28] Its various meanings correspond with necessary stages in the development of a system of psychology; and while the word has largely passed out of use, that is not because conceptual thinking has been proved superfluous, but rather because our concepts have changed. The psychological doctrine of visual perception is surely conceptual in the same way, if not to the same degree, as the physical doctrine of light. Wundt, who is both temperamentally and intellectually averse from a 'psychology of reflection,' and whose greatest service to psychology is his perpetual insistence upon direct observation, has here drawn his bow too strongly. Taught by his own experience and by the history of human thought that concepts are bad masters, he will not allow psychology to employ them as servants.

---

[28] Wundt would reply, again, that psychologists have here shown a regrettable tendency to confuse the standpoints of natural science and of psychology: cf., *e.g., Logik*, iii, 1908, 246 f., 262. Even so, however, the confusion was the result of a felt need for conceptual construction. And what of the theory of actuality itself?

(3) We turn, finally, to the characterisation of the three natural sciences. Since we have ourselves made physics, biology, and psychology typical or representative sciences, we are naturally interested in Wundt's account of the point of view of biology. And it is disappointing to find that the phrase 'point of view' is used in two senses. Physics contemplates the universal, chemistry the specific, in nature: these are two points of view from which material phenomena may be scientifically regarded. Biology, so far, is simply a 'sphere of application' of physics and chemistry, without standpoint of its own. But biology, we are told, also contemplates natural phenomena, in its personal behalf, from the point of view of teleology,[29] This, however, cannot possibly be a third point of view, coördinate with those already assigned to physics and chemistry. The antithetical correlate of teleology, in the Wundtian logic, is causation; teleology is, as we have seen, simply a regressive causation, to which our ignorance compels us when phenomena are complicated and their relations equivocal. If, then, biology is to be marked off from physics and chemistry as teleological, it would seem to follow that these sciences are causal, and that the points of view of 'universal' and 'specific' are sub-headings under the general heading of causation. Wundt, however, acknowledges that physics and chemistry are themselves in part teleological: the whole doctrine of energy, for example, is of that character; and he further assures us that the phenomena of biology not only have their analogues in in-

---

[29] *Logik,* ii , 1907, 276 f.

animate nature but are also, in part, within measurable distance of causal explanation.[30] Again, then, biology is left without a standpoint of its own. It is not an independent science, but a special branch of physics and chemistry whose phenomena, owing to their complexity, must in large measure be systematised provisionally in terms of means and end, and whose causes, for the same reason, must in some cases be taken over bodily from psychology.

If we would understand how Wundt can be content with so lame a conclusion, or rather how he can fail to see that, from the scientific standpoint, his conclusion is, in fact, lame and impotent, we must pay regard to the whole tenor of his discussion. Wundt's interest in biology is, it would appear, less scientific than philosophical. He regards it as less important to distinguish biology from physics and chemistry than to show that the organism furnishes the connecting link between philosophy of mind and philosophy of nature.[31] The connection hinges on the idea of 'evolution.' Since evolution implies progress or improvement (*Vervollkommnung*), it applies primarily to the domain of mind, which is the domain of true final causes. If, then, we must have recourse to this same idea of evolution for the understanding of organic nature, it follows that the forms of life are at once the expressions of complex natural causation and the effects of 'mental forces' (*geistige Kräfte*).[32] Hence, while Wundt is

---

[30] *Phys. Psychol.*, iii , 1911, 665, 691; 702 ff., esp. 717 f.

[31] *System*, ii , 1907, 135.

[32] *Ibid.*, 147; *Phys. Psychol.*, iii , 1911, 733.

an uncompromising opponent of vitalism within biology, he secures all the advantages of vitalism by posit-
ing a psychological teleology at work, as it were, behind or beneath biology. The independence of biology
is thus secured, not scientifically but philosophically:
secured, however, in a way which accounts for Wundt's
characterisation of its 'point of view,' in a scientific
context, as teleological.

The foregoing criticism may be summed up in the
remark, which could otherwise be abundantly sup-
ported, that Wundt's whole thought centres about psychology and that he therefore sees the other sciences
always in their relation to psychology. To say this is
not at all to charge him with psychologism; it is to say,
simply, that he is psychologist in grain, and that psychology is therefore the focus upon which all the lines
of his thought converge. The case is unique: there is
nothing like it in the 'history of philosophy': and
the resulting advantage to psychology itself is greater
than the present generation can assess. Every quality,
however, has its defects. For the matter in hand we receive less help from Wundt than we shall get from a
philosopher who views the sciences, truly without
Wundt's range of knowledge, but also without his
psychological preoccupation.

§ 7. Avenarius was not a man of science. He was
neither a psychologist nor, in any scientific sense of
the word, a biologist; he was essentially a philosopher.
But he stood, as philosopher, in a twofold relation to
science. He accepted, on the one hand, the systematic
work of natural science; he approached his philosophical task as if it were a comprehensive problem in

natural science; his theory of knowledge is a 'biological' or 'biomechanical' theory. He aimed, on the other hand, not only to establish a general *Wissenschaftslehre,* but also to lay the foundation in particular for psychology and for what are called the 'mental' sciences. He is thus recommended to us both by his scientific attitude and by his psychological interest; and his substantial agreement with Mach, an independent thinker who was experimental psychologist as well as experimental physicist, adds force to the recommendation.

Avenarius, like Wundt, comes to his definition of psychology by way of a theory of knowledge. There is, however, a difference, which we may roughly express by saying that Wundt's definition is grounded in, while Avenarius' is grounded on, its author's philosophy. Wundt, we remember, had achieved competence in physiology and psychology before he wrote his *Logic* and his *System of Philosophy.* His thought is saturated with science—with fact and theory, history and method, law and experiment; he moves slowly and cautiously from special science to philosophy; and when he attains a theory of knowledge, it is dyed through and through with the colour of science. Avenarius, on the contrary, began his series of publications with a study of Spinoza; and then, turning away from historical enquiry to constructive philosophising, issued in turn the *Prolegomena* to his principal work and, after an interval of some ten years, that work itself, the well-known *Kritik der reinen Erfahrung.* Not until he has supplemented criticism by system, and supplied form with content—not, in other words, till

he has written *Der menschliche Weltbegriff*—does he
proceed to his definition of psychology. The psychological discussion appears, therefore, as a sort of appendix
to Avenarius' philosophy. In all respects, in trend and
method and outcome, it is, as we have said, grounded
on the *Kritik*; but it is an addition, and may be detached, with the happy result that we may consider
Avenarius' views on the interrelation of the sciences
without setting forth his theory of knowledge.[33]

Psychology, says Avenarius, has no separate subject-
matter. There is nothing empirical, as there is also
nothing metaphysical, to which the adjective 'psychical' may legitimately be applied; nor can we create a
'psychical' subject-matter by means of an inner sense
or a specific method of introspection.[34] Yet there is an
empirical science of psychology, and we may rightly
speak of 'psychological' facts and laws. The science
is, indeed, as wide as experience itself; its subject-matter is the whole of experience, regarded from a certain
point of view; psychology embraces all experience, *die
Erfahrung überhaupt*, in so far as experience is regarded as dependent upon the individual.[35]

---

[33] Readers who may be repelled by Avenarius' terminology will
find a conspectus of his work in F. Raab, *Die Philosophie von Richard
Avenarius: systematische Darstellung und immanente Kritik*, 1912.
This author gives references both to Avenarius' writings and to the
principal criticisms and commentaries.

[34] So I interpret the word *Betrachtungsweise* in Bemerkungen zum
Begriff des Gegenstandes der Psychologie, iii, *Vjs. f. wiss. Philos.*,
xix, 1895, 15.

[35] Bemerkungen, etc., iii, *Vjs.*, xix, 1895, 15 f.; Bemerkungen, etc.,
ii, *Vjs.*, xviii, 1894, 417: "Gegenstand der empirischen Psychologie ist
jede Erfahrung sofern sie in dem Sinne, in welchem sie eine Erfahrung ist, *als abhängig von dem Individuum*, in Bezug auf welches
sie in diesem Sinne eine Erfahrung ist, aufgefasst wird."

This is Avenarius' definition of psychology; and all
its three terms—experience, dependent, individual—
need a word of comment. By 'experience' Avenarius
means literally everything that is 'given,' *vorgefun-
den,* whether it be 'thing' or whether it be 'thought':
each and every datum of the universe, taken in the
precise sense in which it comes to us as datum. The
one and only condition which must be fulfilled, if a
particular object is to be amenable to scientific treatment, is that it be thus empirically given. By 'dependent,' in the second place, Avenarius means 'logically' or 'functionally' dependent: dependent in such
wise that, if the first term of the functional relation
(*i.e.,* the individual) varies, then the second term
varies also. The logical priority of the 'individual,'
as the independent variable of the correlation, is in-
herent in the presuppositions of the empiriocritical
philosophy. For Avenarius sets out, thirdly, from a
'human individual' placed amid partially independent
surroundings, upon which he himself, with all his
thoughts and feelings is dependent; and these surroundings include other human individuals, whose situation
is in principle the same as his own. Experience is therefore, in the first analysis, dependent upon the individual's 'surroundings.' But it is easy to show that
this dependence is not immediate: for a tonal stimulus, *e.g.,* is not registered in experience unless the
auditory nerve and its attachments are intact. It appears accordingly that, in the matter of experience,
the 'human individual' does not stand opposed to
environment, but is in some sense a constituent of
those very 'surroundings' upon which experience is

conditioned, nay more, is in this same sense the direct or immediate condition of experience.[36] The sense is, in the large, biological; in particular, neurological. Avenarius thus finds himself able to substitute for 'the individual' the concept of 'the system C,' as that environmental system upon which experience is directly or immediately dependent. And psychology may now be redefined as the science of experience as a whole, considered as dependent variable of the system C.[37]

There has been much debate whether this system C is the actual, physiological brain, a part of the central nervous system known to anatomists and physiologists. Such debate is really needless; for the meaning of the phrase varies with the context in which it occurs. In philosophical regard, the system C is not the physiological brain; it is, so to say, a logical or functional brain, without spatial configuration or limitation. In the special sciences, it is what these sciences make it out to be; and for the purposes of psychology it is, undoubtedly, the physiological brain—or rather that organ or centre or partial system of the brain which constitutes, in Fechner's terminology, the *locus* of psychophysical processes.[38] Using this language, then, we may say finally that psychology is the science of ex-

---

[36] *Kritik der reinen Erfahrung*, i, 1888, 33. I have spoken here of 'experience' when I should have spoken of *E-Werte;* but see *Vjs.,* xix, 16.

[37] Bemerkungen, etc., ii, *Vjs.,* xviii, 1894, 418: "Gegenstand der Psychologie ist die Erfahrung überhaupt als Abhängige des Systems C."

[38] *Kritik,* i, 35 f.; *Vjs.,* xviii, 418; G. T. Fechner, *Elemente der Psychophysik,* i, 1860, 10.

perience at large, as dependent variable of the psychophysical brain-centres.

Again: just as there is no special class of objects
that we may call psychical (*psychisch*), so also there is
none, for Avenarius, that we may call physical (*phy-
sisch*). Natural science, like psychology, views the
whole of experience from a particular standpoint.
Whenever we consider an item of experience as dependent, not upon the system *C,* but upon something
else—the dependence in question falling under the law
of the conservation of energy—we are dealing with it
as an item of natural science (*physikalisches Objekt*).[39]
More than this Avenarius does not say; and his in-
terpreters merely paraphrase his statement. "If," remarks Wlassak, "I seek to discover the dependence of
a certain environmental constituent *A* upon another
environmental constituent *B,* I am working in physics
[in the widest sense of that term]; if I seek to discover
in how far *A* is changed by a change of the sense-or-
gans or the central nervous system of a living creature,
I am working in psychology." [40] Since there can be no
doubt that Avenarius, in defining psychology, meant to
mark off this empirical science from the other empirical sciences, as well as from philosophy, we must suppose that he looked upon the complementary definition
of natural science as self-evident.

---

[39] Bemerkungen, etc., iii, *Vjs.,* xix, 16 ff. Avenarius distinguishes
three special forms of 'logical dependence': the mathematical (the
relation, *e.g.,* of logarithms to their natural numbers), the physical
(in the sense of *physikalisch, i.e.,* of transformations of energy), and
the psychological.

[40] R. Wlassak, in E. Mach, *Die Analyse der Empfindungen,* etc.,
1900, 38; 1902, 40.

We find nothing in Avenarius' writings concerning
the relation of physics (in the narrower sense) to
biology. His own biology, which has been variously
interpreted, appears to rest upon two rather common-
place principles: that the effective functioning of a system *C* depends on a certain balance between stimula-
tion and nutrition, and that the viable systems, which
have maintained themselves in the struggle for existence, are the vehicles of organic and mental evolution.
There can be no doubt that his sympathies were with
'mechanism' and against 'vitalism.'

§ 8. We may prepare the ground for a critical examination of Avenarius' position by a brief statement
of related views. For while Wundt, with his doctrine
of mediate and immediate experience, stands practically alone, Avenarius' ideas regarding psychology and
its relation to natural science are, in their essential features, shared by various writers, of whom some reached
them independently, and others have derived them
from Avenarius himself or from Mach.

(1) Mach, with whom we naturally begin, is the
apostle of scientific unity.[41] He feels strongly that
physics and psychology must, and in some way can,
be reduced to a common denominator, so that the investigator may maintain his scientific attitude unchanged as he passes from the one science to the other.

---

[41] See esp. *Beiträge zur Analyse der Empfindungen*, 1886, 1 ff.; *Die
Analyse der Empfindungen und das Verhältniss des Physischen zum
Psychischen*, 1900, 1 ff., 28 ff., 35 ff.; *Erkenntnis und Irrtum*, 1906,
5 ff., etc. Külpe (*The Philosophy of the Present in Germany*, 1913,
52 ff.) is mistaken in his belief that the last-mentioned work con-
fesses to a change of view.

After long reflection he adopts the view that the whole world of experience, 'internal' and 'external' alike, is made up of a finite number of 'elements,' homogeneous throughout all the sciences. These elements he inclines to call 'sensations,' though he does not insist upon the term.[42] They are given to us in manifold connections, some transient, some more stable; and common sense, struck by the more stable connections, has been led to a belief in 'things' and 'bodies' and 'selves' as substantially different kinds of experience. If, however, we scrutinise these apparent units, closely and impartially, we discover that they have no substantiality and no fixed boundaries; they prove to be complexes of the indifferent elements, placed in diverse functional relations or relations of dependence. All scientific investigation bears, accordingly, upon the same subject-matter. The sciences are differentiated by point of view, by the direction which enquiry takes, and not by the material upon which it is directed. "A colour is a physical object, so soon as we are concerned to note its dependence, *e.g.*, upon the illuminating light-source (other colours, heats, spaces, etc.). But if we are concerned to note its dependence upon the retina,[43] then it is a psychological object, a sensation [in the narrower sense]." From this standpoint, the opposition between 'myself' and the 'outside world,' between sensation and thing, between psychical and physi-

---

[42] Avenarius had also spoken of 'sensations' in the *Prolegomena* (1876), though he dropped the term in his later works. It is to be remembered that Mach regards spaces and times as sensations.

[43] Mach speaks more or less indifferently in this connection of 'body,' 'nervous system,' and organ of sense.

cal,[44] simply disappears. The man of science runs no
risk of losing his bearings as he passes from physics to
psychology and back again; he merely shifts his attention from one set of functional relations to another.

It is needless to repeat that Mach stands very close
to Avenarius. From different starting-points and by
different roads the two thinkers have come to the same
conclusion.[45] Mach, however, now goes on to do what
Avenarius left undone: to discuss the relation of
physics to biology. In his mode of approach to this
topic he reminds us of Wundt.

To talk of general biology, Mach says, is to raise
the question of causation *versus* teleology. He has himself no objection to an empirical teleology; he has often

---

[44] Avenarius had remarked: "Ich kenne weder Physisches noch
Psychisches, sondern ein Drittes," which we might parody as: I
know neither physical nor psychical, but only a tertial (H. Höffding,
Moderne Philosophen, 1905, 121; *Modern Philosophers*, 1915, 135;
Mach, *Erkenntnis und Irrtum*, 13; R. Avenarius, *Vjs.*, xix , 1895, 15).
Many sentences of the *Analyse* read as if they were Avenarius' own.

[45] There is a difference: a difference which Wlassak remarks, Mach
questions, and Wlassak forgets again, all in three successive pages
of the *Analyse* (1900, 38 ff.). It lies in the fact that Avenarius'
E-Werte are always *Inhalte von Aussagen:* a behaviouristic consequence which follows inevitably, so long as theory of knowledge and
psychology are supposed to be woven of the same cloth, from the
elimination of introjection. Mach defines his own primary aim as
that of the elimination of extrajection (*op. cit.*, 42), and it is certain
that he is psychologically more conservative than Avenarius. Yet I
cannot help wondering (though this will be rank heresy in the eyes
of the empiriocriticists) whether Avenarius, with his 'absolute'
treatment of 'partial experiences,' has not himself drawn something like a line of division between theory of knowledge and special
science. I wonder, at any rate, if the empiriocriticists of the strait
sect, with the banishment of introjection made part of their creed,
were not a little surprised when they learned of the place assigned
to psychology in the *Bemerkungen*.

found teleological ideas useful in scientific enquiries. The idea of science is, nevertheless, a causal (or rather, in his own terminology, a functional) description of the world; teleological considerations are only temporary and provisional. Some day, we may hope, physics will be competent to deal with the organism. Meanwhile there are characters, like organic memory and organic association, that utterly resist the methods of physics. It is possible that the physiology of the senses, in which physics and psychology meet, will bring out a new order of facts, upon which a comprehensive science of the organic and the inorganic may be based.[46]

With this suggestion the discussion ends. Some such suggestion was, no doubt, the natural recourse;[47] Mach was baffled by the problem which he had honestly faced, and fell back upon his faith in the unity of science. In fact, however, his treatment of biology is altogether inconclusive. We are again reminded of Wundt.

(2) It is a far cry from Mach to Ward, from the man of science struggling toward a philosophy to the trained philosopher pouring out the vials of his contempt upon scientific construction. And it may, indeed, be questioned whether Ward's definition of psychology belongs to the present context, or whether it should be regarded as a third type of definition by point of view, coördinate with those of Avenarius and Wundt. On the whole, however, it seems that the definition as such, taken on the middle ground between theory of knowl-

---

[46] *Die Analyse,* etc., 1900, 60 f., 62 ff., 151 ff.

[47] Especially as it was an echo of earlier thinking: *op. cit.,* 73. Cf. also *Erkenntnis und Irrtum,* 1906, 14, 459 ff.

edge and special science, may properly find a place beside that of Mach.

Experience is the source of science. But experience, Ward points out, is used in a double sense. There is the experience of a given individual, and there is the common empirical knowledge of the race, the result of intersubjective intercourse. Experience in the first sense is usually assigned, as subjective, to psychology, and experience in the second sense, as objective, to natural science: so arises the dualism of mind and nature. Yet, as a matter of fact, our primary, concrete, individual experience always implies both subjective and objective factors, and implies them as organically coöperating members of a single whole. Moreover, experience in the other sense, common or collective or generalised or universal experience, has grown out of, is but an extension of, is of one piece with, individual experience. This common experience too, therefore, may be expected to show the duality of subject and object within the single organic unity. We find, accordingly, a transsubjective or universal object, which is only an elaboration of the sensory object; and we find, further, that this universal object is object for an universal subject, which is the subject of individual experience "advanced to the level of self-consciousness, and so participating in all that is communicable, that is, in all that is intelligible, in the experience of other self-conscious subjects. Universal experience is not distinct from all subjects, but common to all intelligents, peculiar to none." [48]

---

[48] J. Ward, *Naturalism and Agnosticism,* ii, 1903, 152 f., 184, 196 f., 282 f., 287 ff.

Psychology and natural science, since they both have to do with experience, have therefore to do, both alike, with subject and object within the unity of experience.[49] Psychology is "the science of individual experience." This does not mean that it is confined to a certain department of experience; "psychology . . . cannot be defined by reference to a special subject-matter"; but "deals in some sort with the whole of experience;" it "must therefore be characterised by the standpoint from which this experience is viewed." In other words, the 'science of individual experience' is the science of experience as viewed from the 'individualistic' standpoint. "By whatever methods, from whatever sources its facts are ascertained, they must—to have a psychological import—be regarded as having a place in, or as forming part of, *some one's consciousness or experience*." "In this sense, *i.e.*, as presented to an individual, 'the whole choir of heaven and furniture of earth' may belong to psychology, but otherwise they are psychological nonentities." This 'some one' or 'individual' is the psychological self, and not the biological individual or organism. The self or psychological subject apprehends and attends, likes and dislikes; and its attitude and activity are known by their effect upon the 'psychical objects,' that is to say, by the changes which they produce in the character and succession of 'presentations.' [50]

---

[49] Both alike, of course, are 'objective' in the sense of 'true for all.'
[50] "Psychological Principles," *Mind,* viii, 1883, 153 ff., 465 ff.; Psychology, in *Encyc. Brit.,* xx, 1886, 38, 39(1), 44(2), 67(1); *ibid.,* xxii, 1911, 548, 550(1), 554 f., 581(2); *Naturalism and Agnosticism,* ii, 1903, 113; *Psychological Principles,* 1918 and 1920, 21 ff., 26 ff., 55 ff.

Natural science is, similarly, the science of universal experience, or of experience viewed from the 'universalistic' standpoint. There is no need to describe its 'objects'; but it is necessary to insist that universal experience implies an intellectual and volitional 'subject.' The universal subject manifests itself precisely as does the individual subject, by its effects upon the objects which are included with it in the unity of experience. We speak of the 'unity' of nature; but that unity is subjective work, the ideal counterpart of the unity of every individual experience. We speak, again, of the 'regularity' of nature; and again we are in presence of a subjective activity; the regularity is an ideal of orderly and systematic knowledge. The 'laws' of nature, in spite of Huxley, are not found in the facts, but are demanded of the facts; man "makes this demand, and looks to its fulfilment to give him prescience and power." [51]

We need not follow Ward's thought further. What is important for us is his teaching that psychology is adequate to the whole range of experience as presented to an individual 'subject,' and that natural science covers the same subject-matter from a standpoint such that the presence or absence of the individual percipient makes no difference.[52] The characterising adjectives 'individualistic' and 'universalistic' sound the note of Avenarius' distinction. The notion of an universal subject which is not the "abstract logical subject," [53]

---

[51] *Naturalism and Agnosticism*, ii , 1903, 235, 248 ff.
[52] Or, as Ward adds to avoid a sorites, makes a difference which is only infinitesimal: *op. cit.*, 196.
[53] *Ibid.*, 197.

i.e., which is not, apparently, Wundt's epistemological subject—that, no doubt, marks a divergence. It involves a teleology which was wholly foreign to Avenarius' thinking.

(3) Two psychologies, those of Külpe and Ebbinghaus, have put Avenarius' definition to the test of systematic presentation. Külpe, indeed, expressly claims that he was the first to make this application.[54] He writes, no doubt, in the spirit of Avenarius; but it is a little curious that he seems never to have grasped the precise meaning of Avenarius' formula.

Külpe sets out from *Erlebnisse,* facts or data of experience, which are as such neither physical nor psychical, but scientifically indifferent. There is, he says, "no single fact-of-experience which cannot be made the subject of psychological investigation." The common property of the *Erlebnisse* which constitutes them the subject-matter of psychology is "their dependence upon experiencing (*erlebenden*) individuals"; psychology is the "science of the facts-of-experience in their dependence upon experiencing individuals." These individuals are corporeal, and in the case of human (*i.e.,* of general) psychology may be reduced to the brain, probably to the cerebral cortex. The problem of psychology is, therefore, the adequate description of those properties of the facts-of-experience which are dependent upon the brain or cortex; and it is such a descrip-

---

[54] O. Külpe, *Einleitung in die Philosophie,* 1895, 63; *Introduction to Philosophy,* 1897, 59.

tion that Külpe essays in the *Grundriss der Psychologie*.[55]

We remember that the *Grundriss* was published before Avenarius began his *Bemerkungen zum Begriff des Gegenstandes der Psychologie*,[56] and we do not underestimate the difficulty of the earlier works. The wonder is, nevertheless, that Külpe, having seen so far, should not have seen farther. There is nothing in Avenarius about a 'common property' of the *Erlebnisse*, and nothing about our describing the *Erlebnisse* 'in their dependence' upon individuals.[57] Avenarius makes psychology the science of experience at large, of the whole of experience, in so far as we regard it as dependent upon the individual. Külpe writes later that "the subject-matter of psychology comprises those factors in, and those properties of, the complete experience of an individual which are dependent upon the individual himself." [58] For Avenarius, however, it is not a matter of factors and properties, but of experience at large; and it is therefore, again, not a matter

---

[55] *Grundriss der Psychologie*, 1893, 1 ff.; *Outlines of Psychology*, 1895 (and later), 1 ff.; *Einleitung in die Philosophie*, 1895, 59, 66; *Introduction to Philosophy*, 1897, 55 f., 62.

[56] The dates are 1893 and 1894-5 respectively.

[57] W. Wundt, *Phil. Stud.*, xii, 1895, 11; H. Ebbinghaus, *Grundzüge der Psychologie*, i, 1897 and 1902, 8; W. Wundt, *Phil. Stud.*, xiii, 1897, 407 f. The controversy misses the main point of the definition.

[58] *Einleitung in die Philosophie* 1913, 74: "Gegenstand der Psychologie ist dasjenige in und an der vollen Erfahrung eines Individuums, das von ihm selbst abhängig ist. Gegenstand der Naturwissenschaft ist dagegen das von ihm Unabhängige." The first of these sentences occurs also in O. Klemm, *Geschichte der Psychologie*, 1911, 172; *History of Psychology*, 1914, 163 ("the object of psychology [is] that aspect of a complete experience of an individual which is dependent upon the individual for its existence").

of 'that which is' dependent, but of our 'taking' of experiences, from a particular point of view, 'as' dependent. Külpe, while he is fully aware that psychology has no specific subject-matter, yet fails to see that his own interpretation of Avenarius brings him perilously near the reinstatement of such a subject-matter. His book, nevertheless, paved the way for Avenarius' *Bemerkungen,* and did a very great service by calling the attention of psychologists to the work of Avenarius himself and of Mach.[59]

Ebbinghaus was strongly influenced by Mach, though he does not accept outright Mach's doctrine of the indifferent elements.[60] In his first edition he defines psychology as "a science, not of any special province of the world, but of the whole world, though only in one determinate regard. It has to do with those structures, processes, relations of the world whose specificity is essentially conditioned by the constitution and functions of an organism, an organised individual. It is also, secondarily, a science of those specific characters of an individual which are the essential determinants of its manner of experiencing the world. . . . The

---

[59] Külpe sees (what not everyone has seen) that Avenarius' elimination of introjection is primarily an affair, not of psychology, but of theory of knowledge (*Die Realisierung,* i, 1912, 111 f.); and it may be that this insight has made him somewhat overconfident of rendering Avenarius' meaning in his own language. In any case, what we are here criticising is Külpe's presentation of the empiriocritical *point of view*: the question of the correlated subject-matter will occupy us later (pp. 265 f. below).

[60] Ebbinghaus mentions Ward, Mach and Külpe, not Avenarius: *Grundzüge,* i, 1897 and 1902, 8. (It is needless to say that Ebbinghaus was also profoundly influenced by Fechner.) As regards the 'elements,' see *ibid.,* 5 ff., 46; *op. cit.,* i, 1905, 2, 50 f.

standpoint of psychology is throughout individualistic; . . . whereas physics tries so far as possible to abstract from the individual, to transcend the limitation which unquestionably inheres in the individualistic standpoint." [61]

It does not appear that Ebbinghaus has seen more clearly than Külpe. The definition which he offers has, moreover, the special disadvantage that it makes nerve-physiology a part, even if only a secondary part, of psychology proper. The second edition shows an improvement in its author's logic, in so far as the definition is omitted and the reference to the nervous system shifted from the beginning to the end of the discussion. This change, however, involves another. The 'bodily organism' which figures at the outset of the earlier exposition is now replaced by the 'individual' or the 'consciousness of an individual'; "save in relation to determinate individuals and their consciousness the facts of psychology simply do not exist." [62] It thus becomes a question whether Ebbinghaus is tending away from Avenarius and Mach in the direction of Ward, or whether the new phrasing is a merely logical consequence of the rearrangement of his text. Since in general, and for that matter in much of the detail, the view taken of psychology and of its relation to natural sci-

---

[61] *Op. cit.*, i , 1897 and 1902, 7, 8.

[62] *Op. cit.*, i , 1905, 2, 4, 5. It seems to be a desire for a larger independence of psychology that has prompted the shift of the paragraph on physiology from 1897, 3, to 1905, 6. Ebbinghaus loses, however, as much as he gains; for the introduction of 'consciousness' gives an air of illogicality to the later paragraph on *unbewusstes Seelenleben.*

ence remains unchanged, we may perhaps incline to the latter alternative. It seems certain, however, that Ebbinghaus had not brought his definition to a state of stable equilibrium, and that, had he lived, he would again have recast his introductory pages for a third edition.[63]

Neither Külpe nor Ebbinghaus throws any new light upon the status and relations of biology.

(4) No one who read James' *Principles* in 1890 would have been reminded of Mach's indifferent sensations or Wundt's undifferentiated *Vorstellungsobjekt.* Psychology, the Preface tells us, "assumes as its data (1) thoughts and feelings, and (2) a physical world in time and space with which they coexist and which (3) they know." [64] The problem of knowledge is here taken posteriorly to the distinction of thoughts and things. But in a series of articles published in 1904 and 1905 James outlines a theory of 'pure experience' which points indubitably to a definition of psychology by point of view.[65]

This 'pure experience' is the primal stuff of which

---

[63] The actual third edition, edited by E. Dürr, transfers Ebbinghaus bag and baggage to the camp of Brentano: *op. cit.,* i , 1911, xiii, 2 f. The introduction (see esp. 7) thus becomes a veritable patchwork.

[64] W. James, *The Principles of Psychology,* i , 1890; vi , 184.

[65] The articles have been brought together by R. B. Perry in a volume entitled *Essays in Radical Empiricism,* 1912. The address delivered by James at the Rome Congress, 1905, is especially valuable as a summary of his doctrine ("La notion de conscience," 206 ff.). The first overt expression of this doctrine occurs, I believe, in the paper "The Knowing of Things Together," *Psych. Rev.,* ii , 1895, esp. 110 *n.* (also in *The Meaning of Truth,* 1909, 49). There are, of course, passages in the *Principles* which partially anticipate it, or connect with it; some of these are noted in the *Essays in Rad. Emp.*

everything is composed.[66] As originally given or *vorge-funden*, it is not uniform, but rather a chaos of pure experiences.[67] We may call it feeling or sensation, and we must recognise that it comprises an indefinite variety of sensible natures.[68] Its items are physical or psychical according to their context of associates; [69] one and the same 'piece' or 'undivided portion' of pure experience may play the part now of state of mind or fact of consciousness or 'thought,' and now of physical reality or 'thing.' [70] Consider, for example, your present surroundings as you read. In the context of your personal biography, these surroundings are your 'field of consciousness'; in the context of the history of house-building, they constitute the 'room in which you sit.' [71] Mental and physical are adjectives of sorting; the given bit of experience goes to this pile or to that according to the relations in which it for the moment stands.[72]

These very relations, moreover, may be ambiguous. Sometimes an item of pure experience will bear relations to its neighbours that are purely aggressive, energetic, interactive: then it belongs unequivocally to physics. Sometimes it will appear, by contrast with the physical, as completely inert, while at the same time its relations constrain it to look back on older experiences, to find them 'warm,' to greet and appropriate them as 'mine': then it belongs unequivocally to psy-

---

[66] *Essays,* 4, etc.

[67] *Ibid.,* 32, 35, 226.

[68] *Ibid.,* 94, etc.; *A Pluralistic Universe,* 1909, 264.

[69] *Essays,* 26 f., etc.   [71] *Ibid.,* 12 ff.

[70] *Ibid.,* 9 f., 37, 137 f., 229, etc.   [72] *Ibid.,* 152 f.

chology. Sometimes, however—and this happens in all cases of appreciation, emotion, desire, thought of purpose—the experience is active both physically and mentally; it stirs the body, and it introduces, holds and regulates the stream of thought. Since we have no pressing need of consistency, we let such affectional experiences "float ambiguously, sometimes classing them with our feelings, sometimes with more physical realities, according to caprice or to the convenience of the moment." [73] There is never, be it repeated, any ultimate distinction of kind. The pure experiences undividedly, *dans leur entier*, whatever their sensible natures, become conscious or physical or which-you-will, according to the context, associates, relations, in which they are set.[74]

Neither James' philosophy nor his conception of the subject-matter of psychology is here in consideration.

---

[73] *Ibid.*, 32 f., 34, 129, 137 ff. (esp. 142, 151 f.), 184, etc.

[74] This appears, emphatically, to be James' doctrine. But there are passages in which he seems to rely upon 'sensible natures,' *i.e.*, upon ultimate differences of kind within the given field of pure experiences. Thus (1) he declares that 'some fires' will always burn and 'some waters' will always quench, while 'other fires and waters' will not act at all (32). The expressions may, however, be short-hand for 'waters in some contexts,' etc. (2) He remarks that an 'evolutionary' theory of knowledge must show how an originally 'energetic attribute' can "lapse into the status of an inert or merely internal 'nature'" (35 f.). The change would seem to be intrinsic. But these two passages occur in James' first essay, and may be coloured by older modes of thought; cf. 140. Yet (3) we read later that the members of mental activity-trains work on one another "by other parts of their nature" than those that energise physically (184). It is clear, I think, that, while his trend is consistent, James' expressions have not settled down to a final form.—Throughout the *Essays* there is a dichotomy of pure experience into physical and mental; there is no third term 'biological.' The 'body' is either physical or (in affectional contexts) ambiguously physical-mental.

We have only to note that he committed himself, toward the close of his life, to a definition of psychology by point of view, and that he apparently hoped, by way of such definition, to come nearer to a 'closed system' of psychology than he had been able to do in the *Principles*.[75]

§ 9. We find, then, toward the end of the nineteenth century, a well-marked reaction against the traditional teaching that psychology is the science of a special class of 'psychical' phenomena or phenomena of 'consciousness.' There is a growing tendency, in reliance upon theory of knowledge, to define psychology by reference to the standpoint which it assumes over against the subject-matter of science in general. It is noteworthy that Wundt, the founder of experimental psychology, shares in this reaction. It is noteworthy that independent thinkers like Avenarius

---

[75] *Principles*, i, vii ; *Essays*, 209 ff.—It is, I suppose, the through-and-through epistemological character of James' discussion that led E. Claparède, at the Rome Congress, to demand the origin of James' mental and physical coördinates (*Atti d. V Congresso Internaz. di Psicologia*, 1905, 154 f.). In other words, if we are simply classifying the sciences, and if we assume a knower common to all sciences and standing, so to say, behind them all, then we may legitimately assume also that the knower is able to take the various points of view which we find, as a matter of fact, to be taken in the sciences. That is the position of this book. If, on the contrary, we send the knower in amongst the known, make the knower a thread like any other thread in the warp and woof of experience, then we are bound not only to enquire concerning the nature of knowing, as thus put into experiential terms (*Essays*, 57), but also and further to explain how the knower gets into grooves, runs into contextual trains, knows from this and that point of view. James' explanation in the *Essays* consists solely, so far as I see, in a general reference to practical bearing upon life (96), to use, need, opportuneness, convenience, purpose (130, 141, 145 ff., 154; so in the Rome address itself, 219, 221, 233).

and Mach and Ward and James reach conclusions which, for all their differences, may still be set down side by side. And it is noteworthy that leading psychologists of the younger generation accept these conclusions, and that the system of psychology thus receives a new orientation.

We were unable to agree with Wundt; [76] and we must now—putting variants and derivatives of his view aside—come back to Avenarius. Psychology, in the definition with which we have become familiar, is the science of experience at large, of the whole of experience, regarded as dependent upon the biological individual or the central nervous system. We are to test this definition, both directly, as an adequate definition of psychology, and also indirectly, as pointing toward characterisations of physics and biology. Let us begin, then, with the negative side, and clear away certain views to which the definition does not commit us.

In the first place, it does not require us, as Wundt supposes, to 'derive' the facts of psychology from the facts of physiology, or to 'explain' the psychological by the physiological. Such aims lie altogether outside of Avenarius' conception. The dependence of which the definition speaks is purely logical, of the same order as the functional dependence of mathematics. If the nervous system is regarded as the logically prior

---

[76] It is not difficult, with some rounding of corners, to find resemblances between Wundt and Avenarius. They both come out, *e.g.*, as heuristic or empirical parallelists. Nor would Wundt have waged so bitter a polemic against Avenarius had there not been a certain kinship between them.

member of the correlation, that does not mean that the subject-matter of psychology can be, either formally or materially, 'derived' from the subject-matter of neurology; and the statement of the correlation itself, as a complete description, is all the 'explanation' that science can give. To say that Avenarius reduces psychology to an 'applied physiology of the brain' is therefore to mistake the aim and to change the universe of his discussion.[77]

Secondly, the definition does not require us, as Wundt again seems to suppose, to follow in the wake of physiology, or (with shift of the figure) to mark time, as patiently as we may, until physiology undertakes a forward movement. We are to look at experience from a certain point of view. When once we have established ourselves at this point of view, our business is, simply, to describe everything that we see. Even, then, if physiology were to stop short at its present level of development, there is no reason why psychology should not advance, and advance indefinitely. The rate of advance would certainly be slowed: for a progressive physiology is of manifold advantage to psychology; special questions are raised, plans of research are quickened, rivalries are excited and controversies begin; and all this activity furthers psychological insight and challenges psychological knowledge.[78]

---

[77] Cf. W. Wundt, Ueber die Definition der Psychologie, *Philos. Stud.*, xii, 1895, 13, 27 f.; Ueber naiven und kritschen Realismus, *ibid.*, xiii, 1897, 409; also *Kleine Schriften*, i, 1910, 498; ii, 1911, 124, 137.

[78] Cf. the dispute between Lipps and Flechsig, *Dritter internationaler Congress für Psychologie,* 1897, 68 ff.

Correlation, functional covariation, is after all what we started out from. Only, again, we must not convert this logical dependence into material, and so deny to psychology the right of initiative which it has constantly exercised in fact, and which the definition, properly understood, does not in the least imperil.[79]

Finally, the definition does not, by its reference to an 'individual,' mark off psychological experience as private or unshareable from the common and shareable experience of the other sciences.[80] If it bade us regard experience as dependent, in some special and intimate way, upon the knowing subject, then that result would follow: in the sense, that is, that a knowing subject is always a personal centre of awarenesses. But the knowing subject bears the same relation to psychology that it bears to biology and physics,[81] and the 'individual' of the definition is itself scientifically defined as the biological individual, the nervous system known to biology. Whenever, then, the excitatory processes of

---

[79] W. Wundt, *Philos. Stud.,* xii, 1895, 19 f.; also *Kleine Schriften,* ii, 1911, 130 f. There is no reason why we should not formulate as "laws" of psychology any uniformities of coexistence and succession in the field of the dependent variable that are correlated with uniformities of occurrence in the nervous system. It is, on the other hand, a little dangerous to speak, as Külpe does, of intrapsychological dependencies.

[80] H. Münsterberg, *Grundzüge der Psychologie,* i, 1900, 72. Psychology does not deal with 'my' anger, 'my' recollection, 'my' expectation, but with experience regarded as dependent upon this, that and the other nervous system—or, rather, upon a generalised nervous system which has a certain margin of variation.

[81] It seems sometimes to be forgotten that the knowing physicist and the knowing biologist are no less 'individual' than the knowing psychologist, and that a physical or biological fact may, in certain circumstances, be observable by only one physicist or biologist.

nervous systems are biologically the same, there the correlated psychological experience is common or shareable. The difference between psychology and natural science, in this connection, is that the statements of natural science have universal validity, and their *plus* or *minus* of variation is ascribed to 'error of observation,' while the statements of psychology have distributive validity, in accordance with the range of variation actually found in nervous systems. In so far as the 'normal' of biology approaches the universal of physics, in so far does the shareableness of psychological experience approach the shareableness of physical: indeed, since the 'abnormal' may in part be realised by the normal, the approach is still closer.[82] It is a very different view of psychology that shuts up the psychologist among 'his own mental processes.'

If, then, we could be satisfied with merely negative tests, we need not hesitate to accept Avenarius' definition as psychologically adequate. Biology and physics, it is true, have still to be considered. But the definition, as it stands, gives the psychologist a positive relation to biology, without thereby tying a physiological millstone about his neck, and also assures to psychology a subject-matter as wide as experience itself, without setting up *tabus* which the 'individual' psychologist may not transgress. All this is satisfactory—and yet we cannot say that we are satisfied. The definition must

---

[82] Thus, we might present to normal vision an environment such as is seen by the partially colour-blind; in this way the abnormal experience would be made shareable.

be qualified or modified, in a positive sense, if it is to square with the results of the preceding Chapter.

For when Avenarius speaks, in a scientific context, of *Erfahrung überhaupt*, of experience as a whole, he puts his own meaning upon the term "experience." The empiriocritical philosophy has no theory of values; it transforms values into the givenness, the found occurrence, of valuations; and valuations appear, accordingly, within its scientific 'experience.' [83] We, on the other hand, have decided the scientific experience is always and everywhere existential. The world of existence is at once the discovery of science, the gift of science to civilisation, and the limitation of science, the only world that science can know.[84] Wundt, who is both physiologist and psychologist, is here a far safer guide than Avenarius, who, as we saw, was neither the one nor the other, but a philosopher.[85] That, however, is as it happens to be: for ourselves, we claim the right, from our previous discussion, to modify Avenarius' formula in the sense of science. Psychology is then the science of existential experience regarded as dependent upon the nervous system.

§ 10.   Our first step is thus taken. Does it point the way to a second, namely, to the characterisation of biology?

Formally, the path lies plain before us. As biology is

---

[83] Cf., *e.g.,* Avenarius' characteristic remark in *Vjs.,* iii, 1879, 71.

[84] Cf. H. Münsterberg, *Grundzüge,* i, 1900, 56.

[85] Cf. p. 113 above. Wundt's attitude in psychology is, if one may so put it, instinctively or temperamentally existential. He is, however, hampered by his view of the relation of psychology to the 'mental' sciences.

logically prior to psychology, so is physics (in the wide sense in which the word covers chemistry and physical chemistry as well as physics proper) logically prior to biology. And as the psychologist deals with existential experience regarded as dependent upon a determinate biological system, so—by analogy of definition—will the biologist deal with existential experience regarded as dependent upon a determinate physical system. The question is, however, whether this formula 'works'; and its working depends upon the determination of the independent variable. The fact that it has not hitherto been proposed, obvious though its logical derivation appears, means that a material difficulty is involved; the 'determinate physical system' has not stood out sharply from the general physical context. Recent enquiry proves, nevertheless, that a system such as the definition requires has all the while been there, under our hands. What the nervous system (or its physiological equivalent) is to psychology, that is the 'environment' to biology.

It will be objected, perhaps, that the term 'environment,' while it is a quasi-technical term of general biology, is still very far from the connotation of a determinate physical system. We reply that, though the objection holds in practice for a large number of biological treatises, it is no longer valid in theory. For Henderson's work has proved the 'environment' to be no less determinate than the nervous system itself.

Henderson approaches his subject from both sides, from the side of biology and from the side of physical chemistry. Setting out from a conception of the 'organism' as complex, durable and metabolic, and reducing the 'environment' by a process of elimination to water and carbon dioxide, he is able to trace the correlation or 'reciprocal relation' of the two variables with extraordinary precision. "No other environment . . . made up of other known elements, or lacking water and carbonic acid, could" in like manner "promote complexity, durability and active metabolism in the organic mechanism which we call life." Setting out, again, from the characteristics of physico-chemical 'systems' and the properties of matter, he arrives at the same conclusion. Carbon, oxygen and hydrogen "possess a unique ensemble of unique properties." These properties "lead to maximum freedom of the evolutionary process in all respects conceivable by physical science. . . . Every other sensibly different distribution of the properties among the elements would involve great restrictions. Thus conditions are actually established (relatively to other imaginable arrangements of the properties of matter) for the existence of the greatest possible number, diversity and duration of [physico-chemical] systems, phases, components and activities." So that the 'environment,' whether it be considered biologically as the complement of the 'organism,' or whether it be considered physico-chemically as a matter of elements and aggregations, has all the marks of a 'system' in Avenarius' sense, and supplies for biology an independent variable which is essentially comparable with the system C.[86]

---

[86] See L. J. Henderson, *The Fitness of the Environment,* 1913, 63 f., 271 f.; *The Order of Nature,* 1917, 209 f. The author draws from his facts teleological inferences which I am unable to accept.

The resulting definition of biology must, of course, be judged by the biologists themselves; the layman can do no more than submit it for expert judgment. It parallels our definition of psychology, and it fills the logical gap that we noted, e.g., in the exposition of J. A. Thomson.[87] It is definitely suggested by Henderson's twofold study of the environment, and it would undoubtedly have occurred to Mach or Külpe or Ebbinghaus had that study been earlier available. Moreover, no other definition of biology by point of view has so far been put forward. These are its claims: and upon them the biologists, as we have said, must decide.

Physics remains: and we may define physics, in Avenarius' way, as the science of existential experience regarded as interdependent. There is here no question of a logical priority. Independent variables are set up within physics, for methodological reasons, and dependent variables are referred to them; but the independent of this investigation is the dependent of the next; and for the science as a whole all variables alike are simply interdependent. The specific logical dependences of psychology and biology, which relate them to more fundamental sciences, are thus replaced by a mutual dependence within the field of physics itself. Or, in other and more concrete phrase, neither psychology nor biology, but only physics, can read the existential universe in terms of energy.[88]

§ 11.   We have now completed the first half of our task, and may summarise the conclusions at which we

---

[87] P. 97.

[88] There can, i.e., be no 'vital' energy, and no intrabiological dependences (no vital 'causality'). Cf. note 60, p. 75 above.

have arrived. We set out to give adequate expression, in behalf of psychology, to three points of view and three corresponding subjèct-matters. For while all science deals with the existential universe, the world of existential experience, there are three typical or representative sciences—physics, biology, psychology— which view this world from different standpoints and thus acquaint us with different aspects of existence; and if we are to determine the point of view and the subject-matter of psychology, we must bring psychology into relation with its coördinate sciences. We have as yet said nothing of subject-matter; but on the side of point of view we may write the required differential formulas as follows:

Psychology is the science of existential experience regarded as functionally or logically dependent upon the nervous system (or its biological equivalent);

Biology is the science of existential experience regarded as functionally or logically dependent upon the physical environment; and

Physics (including chemistry and physical chemistry) is the science of existential experience regarded as functionally or logically interdependent.

The 'nervous system' of the first definition is, as matter of scientific fact, describable only and wholly in biological terms; its precise limits as independent variable for psychology are, however, not drawn beforehand by biology, but are determined by the range of that functional covariation upon which the definition rests. So the 'physical environment' of the second definition is, as matter of scientific fact, describable by physics; but physics as such knows nothing of an intra-physical environmental system; the limits are drawn, again, by the range of covariation of physical and biological. Physics is logically prior to biology, and biology in its turn is logically prior to psychology: but it does not necessarily follow that the 'nervous system' is a system in the sense of biology, or the 'environment' a system in the sense of physical chemistry. The two systems are constituted solely by the reciprocal relation of the independent and dependent variables.

Here, then, are definitions by point of view: working definitions, that make no pretension to finality, but that promise to be serviceable, as they appear also to be adequate, at our present level of scientific knowledge. They are not revolutionary; they neither change our notion of the scientific system nor impugn the facts that we have observed and the laws that we have wrought out from the facts.[89] They do (and it is surely a merit) cut straight across the tangle of certain historic controversies.[90]

---

[89] It may be noted, *e.g.*, that the logical dependence of biological upon physical justifies us in substituting stimulus for excitation in cases where the functional dependence of psychological upon biological is still unknown.

[90] I have in mind such controversies as centre, in psychology, about the terms interactionism, parallelism, epiphenomenalism, and in biology, about mechanism and vitalism; passing mention has been made of some of them in previous notes. These issues, whose discussion in their day and generation was of solid advantage to science, seem to me to have become barren. Hence a new orientation is to be welcomed. Barren issues, nevertheless, have a way of springing up again, with change of form, to renewed fertility: so that we can neither hope ourselves to have said the last word, nor afford on behalf of our pupils to neglect the history of science.

CHAPTER III

THE DEFINITION OF PSYCHOLOGY:
SUBJECT-MATTER

CHAPTER III

THE DEFINITION OF PSYCHOLOGY: SUBJECT-MATTER

§ 1. Since point of view is, by hypothesis, correlated with subject-matter, we cannot rest satisfied with formulas that take account of point of view alone. We must go on to enquire whether and how far the subject-matters currently assigned to physics, biology and psychology correspond with the differentiation of these sciences by point of view; and if in any case the correspondence fails, we must ask further whether our own characterisation of standpoint is at fault or whether the subject-matter in question has been misappropriated. Our first interest lies always in psychology; and our business, in the concrete, is to consider critically the views of those psychologists who define their science by reference to a peculiarly psychological subject-matter. We shall be unable—and it is fortunately not necessary—to deal otherwise than summarily with the subject-matters of physics and biology.

Even with this restriction, the present Chapter might easily run to an inordinate length. For there are many authors who reach their definition of the 'psychical' by the road of philosophy; and if in such instances we should try to do individual justice, and to follow up every shade of meaning and every nuance of implication, we should be bound to examine, not only the consequences of the definition for scientific psychology, but also the philosophical foundation upon which it is based. Seeing that we are concerned with science, and that philosophy lies beyond the scope and competence of our discussion, we shall ignore these individual differences. We shall take up, one by one, the typical definitions of psychological subject-matter, and shall criticise them in terms as general as those in which they are formulated. We thus bring under control a large body of logically heterogeneous material. And if we are obliged to round off the corners of individual exposition, we still need not fear that serious injustice will result: for a definition that proves inadequate when stated in its generalised form will hardly be made adequate by a particular phrasing or derivation.

§ 2. First of all, however, and before we come to the definitions proper, we must note the custom of writers of psychological text-books to appeal to their readers by way of illustrative example. It is usual to introduce the subject by a list, more or less orderly, more or less full, of the phenomena which are to be discussed in the body of the book. Sometimes the list appears as an illustrative supplement to a formal definition; sometimes it is offered as a preliminary and non-committal substitute for the true definition, which will be reached at the end of the work; and sometimes it is put forward in lieu of definition, on the ground that the familiar concrete is preferable to an unfamiliar abstract.[1] Demonstrative gesture thus replaces or reinforces verbal definition.

Were it not that customs persist by a sort of inertia, this pedagogical practice would long ago have been given up; for experience amply confirms what logic plainly shows, that the gesture is equivocal and that recourse to it is therefore likely to be seriously misleading. There are in fact very few psychological terms that are not also employed, in technical senses, by other disciplines; and there are very many terms, employed technically by psychology, that carry a different meaning in the language of everyday life. If psychology deals with ideas, so also does logic; if psychology deals with imagination, so also does æsthetics; and if psychology deals with acts of will, so also does ethics. Here already is risk of confusion. But the risk is vastly increased if we ascribe to psychology, without qualification, the meanings of current speech. When we are told that psychology has to do with our doubts and errors, our principles and ideals, our wishes and opinions, the statement, so far from orientating us toward science, serves simply to confirm us in our natural commonsense attitude. Nor does it help if a few quasi-technical terms are added. A reader, for example, who, approaching science from the standpoint of commonsense, finds himself confronted by a list which brackets together 'ideals' and 'sensations of colour,' will be

---

[1] F. Brentano, *Psychol. vom empirischen Standpunkte*, i, 1874, 103; H. Münsterberg, *Grundzüge der Psychol.*, i, 1900, 67 f.

the more bewildered the more earnestly he strives to understand.[2]

The truth is that the psychologist who makes out such a list has already done for himself what the string of examples purports to do for the beginner. He has already formulated his definition; he has discerned the common property, or adopted the single point of view, which holds all the various items of his list together. He knows that his index will not contain the word 'error,' but only the conventionally technical 'illusion'; not the word 'principle,' but only the technical terms 'problem' and 'determination.' To him, this transformation seems harmless and obvious; it was accomplished before he wrote his introduction.[3] The reader, however, is in less happy case. The question of the subject-matter of psychology, which he might have faced once and for all, is presented to him in the form of a series of special questions, all of which must, by some unknown trick of method, be made to yield the same answer.

It does not follow that the demonstrative gesture itself need be given up. It follows only that the gesture, if employed, must be deliberately shaped to accord with the writer's formal definition, expressed or implied, of the subject-matter of psychology. Temperament will decide whether a book is to open with the

---

[2] Brentano, *loc. cit.*; H. Ebbinghaus, *Grundzüge der Psychol.*, i, 1905, 1.

[3] The special reference is to E. Dürr's edition of Ebbinghaus, *Grundzüge,* i, 1911, 1; ii, 1913, Sachregister. Brentano (*loc. cit.*), makes use of the list of examples to anticipate his own classification of psychical phenomena.

formula of definition or (let us say) with the Müller-Lyer illusion: the point is that, in the latter event, the treatment of the illusion must be strictly psychological.

§ 3. It is but a short step from the rough, illustrative list of psychical phenomena to the distinction of two worlds, an 'inner' and an 'outer,' as the respective provinces of psychology and natural science. Common-sense, as we remarked in the instance of 'ideals' and 'sensations of colour,' finds the list bewilderingly heterogeneous, and taking it as a whole can make nothing of it. The psychologist, therefore, breaks it up. He points out that there are certain items—thoughts, feelings, wishes, resolutions—which fall into a group, show a certain kinship with one another, belong to one another; if it is difficult to say, forthwith, what it is that they have in common, they at any rate have no likeness whatever to the objects of the physical world. And since material things are things outside of us, objects of 'external' nature, it is natural to mark off this other group as 'internal,' as the objects of an inner world. Indeed, when the name has once been given them, it seems to fit them very well.

The 'sensations' are still a puzzle: colours and sounds, temperatures and resistances, appear in some way to belong to both worlds alike. Here, then, the psychologist must come again to the help of common-sense, and this time he draws a technical distinction. When sensations are regarded as matters of individual experience, he explains, they are strictly 'internal' affairs, and belong to the group of thoughts and feelings. When, on the other hand, they are regarded for themselves, independently of any individual experience, they form part of the subject-matter of natural science.

The two scientific worlds are thus made up of radically different objects, objects as different as my desire to be wealthy and the copper-mine whose possession would make me so, and objects of the first kind are as obviously 'internal' as those of the second kind are 'external.' There is, nevertheless, a region of overlapping, which makes necessary some further explanation. The colour and hardness of the copper, as I see and feel them, are no less internal than my wish to own the mine; the same colour and hardness, as referred to the reflection of light and the density of a material body, are altogether external. If this twofold relationship of the sensations makes things a little complicated, still it has its reassuring side: the two worlds, though they are strictly delimited, are nevertheless not wholly separate; the overlapping of the subject-matters gives us a hint of the essential unity of science. Psychology, in particular, is brought down from the clouds of speculation and becomes the scientific complement of physics.[4]

Attractive as this exposition is, it yet cannot bear examination. Even if we discount the more or less overt appeal to common-sense, it has two fatal weaknesses.

The first, of course, is the recognition of the overlap between the inner and outer worlds. The colour

---

[4] This account is substantially that of Ebbinghaus, *Grundzüge*, i, 1905, 2 ff. On the epistemological side, see Münsterberg, *Grundzüge*, i, 1900, 68. On the distinction of 'inner' and 'outer' in general, cf. Avenarius, *Vjs.*, xviii, 1894, 142, 150 ff.

seen, the experienced copper-red, shows no sort of phenomenal resemblance to the reflected train of light-
waves which is the physical colour. So the question at
once arises: What is the reason for recognising any
overlap at all? And thereupon the counter-question
comes up: If we do recognise an overlap, why should
we restrict it to the sphere of sensation? Both these
lines of argument have, as a matter of fact, been taken.
There are psychologists who reject all notion of a community; the 'sensations' are either turned back, bodily, to natural science, or are made the subject-matter
of a neutral 'phenomenology' which serves as point of
departure both for physics and for psychology. There
are others who urge that the phenomenal difference
between physical and psychological colour is no less—
if indeed there can be any question of magnitude in
the case—than is the difference between thought and
the neural processes upon which thought is admittedly
'conditioned'; and that if in the one instance the
phenomena that we classify as inner and outer are
'ultimately' the same, so may they be also in the other.
We need not accept either of these conflicting views;
but the fact that they have been put forward indicates
that the splitting up of 'sensation' only cuts the knot,
and leaves the tangle as it was before.

But there is a further difficulty. Let us grant for
the moment that thoughts and feelings constitute a
natural group of related phenomena, and let us agree
to mark off this group as 'internal' from the phenomena of an outside world: still we have made no
advance toward a true definition of the subject-matter
of psychology. 'Inner' and 'outer' are pictorial terms,

carrying a spatial metaphor; they are indicative, and not descriptive. If they are to acquire scientific significance, they must be correlated with some attributive difference, made out by observation of facts on the scientific level; and if such a difference can be found, we shall have no need of pictorial terms to express it. The bare distinction of 'inner' and 'outer,' though it takes us a step beyond the medley of crude examples, does not set us upon the path that shall lead to our goal.

§ 4. It is often said—and now we arrive at what purports to be a definition—that the attributive difference between physical and psychical is given with the presence or absence of the character of space. "The department of the Object, or Object-World," writes Bain, "is exactly circumscribed by one property, Extension. The World of Subject-experience is devoid of this property. . . . Thus, if Mind, as commonly happens, is put for the sum-total of Subject-experience, we may define it negatively by a single fact,—the absence of Extension." [5]

This division of the world of human experience into an Extended, popularly called matter, and an Unextended, popularly called mind, seems ordinarily to be regarded as a straightforward application of the logical law of excluded middle. That law, however,

---

[5] A. Bain, *Mental and Moral Science*, 1881, 1 f.; *The Senses and the Intellect*, 1868, 1 f.; H. Münsterberg, *Ueber Aufgaben und Methoden der Psychologie*, 1891, 7; *Grundzüge der Psychologie*, 1900, 69 f. Localisation is coupled with extension by F. Brentano, *Psychologie vom empirischen Standpunkte*, i , 1874, 111 ff.; A. Höfler, *Psychologie*, 1897, 4, 349 f.

yields nothing, not even a negative determination, for psychology. We may say, of course, with all logical correctness, that the universe is either Extended or Not extended. But if we change the either-or into a both-and, we have left the ground of formal logic. And if we further attribute to the both-and the exhaustiveness of classification which belongs to the either-or, we expose ourselves still more openly to the challenge of facts. The universe now consists of two and only two sorts of phenomena: the extended or physical, whose sum-total is matter, and the unextended or psychical, whose sum-total is mind. In behalf of science at large, we must raise the question whether this classification is in truth exhaustive. In behalf of psychology, we must ask whether the line of division has been significantly drawn, and whether the unextended is sufficiently homogeneous to form the subject-matter of a single science.

As regards the first question, it is clear that the classification is not exhaustive unless vital phenomena, whose sum-total is life, are demonstrably material, so that biology disappears in physics. Bain himself, in his classification of the sciences, declares that "biology enters upon an entirely new field of phenomena," inasmuch as living bodies obey not only the laws of physics but also "their own specific laws as living bodies." [6] This statement, which accords with our own position in the preceding Chapter, forbids a dual division of experience with matter and mind.

The second question, whether the line of division

---

[6] A. Bain, *Logic: i. Deductive,* 1895, 27.

between matter and mind has been drawn significantly for psychology, brings to light an ambiguity in the word Extension. We may take the term to mean, in the most general sense, any sort of spread or diffusion, without specific reference to the centimeter-space of the text-books of physics. In that case Bain's distinction is not significant. We cannot say a priori that "the world of Subject-experience is devoid of this property"; the history of psychology records the contrary opinion, and the appeal lies to psychological observation. But we may also suppose that Extension is used in a narrower sense, to mean material or 'external' spatiality, the uniform and measurable space of physics. Under this interpretation of the word, however, we cannot speak in strictness of the circumscribing of the object-world by a single property. Extension appears rather as one only of the constitutive properties of matter, as one among others; and there is no reason a priori to give it precedence over, let us say, time and inertia. Unless, then, we are prepared to regard the psychical as possibly temporal and possibly inert—taking both adjectives in their physical sense—we still cannot accept Bain's distinction as significant.[7]

There remains the question of the homogeneity of the unextended. Here it is enough to point out that the relation of psychology to the 'mental sciences' has long been, as it continues to be, a matter of controver-

---

[7] If there is a logical incompatibility in such expressions as 'a three-cornered satisfaction,' 'a yard-long reflection,' so is there also in 'a solid satisfaction,' 'a half-hour's reflection,' provided that the solidity and the half-hour are taken in the sense of physics.

sial discussion. Bain, in particular, may again be quoted against himself: in his classification of the sciences he marks off logic from psychology as occupied with a "distinct department of phenomena." [8] But if this division holds, it is plainly impossible for him to identify the not-extended with mind, and mind with the subject-matter of psychology.

We conclude, accordingly, that the 'negative definition' of psychical phenomena as those which lack extension is by no means the logical innocent that its advocates make it out to be. We may ignore its philosophical origin; we cannot, if we reflect at all, fail to see that it rests upon assumptions which are logically inacceptable.

§ 5.* In the dichotomy by Extension, physical phenomena receive positive, and psychical phenomena receive negative, determination. In another dichotomy, which is perhaps even more familiar, this relation is reversed: the universe of experience is divided into the Conscious and the Not-conscious, and psychical are identified with conscious phenomena, mind with the totality of consciousness. Psychology thus receives at length a positive definition.[9]

---

[8] *Op. cit.*, 25 f.

* [§§ 5-19 inclusive have been published in two installments under the title Functional Psychology and the Psychology of Act in the *Amer. Journ. Psych.*, xxxii, 1921, 519 (§§ 5-8) and xxxiii, 1922, 43 (§§ 9-19). See Preface, p. vi. With § 20 the author returns to the definition of psychology by point of view and the relation of psychology to physics and biology. H. P. W.]

[9] Moreover, the Not-conscious may be further subdivided, in the interest of biology, into a Living and a Not-living. There can be no doubt that, formally regarded, this classification is superior to that by Extension.

The word 'consciousness' is, however, notoriously ambiguous,[10] and the question whether the adjective 'conscious' suffices to mark off a special class of phenomena must therefore be discussed with great care. It must, moreover, be discussed in two separate contexts. For the psychologists who recognise the independent existence of 'phenomena of consciousness,' as the given objects of psychological investigation, fall at the present time into two principal groups. The one of these emphasises, in a psychology of 'function,' the biological aspect of empirical psychology; the other, in a psychology of 'act,' emphasises its intentional aspect.[11] Both alike may therefore trace their descent from Aristotle.[12] But in spite of much that they hold in common, the difference of motivation makes it necessary to consider the two groups separately.

In dealing with 'functional' psychology, we shall first examine a single representative system, and shall then bring together, for critical review, what appear to be the major tenets of the school. Systems that are based upon the concept of consciousness, even if this be

---

[10] The *locus classicus* is A. Bain, *The Emotions and the Will*, 1880, 539 ff. Cf. also R. Eisler, *Wörterbuch der philosophischen Begriffe*, i, 1910, 177 ff.

[11] Functional psychology, in this sense, is especially American, and the psychology of act especially German. Recent English psychology, through G. F. Stout (*Anal. Psychol.*, i, 1896, 36, 40), has been influenced by Brentano.

[12] Intentionalism is ascribed to Aristotle on the ground of his doctrine of the relation of sensation to object of sense (*De anima, 424a, 425b*), and of thought to the object of thought (*ibid., 429a, 430a, 431b*). Cf. also his statement that the objects of memory and imagination (*De mem., 450a*) and those of thought and desire (*De an., 433a; Met., 1072a*) are identical.

taken under a single aspect, will inevitably differ; and
we find accordingly that the biological emphasis falls
differently in different functional psychologies. For
Ladd, the 'stream of consciousness' is a life, and mind,
the totality of consciousness, is an organism, "a unique
and living totality in a course of development"—an
organism living a life of its own, which is always connected with the bodily life, but yet is "in some sort
independent of" the body; and functional psychology
is the science of the functions or activities of this psychical organism.[13] Angell, on the other hand, regards
consciousness as an organic function,[14] a phenomenon
of control;[15] "mind," he declares, "seems to involve
the master devices" whereby the "adaptive operations
of organic life may be made most perfect."[16] Judd,
again, appears to combine both views. At first, consciousness is represented as an organic function, as
something which, like the digestive or locomotive function, plays its part in the economy of the organic life
under the conditions of the biological struggle for existence; it is thus one of the 'attributes' of man, consid-

---

[13] G. T. Ladd, *Psychology, Descriptive and Explanatory*, 1894, 638,
659 ff.; *Philos. of Mind*, 1895, 400 ff., esp. 405; G. T. Ladd and R. S.
Woodworth, *Elements of Physiol. Psychol.*, 1911, 656 ff.

[14] J. R. Angell, *Psychology*, 1904, 79. In 1908, 95, the phrase is
dropped, but the meaning of the passage appears to remain the
same.

[15] Angell, "The Province of Functional Psychology," *Psychol. Rev.*,
xiv, 1907, 88.

[16] *Psychol.*, 1908, 8. In 1904, 7, "mind seems to be the master de-
vice." Cf. also 1904, 50,86; with 1908, 64, 103. In both editions mind
is "an engine for accomplishing the most remarkable adjustments of
the organism to its life conditions": 1904, 379; 1908, 436.

ered as the highest animal.[17] Later, consciousness is 'possessed' by a knowing self, an unitary being which finds its nearest analogy in the living organism.[18] Differences of this sort find their natural expression in the classifications and arrangements and relative emphases of the writers' systematic works. But they have little if any bearing on the question immediately before us; they do not destroy the essential unity of the functional school.

The psychology of 'act' cannot be treated in the same comprehensive way. For here, as we quickly recognise, individual differences are not only inevitable but also fundamental and constitutive, so that the principal systems and programmes must be separately considered. Brentano, of course, furnishes both our starting-point and our constant point of reference. Besides Brentano, we pass under review, either in their own person or in that of some member of their school, Meinong, Stumpf, Lipps, Husserl and Külpe. We then interrupt the course of the exposition, in order to compare and contrast two experimental text-books of intentionalistic psychology, Witasek's *Grundlinien der Psychologie* (1908), which systematises Meinong's views, and Messer's *Psychologie* (1914), which we may regard as, in large measure, a systematisation of the later views of Külpe. The digression will be useful: it will reveal likeness and difference, in kind and in degree, and will thus prepare us for a broader survey of

---

[17] C. H. Judd, *Psychology*, 1917, 4, 161; "Evolution and Consciousness," *Psychol. Rev.*, xvii, 1910, 84.

[18] *Psychology*, 274 ff. Cf. below, p. 177.

the act-systems. But here, we repeat, it proves impossible to follow the lines laid down by our study of functional psychology. We shall rather enquire, first, into the significance for these systems of the classification of psychical phenomena, and secondly into their treatment of two modes of such phenomena, namely, sensation and attention. The choice of topics is not arbitrary. It is suggested by the foregoing review of the principal systems; and it leads us to certain general conclusions with respect to intentionalism at large.

§ 6. We may take, as broadly typical of the functional systems, Ladd's definition of psychology: "the science which describes and explains the phenomena of consciousness, as such." [19] Consciousness, Ladd says, cannot in strictness be defined. Its meaning may, however, be brought out by contrast. "What we are when we are awake, as contrasted with what we are when we sink into a profound and perfectly dreamless sleep, or receive an overpowering blow upon the head—*that* it is to be conscious. What we are less and less as we sink gradually down into dreamless sleep, or as we swoon slowly away: and what we are more and more, as the noise of the crowd outside tardily arouses us from our after-dinner nap, or as we come out of the midnight darkness of the typhoid-fever crisis—*that* it is to become conscious." [20] For the rest, he commits his case to the "reflective mind of all mankind." "The distinction between external facts and facts of consciousness, as actually made by every man, furnishes

---

[19] G. T. Ladd, *Psychology, Descriptive and Explanatory*, 1894, 1.
[20] *Ibid.*, 30.

. . . the one peculiar and abiding standpoint of psychology." [21]

It would be foolish, certainly, to require a definition of the indefinable. If we are to deal with the indefinable, we can ask only that it be exhibited. We must insist, however, that it be exhibited clearly and unequivocally, in such wise (to put the matter a little paradoxically) that we can assure ourselves of what the writer's definition would have been, had he been able to formulate it. Ladd, as we have just now seen, attempts to exhibit the conscious by contrast with the not-conscious. We note, however, with some disquiet that —while psychology is to deal with the facts or phenomena of consciousness—it is 'we' and not these facts that are conscious, and that consciousness is made susceptible of degree, of less and more. If there is an universally realised difference between "external facts and facts of consciousness," in their status as data for scientific treatment, then surely the difference should be demonstrable from the face of the facts themselves, and 'we' who discern it should be left aside. Moreover, the facts, if they are data for scientific treatment, must surely either be or not be "facts of consciousness," and cannot vary their nature by more and less. Man is not more biological than amoeba, or the mountain brook less physical than Niagara.

Ladd's illustrations are therefore by no means free from objection—so far, at any rate, as regards a science of "the phenomena of consciousness, as such."

---

[21] *Ibid.,* 3.

We must, however, take them as they stand, and see what Ladd makes of them when he comes to technical exposition.

A man of ordinary education and intelligence, looking back on his recovery from swoon or fever-crisis, would, no doubt, be likely to report a gradual restoration of 'consciousness': by which he would mean an increasing awareness, an increasing realisation and appreciation and command, of himself and his surroundings. It is precisely this varied awareness, now, that Ladd intends by his own technical use of the word 'consciousness.' [22] Every 'state of consciousness' with which a scientific psychology has to do is, he tells us, at one and the same time "fact of intellection, fact of feeling, fact of conation." [23] Intellection is evidently a mode of awareness: whether intellection mean that universal discriminating activity which has its root in the awareness of resemblance,[24] or whether it be taken to embrace the whole series of psychoses that runs from the abstract 'sensation' through perception and ideation to judgment.[25] In so far, then, as every state of consciousness involves intellection, consciousness is always, in this narrower intellectual sense, awareness. Feeling too, however, is a mode of awareness; it is our

---

[22] The two terms are not seldom used interchangeably. See, *e.g.*, *op. cit.*, 166, 290, 293 ff., 296 f., 300, 310, 322, 328 f., 331 ff., 379, 422, 517, 523 f., 530 f., 636; Ladd and Woodworth, *Physiol. Psychol.*, 430, 512, 681, 685. They appear, indeed, from such passages as *Psychol.*, 11, to be strictly coördinate.

[23] *Psychol.*, 33, 58, 172, 264, etc.

[24] *Ibid.*, 33, 288 ff., esp. 293.

[25] *Ibid.*, 93, 235, 251, 357, 430, etc.

very being become aware;[26] and conation also is a mode of awareness, awareness of activity.[27] Every state of consciousness, therefore, is at once fact-awareness, value-awareness and activity-awareness—the unitary awareness-resultant of three irreducible awareness factors.[28]

Ladd thus obtains a starting-point for his system: but he has not adhered rigorously to his illustrations. For these states of consciousness, which are the primary data of psychology, while they all belong to some 'self' or 'I,' and indeed cannot be 'thought of' out of that connection, yet do not necessarily carry the reference to 'self' within or upon them; their consciousness is not necessarily a self-consciousness.[29] The convalescent of Ladd's illustrations, on the other hand, would assuredly maintain that 'he' became increasingly conscious, 'he' and not his 'states.' It is the observer who may become increasingly aware: the 'state' or 'fact' or 'phenomenon of consciousness' is, as we saw, simply conscious, and cannot become increasingly or decreasingly what it essentially is.

We are, however, not yet at the end of Ladd's ac-

---

[26] *Ibid.,* 170. Cf. the doctrine that feeling may precede or outlast ideation (181); the illustrations offered in support of a manifold of affective qualities (*e.g.,* 170); and the doctrine that feeling is an integral factor in (not merely a determinant of, or an influence upon) knowing (53, 510 ff.; *Philos. of Knowledge,* 1897, 95, 124, 165 f.).

[27] *Psychol.,* 83, 216, 219; *Philos. of Mind,* 1895, 87 ff.

[28] 'Fact' must be understood, not in the sense of our own previous discussion, but rather in the manner of common sense; cf. the illustrations, *Psychol.,* 17, 19, 50 f., etc. For value, cf. *Philos. of Knowledge,* 124.

[29] *Psychol.,* 31 f., 523.

count. The state of consciousness which is to be the
subject-matter of psychology must, he points out, do
more than merely exist; it must become an 'object of
knowledge.' [30] But it can become an object of immediate knowledge only by way of introspection or self-
awareness;[31] and since this observing activity is itself
a phenomenon of consciousness, the total state of consciousness, as object of psychological knowledge, is not
just awareness, but rather self-awareness, awareness
of awareness. The state remains unitary. If, however,
we have recourse to logical abstraction, then the second
awareness, the "phenomenon [of consciousness] known
as fact," may be distinguished as 'content' from the
activity of observation, the "knowing of the phenomenon [of consciousness] as object." [32] In this way the
observer is brought within the conscious field, and
degrees of consciousness are so far justified.

Still we are not at an end. The 'content' thus ab-
stractly marked off from the activity of consciousness
remains consciousness, and must therefore in its turn
admit of the same distinction of activity and passivity.
Sensations, ideas, feelings, conations may be regarded,
passively, as 'content' of consciousness.[33] Their description and explanation make up half of the detailed
psychological story. In the other half, consciousness

---

[30] *Ibid.*, 1 f., 4, 7, 9, 32, etc.

[31] *Ibid.*, 9, 15, 523, etc. Introspection is also called self-consciousness
and reflective consciousness.

[32] *Ibid.*, 32 f.; cf. 37, 49, 289 ff. Ladd varies in his use of the terms
'active' and 'passive': see 46, 83, 96, 214, etc.

[33] *Ibid.*, 309. There seems to be inconsistency as regards feeling:
cf. 19 f., 163, 523.

(conscious content in the broader sense) is regarded actively: as intellection (or awareness of likeness and difference), as reactive feeling (mental tension, conviction), as attention.[34] Ladd is emphatic that "the task of a scientific psychology is as truly the description and explanation of the phenomena of consciousness, considered as forms of active functioning (of consciousness 'function-wise'), as it is the description and explanation of the particular qualities and quantities of the phenomena regarded as passive states (of consciousness 'content-wise')." [35] And he expressly applies this dictum to the "single state of consciousness, so far as we can catch it and separate it from the stream of conscious life," *i. e.,* to what he has called the phenomenon known as fact, no less than to the "stream of conscious life in which every such state occurs," *i. e.,* to the total consciousness which includes the knowing along with the known.[36]

It appears, then, that Ladd operates with two distinct notions of 'consciousness': the notion of consciousness as the sum-total of conscious states which make up the experience of an 'I,' and the notion of consciousness as the observing activity of this 'I' itself. If the states alone are conscious, there should be no more or less of consciousness: but Ladd, assimilating the conscious character of the states, their essential nature as awareness, to the conscious character of the observing self, is able to speak of degrees of conscious-

---

[34] *Ibid.,* 288 ff.; 308 f.; 213, 289.
[35] *Philos. of Mind,* 86.
[36] *Psychol.,* 290 f.

ness at large. The complete datum of psychology, awareness of awareness, he regards as intrinsically unitary, but as separable by logical abstraction into awareness knowing and awareness known, activity or function and content of consciousness. The awareness known, the content-awareness, he then divides again, by the same abstraction and in the same terms, into activity or function and content. These divisions are confessedly artificial: there is no real line of division within the psychical fact: and we must suppose—since there seems to be no logical reason why they should not be repeated *ad infinitum* [37]—that they are carried only so far as is necessary for systematic exposition. Ladd himself justifies them, partly on the ground of convenience, but also, in the general portion of his treatise, because they indicate that psychology, the science of the phenomena of consciousness as such, is far more than description and explanation of merely passive 'content.' [38]

§ 7. In seeking to appraise Ladd's definition of the psychical, as subject-matter for a science, we shall confine ourselves to a few broad lines of criticism. And

[37] Brentano (*PES*, i, 1894, 167) avoids the infinite regress by means of his *eigenthümliche Verwebung:* cf. my *Exper. Psychol. of the Thought-processes*, 1909, 47 f. Ladd (*Psychol.*, 35) comments critically on Brentano's fourfold act, but does not appear to recognise the logical difficulty in which he is himself involved. I do not know that every logical regress is necessarily vicious. But in this case Ladd's system is not intelligible without the regress, while the nature of the regress itself is (as it seems to me to be) unintelligible.

[38] It follows, of course, that Ladd's 'physiological psychology' is, as psychology, only a portion of a science, and not an organized scientific whole: see Ladd and Woodworth, *Physiol. Psychol.*, 381, 430, 542, 597, 625, 656, 664 f.

we begin by considering (1) the place or position to which the definition assigns psychology within the group of the acknowledged sciences.

Observation, the immediate awareness of fact, seems in Ladd's view to be identical over the whole range of science. He draws no distinction of kind between inspection and introspection.[39] When, however, we turn to the relation between this direct method of acquaintance and the object upon which it is directed, we find that psychology is "peculiar, and indeed unique." For observation, being itself a fact of consciousness, merges into, or fuses with, the facts of consciousness observed; "it is separable, neither in reality nor in time, from the phenomenon observed as fact." [40] Our own discussion of psychological method must be postponed.* Here we note only that, as regards the relation of its primary method to its subject-matter, Ladd marks off psychology, as unique, from all the other sciences.

The subject-matter of psychology, in what (for want of a better phrase) we may call its logical constitution, is also, for Ladd, unique. The state of consciousness, it will be remembered, is always, at one and the same

---

[39] *Psychol.*, esp. 17 f. Even the fact that psychical phenomena are "alterable—swiftly and largely—by the very act of attention which makes them objects of knowledge" seems to be paralleled on the side of inspection: see 18 (§ 3), 305 f., 318 f., 367 f., etc.

[40] *Ibid.*, 32 f., 319, 530, etc. Cf. *Philos. of Mind*, 160: "The knowing subject and the object are . . . woven into a vital oneness of being."

* [In the original MS. this sentence closed with the words, "to the following Chapter." The reference is to the chapter on Method which, as has been said, was never written. See Preface, p. v f. H. P. W.]

time, fact of knowledge, fact of feeling and fact of conation. "This unity in variety, which belongs to all states of consciousness as such, is of unique character —and this, whether we lay emphasis on the unity that comprises the variety, or upon the variety comprised in the unity." [41] This uniqueness of constitution, exemplified by the single state of consciousness, is attributed by Ladd to the entire course of the mental life.[42]

Not only in logical constitution, however, but also in its self-determination, is the subject-matter of psychology unique. Descriptive and explanatory psychology leads us "to recognise a unique and self-active being" as, within limits, "interiorly determining, in a quite inexplicable way, its own course." [43] The presence among its data of this incalculable surd—whatever the limits of its operation may be—again separates psychology from the other sciences.

Here, then, are three points at which scientific psychology is wholly and necessarily out of touch with what should be its fellow-sciences. It is clear that the

---

[41] *Psychol.*, 36, 172 f.

[42] There is, namely, a "principle of continuity which gives its unique character to what we can observe of mental development. In all forms of organic physical evolution . . . the factors and stages of the evolution have some existence and value considered *in themselves*, as it were. But the case of mental development is not so. . . . Each factor, faculty, and stage exists for consciousness as in and of its own continuously flowing life-movement"; *ibid.*, 659 f. The unity and variety of states of consciousness "are illustrations of this very principle of continuity as lying at the base of mental development": 661.

[43] *Ibid.*, 638, 662. We might append, as a fourth point, the fact that psychology sustains a "quite unique" relation to philosophy: *ibid.*, 638; *Philos. of Mind*, 71.

word 'science,' if it is to be retained at all, must be given an extraordinarily elastic meaning. In fact, the position which Ladd assigns to scientific psychology is a position, not within, but without the circle of the acknowledged sciences.[44]

(2) Ladd, however, has his own definition of science. "There is science," he says, "wherever there are ascertainable facts that may be described and explained in their relation to one another and to other classes of facts." [45] We must therefore consider, secondly, the nature of the 'facts of consciousness' that appear in his pages as the data of a scientific psychology.

Throughout his psychological writings Ladd is insistent that the phenomena of consciousness be regarded both content-wise, as facts of passive existence, and function-wise, as facts of activity.[46] The task that he sets himself is, accordingly, twofold: he must de-

---

[44] Ladd can be sufficiently severe upon these 'acknowledged' sciences: e.g., Philos. of Mind, 6 ff. The point here, however, is that he distinguishes psychology by its three (or four) unique characters from the other sciences, not as seen by themselves, but as he sees them.

[45] Psychol., 658. The 'affirm' of the following sentence should apparently be read 'deny.'

[46] Ladd observes that "a psychosis without content is equivalent to no psychosis at all; there are no phenomena of consciousness in general" (Philos. of Mind, 85; cf. Philos. of Knowledge, 200, and Psychol., 30 f.). Yet he frequently speaks, in the Psychology, as if consciousness were, after all, something 'apart from' and superadded to the 'actual psychic facts'; we read of 'conscious psychic activity' (214), 'conscious intellection' and 'conscious mentality' (296), 'the conscious mind' (305), 'conscious mental life' (321, 469), 'conscious feeling' (583, 587), 'conscious ideation' (600), 'conscious conation' (623), 'conscious acts of will' (657), and 'conscious attention' (666 f.). Similar phrases occur in Ladd and Woodworth, Physiol. Psychol., 380, 463, 642, 671, 676, 679. These slips give further evidence of the instable nature of Ladd's concept of consciousness.

scribe and explain both the content and the function of every typical psychosis; and, indeed, he must describe and explain the particular content as adequate vehicle of a particular function, and the particular function as correlated activity of a particular content. This of itself would be a sufficiently difficult programme; but Ladd is hampered in his undertaking by his double use (to which we have already referred) of the term 'consciousness,' which means both 'my' awareness and also the awareness intrinsic to a psychosis as such. Consider, for example, that "convenient abstraction," the sensation. Every sensation is at once active and passive, a "psychical activity" and a passively received "impression." As active, it should be actively aware, actively cognisant of the "quality belonging to the object of sense." In Ladd's account, however, it becomes, even while regarded as intrinsically active, an "item of information" to 'me'; 'my' sensations "become objectified, as my feelings and thoughts cannot, in the form of qualities of perceived *things*." The function which should be the sensation's own is thus transferred, from the sensation, to the 'me' to whom all sensations belong.[47]

In this case, then, there is loss to be noted; in the case of primary intellection, on the other hand, we have a superfluity. Intellection, as actively discriminating consciousness, is "within," is "an integral part of," every state of consciousness, so that a concrete psychosis is by its very nature self-discriminating and self-discriminated. Yet if I make a state of consciousness

---

[47] *Psychol.*, 93 ff.

the object of my regard, discriminating consciousness is found to "accompany" the now passive fact. It is perhaps intelligible that 'my' discriminating consciousness should be needed to discern the discriminating activity which is native to the psychosis (though it must be remembered that, as such, these two activities are identical); but it is surely not clear how this attendant discrimination of mine helps toward the discernment of the already self-discriminated 'content.' Two discriminating activities, of precisely the same kind, are here set to work in circumstances where it seems that one would be sufficient.[48]

In still other cases, the duplication of consciousness leads to sheer logical confusion. Suppose, for instance, that I, by way of primary attention, make a state of consciousness the passive object of my consideration: primary attention is then the degree of psychical energy "expended upon" the different aspects or moments of the state. Yet every mental state, as active, has its own degree of this same psychical energy, upon which attention, in its present turn, is constantly dependent. Ladd tries to save his logic by the remark that these two statements "only serve to approach the same truth from different sides." But the truth, as he leaves it, seems rather to be a matter of alternatives.[49]

Difficulties of this sort recur again and again to baffle the student of Ladd's psychology. The 'facts of consciousness' with which the system deals are both

---

[48] *Ibid.*, 33 f., 288.
[49] *Ibid.*, 74 f., 78, 83, 621. On 'psychic energy' (of which **Ladd** gives no definition), see 39, 41, 44, 64 f., 78, 83, 132, 261, 386, etc.

ambiguous and instable. They are active and they are passive, they are forthputtings of a mind and data of a science, they are conscious and I am conscious of them. Moreover, they play their systematic parts with so little regard to omission and repetition and contradiction that the plot of the play tends to be lost.

(3) This plot itself, we must add—the systematic working up of the psychological materials—shows a like ambiguity. Ladd declares, for example, that the mental life, from its very beginnings, carries the plain promise of a plan, so that "no *science* of the life of mind is possible without recognising the presence of final purpose"; yet he affirms also that "in attempting a scientific account of the mental life psychology is justified in laying emphasis, at first, upon the passive and, as it were, externally determined side of the total development," as if no plan were visible or operative.[50] Here is no distinction of function and content within consciousness, but the recognition of two radically different psychological attitudes toward mind in general. The same attempt to have things both ways is seen in the treatment of the faculties: Ladd, in all literalness, both accepts and rejects the doctrine of faculties. He speaks, in formal reference, of the 'so-called' faculties; he explains that the term (faculty) is both futile and dangerous; and still he employs the concept, repeatedly and constructively, in his psychological exposition.[51]

---

[50] *Ibid.*, 266 f., 286 f., 414, 664 f., 668; *Philos. of Mind,* 203; *Philos. of Knowledge,* 473, etc.

[51] *Psychol.*, 33, 45 f., 49 ff., 60, 288, 317 f., 380, 409 f., 455, 490, 612, 659, 664. In particular: (1) Ch. iv is headed "The So-called 'Mental Faculties.'" Ladd's use of 'so-called' is a mannerism, which began

And, as a final instance, the same criticism holds of Ladd's treatment of mental composition. He makes free use of the terms 'mixture' and 'blending' and 'fusion' and 'association,' while yet he assures us that this language is figurative, adopted only for the avoidance of "almost unending periphrases." But is taste, or is it not, a complex of "gustatory, olfactory and tactual elements"? And is there, or is there not, in stereoscopic vision, a 'combination' of visual with tactual and motor sense-complexes? The reader looks in vain for a single periphrasis to clear his mind, and is forced to the conclusion that Ladd's logic is trying to say both Yea and Nay of the same subject-matter.[52]

(4) Where both data and applied logic are thus ambiguous, it is perhaps unnecessary to urge that the resultant is not an organised system. Since, however, we are presently to discuss the working concepts of 'function' and 'content' in their general applicability to the subject-matter of psychology, we cannot afford

---

perhaps as a defensive reaction against the possible charge of looseness of language. Since it has come with him to mean anything from 'what is ordinarily called' to 'what is falsely called,' it does him little service. (2) The adjectives 'futile' and 'dangerous' are not too strong. For we are told (51) that words like 'faculty' do not explain; that they help but little in classification; and that their use, however guarded, is "likely to occasion . . . a generally inadequate and misleading account of the development of mental life." (3) For the seriousness with which the concept is taken, see such passages as 380, 490.

[52] The following sentence (*ibid.*, 235) is characteristic: "The introspective and experimental analysis of modern psychology cannot be abandoned, because, in spite of repeated explanations, some readers will persist in misunderstanding our necessarily figurative terms." Cf. 18 f., 23, 37, 38 f., 89 ff., 94, 102 f., 106, 115, 118, 132, 141 ff., 146, 160, 180, 186, 209, 253 ff., 318 f., 323, 349, etc.

to neglect this formal point of criticism. We note briefly that Ladd's system breaks bounds on every side.

Ladd starts out with the threefold unity of intellection, feeling and conation, all of which 'moments' or 'aspects' of consciousness are to be taken both as content and as function. These are the material postulates of his psychological system. But they prove to be inadequate. The study of intellection, for instance, brings us in time to the problem of recognitive memory; and here our scientific advance is arrested; recognition is "a form of mental reaction *sui generis,* which, while depending upon conditions . . . , has still a unique character that transcends the conditions on which it reposes." [53] In like manner the study of feeling brings us to the feeling of obligation and the sentiment of moral approbation or disapprobation. "These two forms of moral feeling are unique. Why they arise in the individual, and why they have that nature and connection with each other, and with the development of intellect, which they actually have— these are questions which psychology [even as explanatory] cannot answer." [54] Lastly, the study of conation brings us to volition, where "psychologically considered, it is no less true that I will the influential ideas, feelings and desires, than that the ideas, feelings and desires influence the final 'I will'." [55] So that there is no single aspect of mind, no single strand of mental development, for which the complication of function

---

[53] *Ibid.,* 382, 397, 399, 401.
[54] *Ibid.,* 581 ff.
[55] *Ibid.,* 618 f., 625 f., 635, 638.

and the compounding of content are sufficient. The system is disrupted on the side of intellect, on the side of feeling, and on the side of will.

There can be little question, then, that Ladd has failed to erect a science of psychology on the basis of a special class or department of "phenomena of consciousness." We looked at his 'so-called' science in its general status and relations, and we found it to stand apart from all acknowledged sciences. We glanced over the contents of his exposition, and we found that his programme has not been carried out. We considered the logic of his system, and we found it no less ambiguous than the materials to which it is applied. We have now examined the result to which his systematic labours have attained, and we find him hopeless of a system. It remains to ask whether his failure is the failure of a particular author, or whether it is the failure of his psychological position 'as such.' [56]

---

[56] The systems of Angell and Judd can be less certainly appraised, partly because they have so far been carried out only at the text-book level, and partly because their writers are more interested in function and genesis than in content. We may, however, note the following points.

For Angell, psychology is the science of consciousness, and consciousness is awareness (*Psychology*, 1908, 1, 222, 366, 442; cf. 5, 150, 185, 199, 228, 246 ff., 337, 364 f., 370, 373, 383 ff., 399, 426 ff., 430, 441 ff., 444, 446). On its subject-side, consciousness is the observing activity of a self; 'we' are immediately aware of thoughts and feelings, of perceptions, images and emotions (2, 442 f.; cf. 84, 302, 401, 408, 431, etc.). In its object-half, or on its content-side (content being taken in the broader sense), consciousness shows the two aspects of structure or content (in the narrower sense) and function (*e.g.*, 201). States of consciousness are functionally unitary, but by logical abstraction may be divided into cognitive and affective (302, 436 f.). [The position of attention is ambiguous. Attention appears to be a function of subject-consciousness, with a structure on the side of

§ 8. We pass, accordingly, to a consideration of the features common to functional systems in

---

object-consciousness; there is apparently no discriminable attentive function within object-consciousness: 80 ff.] Both the cognitive and the affective functions are, in their own right, modes of awareness: the cognitive are informative (109, 170, 198, 201, 222, 248), the affective are evaluative, awarenesses (302, 320, 322, 327, 378, 382). In general outline, therefore, Angell's system is very like Ladd's.

For Judd, likewise, psychology is the science of consciousness (*Psychology*, 1917, 1, 5, 10, 12, 38, 145, 309; behaviour is to be studied for the understanding and explanation of consciousness), and this consciousness is awareness (2 ff., 6, 12 f., 142, 238, 329; cf. 27, 65, 73, 160 f., 166, 169, 183, 190, 212, 233, 246, 270, 276, 291, 345). Awareness, however, is always the awareness of 'someone'; it is 'one' or 'the observer' or 'the individual' or 'the child' that is conscious (1, 141 f., 155, 169, 189, 241, 272, 301, etc.). 'Conscious processes,' which are classified according to nervous processes (64 ff.), show the familiar duality. Over against sensations (73, 188), which are discussed contentwise, stand the attitudes of feeling and attention (66 f., 146 ff.), which are discussed functionwise. Perception includes, on the side of function, the activities of fusing, locating, distinguishing, recognising, in a word, of relating sensations (163, 166, 169, 186, 189 191), and on the other side the product or resultant of these activities, the percept of relational fact, a content of a higher order (169, 175, 186 f., 189, 191 f.). The content of memory consists in images, which are primarily substitutes for sensations and percepts (241 ff.), and its activity consists in recall according to the laws of association (244 ff.). Ideation furnishes us with contents of a still higher order, difficult of precise description (246), and with such activities as conception, abstraction, generalization, judgment and reasoning (263 ff.). Lastly, in voluntary choice we have a personality, an organized whole of mental activities (308), directed upon 'ideas' which are themselves organized "composites of experience" (306, 309).

There remains the question of the 'someone' who is thus in manifold ways and degrees aware. Judd's teaching is that we must conceive the knowing self, to which the study of conscious processes leads us, as an unitary being—a 'conscious being' which, like the 'living being,' is an organized unity (274 ff.; cf. 263). The self possesses and, by unifying, modifies conscious states (274). It is, however, difficult—since the terms 'self' and 'personality' are used interchangeably—to reconcile the statement that "the self is a being which perceives and forms concepts" (274) with the statement that "personality is the name of that individual nature which has been

general.[57] There seem to be four main tenets or tendencies which we may regard as characteristic of the school.

---

developed out of the play and interplay of impressions and instincts and conscious comparisons and imaginations" (308). See p. 160 above.

[57] This is not the place for a bibliography of functional psychology. I give a few early references, and name two papers of objective import—W. James, "On Some Omissions of Introspective Psychology," *Mind,* ix, 1884, 18 f.; *The Principles of Psychology,* i, 1890, 478; H. Ebbinghaus, *Grundzüge der Psychol.,* i, 1897, 161 ff. (i, 1905, 176 ff.; changed by Dürr, i, 1911, 175 ff.); E. B. Titchener, "The Postulates of a Structural Psychology," *Philos. Rev.,* vii, 1898, 449 ff.; "Structural and Functional Psychology," *ibid.,* viii, 1899, 290 ff.; C. A. Ruckmich, "The Use of the Term '*Function*' in English Text-books of Psychology," *Amer. Journ. Psych.,* xxiv, 1913, 99 ff.; K. M. Dallenbach, "The History and Derivation of the Word 'Function' as a Systematic Term in Psychology," *ibid.,* xxvi, 1915, 437 ff.

Angell remarks (*Psychol. Rev.,* xiv, 1907, 63) that 'structural psychology was the first to isolate itself.' In a broad sense, that statement is true; functional psychology claimed the whole field. In historical detail, however, things are less simple. There had already appeared in America the two overtly functional systems of J. M. Baldwin (*Handbook of Psychology,* 1889-91) and Ladd (1894). Moreover, it was as early as 1887 that Ladd, in his *Physiological Psychology,* sought deliberately to subsume the whole body of experimentally observed facts to a functional view of 'the nature of mind.' So that functional psychology had been a little uneasy, a little self-conscious, for a whole decade before the catch-word 'structural' came on the controversial scene. And the first note of revolt (E. W. Scripture's *New Psychology,* 1897) was struck in the physical, not in the biological, key. Scripture's attempt proved abortive, partly because the physical concepts of time, space and energy were inadequate to the psychological data, and partly because he represented his new psychology as a straight development from the old: "there is no difference in its material, no change in its point of view" (453). 'Structural' psychology, as its name implies, recognized the existence of a correlative psychology of function; it isolated itself only to the degree that it demanded equal rights for content and activity, and by so doing protested against the autocracy of function. In the 'biological' atmosphere of its time the phrase did good controversial service. If the view of my book is accepted, both 'functional' and 'structural,' as qualifications of 'psychology,' are now obsolete terms.

(1) The distinction between the 'activity' or 'function' and the 'content' or 'structure' of consciousness is recognised, explicitly or implicitly, by all the psychologists of function. It reflects, of course, the biological distinction of organic function and organic structure, of physiology and morphology. We say 'biological,' in deference to current usage: in point of fact, the distinction is rather technological than scientific. It belongs of right to the great technology of medicine; it was accepted, and found useful, by human physiology; it remained serviceable in the beginnings of comparative physiology. On the strict ground of science, it is no longer adequate to our knowledge; [58] and if it still persists in biological text-books, the reason is again largely technological: the distinction recommends itself for pedagogical purposes. Even in medicine, its encouragement of a rigid specialisation lays it open to criticism.

There is, nevertheless, in the 'biological' context, a certain appeal to common sense, a certain plausibility, about this correlation; heart and lungs and hand and brain, regarded as machines, are obviously 'adapted'

---

[58] As appears, *e.g.*, from such works as H. S. Jennings' *Behaviour of the Lower Organisms* (1906), and J. S. Haldane's *Organism and Environment as Illustrated by the Physiology of Breathing* (1917); cf. also B. F. Kingsbury, "The Fitness of Organisms from an Embryologist's Viewpoint," *Science*, N. S. xxxviii, 1913, 174 ff.; "The Interstitial Cells of the Mammalian Ovary; Felis domestica," *Amer. Journ. Anat.*, xvi, 1914, 79; "The Development of the Human Pharynx," *ibid.*, xviii, 1915, 374 ff. It is obvious that those who identify biological phenomena with physicochemical processes have no need of the concept of function (see, *e.g.*, J. Loeb, *Forced Movements, Tropisms and Animal Conduct,* 1918); but this view is not here under consideration.

to the 'ends' which they subserve. We search in vain for any such plausible coördination of conscious content and conscious function. The "forms of receptivity," according to Ladd, stand in "bewildering and unclassifiable variety" over against the "relatively few forms of organising activity displayed in all mental states." [59] If content is to be made adequate to function, then (as in the instance of the 'representative image') function must be read into content, so that the content becomes an hypostatised function.[60] Nowhere is the attempt made to show that the strictly observable 'contents' are the suitable vehicles or instruments or substrates of the various modes of psychical activity.

Why, then—it is natural to ask—why, and with what hopes, did psychology submit itself at all to 'biological' guidance, and seek within its subject-matter for the analogues of organic structure and organic function? The answer refers us to historical conditions. Historically viewed, the functional psychology of which we have taken Ladd to be representative is a plea in avoidance offered before the court of science on behalf of empiricism. The continually growing body of experimental facts, menacing even while unorganised, had to be reckoned with; and the distinction of function and content afforded a means whereby it

---

[59] *Psychology,* 53 ff., esp. 57.

[60] *Ibid.,* 234 ff., 244 ff., 376. D. S. Miller ("The Confusion of Function and Content in Mental Analysis," *Psych. Rev.,* ii, 1895, 536) meets the difficulty by a reference to the unlikeness of physical cause and physical effect. But content does not stand to function as cause to effect, and physical causes and effects are alike energetic.

might be duly subordinated to the empirical system.
If the worst should come, and experimental psychology
should be able presently to organise itself as an independent science, still the empiricist had gained time, a
breathing-space for adjustment, and had gained also a
set of working concepts by whose aid the break might,
so to say, be eased and graded. What he expected,
however, as is clear from all of Ladd's work, was a
new lease of life for the traditional empiricism. The
particular line which his reconstruction followed was
settled for him by the status of science at the time.
Not mathematics, not physics, was the characteristic
modern 'science,' but biology; and if biology thought
and spoke in terms of structure and function, psychology need not scruple to think like thoughts and to use
like language. So there arose a new empirical psychology, in all essentials at one with the old, but more or
less effectively disguised under the cloak of contemporary science. After the event, we can see that psychology borrowed in haste, without assurance that the
loan could be turned to properly psychological account.
We can see, further, that the biology to which psychology appealed was not in truth a scientific biology, but
a biology conventionalised and popularised. At the
time, nevertheless, it was only natural that the
contents and functions of this new empirical psychology should seem to bear the authentic stamp of
science.

(2) In the second place, functional systems are disposed to correlate the phenomenon of consciousness
with unreadiness or inadequacy of the nervous system;

"consciousness is only intense," remarks James, "when nerve-processes are hesitant." [61] As soon as the organism is confronted by a problem which its existing neural organisation is unable to meet, consciousness steps in to dispel the perplexity; "straightway appears consciousness, with its accompanying cortical activities, taking note of the nature of the stimulus and of the various kinds of muscular response which it called forth." [62] The point must be taken, it would seem, with a certain reservation: for it is not unreadiness or inadequacy in general that is responsible for the appearance of consciousness, but rather such unreadiness and such inadequacy as require, within the biological limitations of the particular organism, only a certain additional prompting or urging to change into readiness and adequacy. With this reservation more or less expressly made, some authors, like Angell, declare in round terms that "conscious activities emerge at the point where reflex acts are found inadequate to meet the needs of particular situations"; "if the reflexes and the automatic acts were wholly competent to steer the organism throughout its course, there is no reason to suppose that consciousness would ever put in an ap-

---

[61] *Principles,* i, 1890, 142. James, although he favoured a functional as opposed to a structural psychology ("The Energies of Men," *Philos. Rev.,* xvi, 1907, 2), does not give us in the *Principles* a system of functional psychology. He gives us a work on the principles of knowledge, written from a psychologistic standpoint. If his volumes are read with this interpretation in mind, the critics' charge of lack of plan (which James repelled: *Text-book,* 1892, iii f.) will be found groundless.

[62] Angell, *Psychology,* 1918, 64.

pearance." [63] Others, like Dewey, argue that difficulties in the way of nervous conduction heighten the clearness of consciousness, but do not commit themselves outright to a theory of its first appearance.[64] There are thus differences of detail.[65] It would, however, be widely agreed that, at any rate in the case of man, the 'condition' of consciousness is a temporary and corrigible imperfection of nervous organisation.[66]

---

[63] *Loc. cit.* Angell confines his discussion, in these passages, to the human consciousness. The question 'why' the human infant should be limited to a certain group of inherited coördinations he hands over to 'the biologist' for answer. So one might hand over many other questions: 'Why,' since in the last resort the environment is for all organisms the same, should any infant embark on a career for which his inherited coördinations are insufficient? and 'why,' having thus embarked, should he again meet with limitations to his conscious powers? and so on. The biologist, in so far as he is man of science, will maintain a discreet silence.

[64] So at least I understand these discussions. See J. Dewey, "The Theory of Emotion," *Psychol. Rev.*, i, 1894, 553 ff.; ii, 1895, 13 ff.; "The Reflex Arc Concept in Psychology," *ibid.*, iii, 1896, 357 ff.; "The Psychology of Effort," *Philos. Rev.*, vi, 1897, 43 ff.

[65] The same general idea has been expressed in various places by W. McDougall. See, *e.g.*, "A Contribution towards an Improvement in Psychological Method," *Mind*, N. S. vii, 1898, 159 ff.; "On the Seat of the Psycho-physical Processes," *Brain*, xxiv, 1901, 607 f.; "The Physiological Factors of the Attention-Process," *Mind*, N. S. xi, 1902, 341 f.; *Physiological Psychology*, 1905, 59 f.
It is possible that Ladd is adopting a like view when he makes conation or conscious striving "the most fundamental of all psychic phenomena" (*Psychol.*, 219). Ladd and Woodworth, however, combat the theories of Dewey and McDougall (*Physiol. Psychol.*, 1911, 610 ff.).

[66] Judd ("Evolution and Consciousness," *Psychol. Rev.*, xvii, 1910, 77 ff.) forms a marked exception to the rule. Consciousness appears only when the organism has attained a certain stage of complexity of inner organization (94). The question of first causes—where this consciousness comes from—is not raised (92). Having appeared, however, consciousness functions as a centre of reorganization (93 f.). The more highly organized, *i.e.*, the more self-sufficing the organism,

A view of this sort seems, indeed, to be logically bound up with the view that consciousness is primarily and actively a matter of function, and only secondarily and passively a matter of content. For if consciousness is to do us some organic service, it will find its natural opportunity in some defect of our given (non-conscious or extra-conscious) organic equipment; and this, in the categories of our current thinking, means some defect in the functional capacity of the brain. Positive evidence, however, is found in the experience of every adult. We have learned to write, to use a typewriter, to ride a bicycle, to play a piano, to drive a motor car; and we know that, as the original problems cease to baffle us, and the skilled movements become habitual, the need of conscious 'control' grows less and less; we find that consciousness 'intervenes' less frequently and less imperatively, until it may finally disappear. Could there be more convincing proof of the instrumental function of consciousness? and is not the formation of a habit typical of the general course of the mental life? [67]

We must here meet the psychologist of function on his own ground; we must, that is to say, grant him his assumption that consciousness, the subject-matter of psychology, is awareness. The question then arises whether our conscious life is, as a matter of fact, noth-

---

the greater is the rôle and the higher the development of consciousness (80 f., 88). In a word, consciousness is at once the product, the index, and the cause of organization.

[67] Judd is here consistent. "Too often the psychology of habit has been guilty of the statement that habituation leads to unconsciousness. This is not the case" (*Psychol.*, 1917, 207).

ing more than a recurrent grappling with problems. Are we aware only when and in so far as we are searching, reconciling, reducing to familiar terms, trying to understand—or whatever other words there may be that imply the setting of a problem and the urgency of its solution? Surely we are not; surely there is a contemplative as well as an acquisitive awareness. We are not always learning something new, or practising this new until it becomes old. There are times when we sun ourselves, as it were, in the full light of consciousness—times when, without any "felt necessity for further nicety of adaptation to surroundings," [68] we are none the less keenly and competently aware. There is a consciousness militant, but there is also a consciousness triumphant: more than that, there is a consciousness that, in the midcourse of its campaigning, rests quietly upon its arms, and surveys the terrain it has occupied. A narrowly instrumental theory of consciousness comes very near to a *reductio ad absurdum* of the biological 'struggle for existence.'

(3) The two characters that we have so far discussed—the distinction within consciousness of content and activity and the assignment to consciousness, especially in its active phase, of a value for organic survival—lie on the surface of the functional systems. Underneath, always and everywhere, runs the steady current of teleology. It is one of the ironies of the history of science that the great biological generalisation which

---

[68] Angell, *Psychol.*, 1908, 74. Note the implication of the phrase! Consciousness, which might on Angell's terms be described, roughly, as the "felt process of adaptation," here anticipates its own function.

was to free us of teleology in our study of the phenomena of life should give rise, in post-Darwinian days, to an unbridled license of teleological 'interpretation.' [69] Biology has suffered, and is still suffering, from that license. Biology, nevertheless, again furnished psychology with the obvious scientific parallel. Biologists spoke in terms of final cause, the whole system of biology was pervaded by teleology, and psychology again had no call to be more scientific than science. We have seen the outcome in Ladd's thinking: a teleological activity of organisation plays upon a causally (or quasi-causally) determined content, to the inevitable confusion of the concept of consciousness which is fundamental to his psychology at large. We find a like ambiguity in Angell's book. Mind, as we have said, there "seems to involve the master devices" through which the "adaptive operations of organic life may be made most perfect," and "the real business of consciousness is to be sought amid the adaptive responses of the organism to its life conditions." [70] But when we go in search of master-devices and real business we are told that the basal distinction is that "between certain kinds of nervous activity overtly involving consciousness . . . and certain other kinds not overtly involv-

---

[69] "If we apprehend the spirit of the 'Origin of Species' rightly, then, nothing can be more entirely and absolutely opposed to Teleology, as it is commonly understood, than the Darwinian Theory": T. H. Huxley, "Criticisms on 'The Origin of Species'" (1864), *Lay Sermons, Addresses and Reviews*, 1887, 264. It is a mind "stored with the choicest materials of the teleologist that rejects teleology "—so J. Tyndall speaks of Darwin (*Report B. A. A. S., 1874*, 1875, lxxxvi). Cf. E. du Bois-Reymond, *La Mettrie*, 1875, 23.

[70] *Op. cit.*, 8, 95.

ing it"; consciousness is only the "index" of "problem-
solving adaptive acts." Nay more: if we speak "as
though mind might in a wholly unique manner step in
and bring about changes in the activity of the nervous
system," we are employing "convenient metaphors,"
"a convenient abbreviation of expression," which must
not blind us to "the fundamental facts which lie behind." [71] Such are the logical sacrifices that teleology
demands of her children!

May it not be, however, that the fault lies with the
children? May it not be that the psychologist of function takes his teleology a little carelessly? It has come
down to him from the older empiricism; it is guaranteed by philosophy and technology; it is justified by
biological example. Small wonder, then, that he should
slip easily, even heedlessly, into the teleological attitude! But are we on that account ruthlessly to banish
teleology from a scientific psychology?

One could wish, certainly, that the functional systems were somewhat less confident of their position.
For it is one thing to affirm broadly that "the stream
of consciousness appears . . . as a current designed
from the beginning . . . to the fit performance of a
certain work," [72] and quite another thing to build psychological facts and laws, the details of psychology,
into a coherent system of means and ends. The teleology which is used in psychology as a tool of scientific
construction is, as a matter of fact, both clumsy and

[71] *Ibid.,* 59 f., 300.
[72] Ladd, *Psychol.,* 668 f.

double-edged. The psychologist may insist on final causes as he will, but he never makes them adequate to the refinement of observation;[73] and he may answer any number of Whys, but he is still faced by unanswerable Why-nots that throw doubt upon his positive explanations.[74] Yet we must insist that final causes, if they are at all recognised in psychology, be recognised primarily for psychology's sake. It is not enough to infuse just so much of teleology into the psychological system as shall orientate us toward ethics or history, or place us within a generally biological context, or blur the difference between 'pure' and 'applied' sci-

---

[73] "Fortunately for science," writes Judd (*Psychol.*, 90 f.), "there have been a few cases in which the same person has been able to observe directly both the normal color sensations and the partially color-blind series." Fortunately for descriptive science, truly: but how fortunate for psychology in Judd's sense? How has the development of red-green vision aided man in the struggle for existence (4)? or what has man gained by the "unique compromise process" (92) which gives rise to the purple sensation? These and like questions are not touched.

[74] "It is because we have . . . no special organ affected by weak currents of electricity that men overlooked for so long a period both the prevalence of forms of electrical energy and the close relation between light and electricity" (Judd, *op. cit.*, 72). But, granted that the facts are as stated and granted that this furtherance of knowledge is useful, why have we not the special organ? For it is surely evident that biological conditions, which have produced the 'electric fishes,' are also competent to produce an electrical sense-organ in man.

Again: "We do not have microscopic eyes like the fly. Nor . . . do we have distance vision like the eagle's. . . . The range of human vision has been determined by the range of possible human reactions" (132); cf. W. H. Hudson, *Idle Days in Patagonia*, 1893, 183 f. But has not man extended his reactions by microscope and telescope, and are not tools (249) sensory as well as motor? Cf. H. Spencer, *Principles of Psychol.*, i, 1881, § 164, p. 365; O. Wiener, *Die Erweiterung der Sinne*, 1900.

ence. Psychology has its own claims in behalf of every item of its subject-matter.[75]

There is, however, no reason to suppose that these claims could be met by any teleology, even the most self-conscious and the most persistent. The whole history of science argues to the contrary. We may freely grant that teleological ideas have the occasional heuristic value which certain investigators have claimed for them.[76] It remains true, notwithstanding, that these same investigators have only by exception had recourse to teleology, and have not been encouraged to adopt it as a guiding principle of research. It remains true that final causes have long been banished from the domain of the older sciences, and that they flourish only where (and in proportion as) exact knowledge is wanting. It remains true that interpretation by means and end tends to close enquiry and thus to bar the progress of scientific knowledge. In particular, it is highly significant that biology, after full trial of teleological principles, is in these latter days resolutely turning away from final causes to the laborious planning of experiments and the patient accumulation of observed facts—so that 'evolution' and 'heredity' and 'adaptation,' once the means whereby we conjured ends, are now coming to be mere descriptive labels for labora-

---

[75] How utterly this subject-matter may drop out of sight, under the prepossession of teleology, appears in the discussion by A. E. Taylor, *Elements of Metaphysics*, 1903, 306 f.

[76] E. Mach, *Die Analyse der Empfindungen*, etc., 1900, 60 f. The instance cited is not physical but biological. I do not find in the *Erkenntnis und Irrtum* (1906) any acknowledgment of the heuristic value of teleology in physics, though the book as a whole contains a good deal of teleological thinking.

tory note-books. The whole history of science thus goes to show that teleology is essentially non-scientific. And, if that is the case, there can be no room for "teleological import" within a "*science* of the life of the mind." [77]

(4) Finally, this teleological attitude threatens the stability of psychology as an independent branch of knowledge. The psychology of the functional systems appears as transitional, as a stage either upon the difficult ascent toward philosophy or upon the level road that leads to various application; always it appears as a half-way house on the journey to something else, and not as an abiding-place. The individual psychologist may look forward to the one goal or to the other, or may perhaps keep both in view; that is a matter of temperament and training. It is at any rate characteristic of the school that they are not content to rest in psychology. Their psychologising, with whatever pains and seriousness it is done, seeks to transcend itself, as if in the last resort it were done not for its own sake but for the attainment of some foreign end.

Ladd, for instance, bears witness on the side of philosophy. "The problems of philosophy," he tells us, "all emerge and force themselves upon the mind in the attempt thoroughly to comprehend and satisfactorily to solve the problems of a scientific psychology; and the attempts, along the different main lines of research in psychology, to deal scientifically with its problems all lead up to the place where this science hands these same

---

[77] Ladd, *Psychol.*, 668.

problems over to philosophy." [78] Psychology is therefore of value as a propaedeutic to philosophy, in so far as philosophy is too difficult and too intricate to be approached directly and without an introductory easement; but the psychologist cannot, in scientific status, compare with the physicist or chemist or biologist. On the contrary! The longer he works in psychology, the more clearly does he confess his inability to tackle his problems at first hand; and the more able he is, the briefer will be his psychological apprenticeship to philosophy.

Judd, on the other hand, lays stress on the importance of psychology for the understanding and consequent control of human life and human institutions. He devotes a chapter of his general *Psychology* to the maxims of 'mental hygiene,' by following which the individual may attain to the highest level of organisation, "when mental development becomes a matter of voluntary control." He devotes another chapter to the institutional applications of psychology, its usefulness in literature and the fine arts, in the social sciences and anthropology, and especially in education. He recognises, to be sure, that psychology's relation to philosophy is "closer than that of any of the special sciences," but the recognition is formal and carefully qualified. The main interest of the study of consciousness is that it gives the key to human nature, and thus enables us

---

[78] *Philos. of Mind*, 1895, 73; *Psychol.*, 12. Cf. J. R. Angell, "The Relations of Structural and Functional Psychology to Philosophy," in *The Decennial Publications of the University of Chicago*, iii, 1903, 55 ff.; *Psychol.*, 1908, 9 ff.

intelligently to guide the course of the individual and of society.[79]

There is no need of further examples, but there is great need that the reader clearly understand what these particular examples are meant to show. The point here at issue is not that the author of a scientific text-book should shut himself up within the four walls of his specialty, and look neither above nor about. Where we find such narrowness of vision, we are likely to find also confusion of thought. The point is rather that we note a marked difference of emphasis between text-books of functional psychology and text-books of other sciences. A text-book of physics will discuss various types of engines and machines, but it will discuss them as illustrative of physical laws. A text-book of physiology may discuss various types of pathological phenomena, but it will discuss them in connection with physiological methods and physiological principles. The text-books of functional psychology, on the other hand, tend—it is true, in varying degree—to make of psychology either an introduction to philosophy or an aid to individual and social welfare. In so far as these tendencies prevail: in so far as functional psychology, in its exposition of psychology proper, goes out to meet the problems of philosophy or of our customary human life: in so far there is real danger that the pains and seriousness which are the due of psychology as science are withdrawn from psychology and expended in those other fields.

These, then, seem to be the four main characteristics

---

[79] *Psychol.*, 1917, 314 ff., esp. 324, 344 ff.; cf. 10, 208, 268, 299 f., 309.

of the functional systems. The subject-matter of psychology is duplicated, though function is preferred to content; consciousness is a solver of problems; the whole course of the mental life is regarded teleologically; and psychology is written as a preface to philosophy or to some practical discipline. We have already indicated that these characters are not logically coördinate. A logical arrangement might, however, have appeared to prejudge the case, whereas our topical presentation has required that every character be discussed on its individual merits. In any case it should now be plain that functional psychology has its roots in the Aristotelian empiricism, and that while it has taken color of modernity from the surrounding sciences it has not adopted the modern conception of science itself. For this reason Ladd's deliberate and sustained effort to maintain the continuity of psychology as science was foredoomed to failure. His loyalty to the past is incompatible with his open-mindedness toward the future. He recognises, frankly, if a little anxiously, the gradual emergence of the scientific problem, yet he cannot bring himself to discard, even in what he defines as science, the constructions of pre-scientific thinking. He is thus betrayed into an illogicality which, in any other context, he would have been among the first to discern.

§ 9. We have now to set a new scene. For while the psychologist of function works, as we have shown, in a biological atmosphere, the psychologist of act, with whom we have next to deal, lives and moves in an atmosphere of logic or theory of knowledge. Functional psychology—so we might say, twisting Fechner's famous phrase—is a psychology from below, a psychology to which we work upward from the more fundamental science, and the psychology of act is a psychology from above, to which we work downward from the superior discipline of logic.

'Function,' Ladd remarks, is "a vague and sufficiently indefinite term," [80] and the statement holds, unfortunately, of biology as well as of psychology. 'Act,' on the other hand, is a term which, whether it occur in logical or in psychological context, may be defined with some rigour. If we cannot frame a definition at the outset, the fault lies not with any ambiguity of 'act' itself, but with the multiplicity of contexts in which the technical term appears. We shall do best to proceed chronologically, and thus to obtain materials for a retrospective survey.

The importance of the 'act' in modern psychology derives from the work of Brentano. And we may begin by quoting the sentences in which Brentano distinguishes psychical from physical phenomena.

"Every psychical phenomenon is characterized by what the scholastics of the Middle Age have termed the intentional (or, sometimes, mental) inexistence of an object, and what we (although the expressions are not wholly free from ambiguity) should term reference to a content, direction upon an object ('object' not meaning here a 'reality'), or immanent objectivity. All alike contain within them something as their object, though they do not all contain the object in the same way. In idea something is ideated, in judgment something is accepted or rejected, in love something is loved, in hate hated, in desire desired, and so on.

---

[80] *Philos. of Mind,* 1895, 300.

"This intentional inexistence is the exclusive property of psychical phenomena. No physical phenomenon shows anything like it. And we may accordingly define psychical phenomena by saying that they are phenomena which intentionally contain an object." [81]

Physical and psychical phenomena, the subject-matters of physics (in the widest sense) and of psychology, are thus differentiated by means of the character of intentional inexistence. Phenomena which 'intentionally contain an object'; are however, in Brentano's terminology, 'acts;' [82] and psychical phenomena are consequently, one and all, 'psychical acts.' [83] Their 'contents' are primarily physical (sensory and imagi-

---

[81] *PES*, 115 f.; cf. 127, 133, 238, 250, 255, 260, 313. I have called attention (p. 9, note 13) to Brentano's change of view regarding the reality of the mental object. The preface to *Von der Klassifikation der psychischen Phänomene* (1911, iv) declares: "Eine der wichtigsten Neuerungen ist die, dass ich nicht mehr der Ansicht bin, dass eine psychische Beziehung jemals anderes als Reales zum Objekt haben könne"; cf. 149.

[82] The term *Akt* is a translation of the scholastic *actus,* which in turn is a translation of the Aristotelian ἐνέργεια. It is likely to carry a suggestion of activity, in the sense of 'voluntary acts,' 'acts of kindness,' etc. The reader may therefore be cautioned to take it strictly as defined by the writer who employs it. "Der Gedanke der Bethätigung muss schlechterdings ausgeschlossen bleiben," writes E. Husserl (*Logische Untersuchungen,* ii, 1901, 358)—and then, a few pages later, slips into the phrase "psychische Bethätigung" (427).
It is strange that the 1910 edition of R. Eisler's *Wörterbuch der philos. Begriffe,* s. v. *Akt,* has nothing to say of the act-psychology.

[83] For *psychischer Act,* see *PES,* 132, 162, 188, 202, etc.; *Act des Bewusstseins,* 296; *Vorstellungsact,* 231, 347; *Act des Vorstellens,* 103, 230; *Gefühlsact,* 189; *Act des Interesses,* 263; *Act der Liebe,* 322, 330. I have not noted *Urtheilsact:* if it does not occur, that is only because *Urtheil* by itself is obviously an act-name. For infinitives, see, *e.g.,* 208, 261 (*Vorstellen*), 214, 262 (*Urtheilen*), 263, 314, 329, 350 (*Lieben und Hassen*).

nal contents are, for Brentano, physical objects), and secondarily psychical, *i. e.,* other acts or unitary blends of other acts. The acts themselves fall into three irreducible classes, ideating, judging, loving-hating, which represent our ultimate 'modes of being conscious.' [84] They stand, nevertheless, in the order given. By the tests of simplicity, independence and generality, ideation ranks before judgment, and judgment before loving-hating.

Brentano's special psychology was, as we know, never written.[85]

§ 10. Brentano claims, in support of his view of the psychical phenomenon, the testimony of a long series of psychologists, from Aristotle to Bain.[86] His definition of the psychical act is, however, challenged, and on substantially the same ground, by Meinong (1899) and Husserl (1901). These critics point out that the 'content' and the 'object' of act, which are identified by Brentano, must in fact be kept apart. When I perceive a house, for example, I most certainly am not ideating my sensory contents (Brentano's physical object). I am rather ideating, by and through these sensory contents, a transsubjective object, namely, the house in question. Brentano's concept of 'immanent

---

[84] *Weise des Bewusstseins,* 266, 295, 345.

[85] Cf. our introductory discussion, pp. 1 ff. The new matter of the *Klassifikation* (131 ff.) shows clearly that Brentano had not in 1874 thought out, even summarily, the contents of his projected second volume.

[86] *PES,* 233 ff., 260.

objectivity' is therefore not adequate to a descriptive psychology.[87]

The effect of this criticism presently appears in the psychological writings of the Meinong school. Höfler (1897) remarks that, while a theory of knowledge must discriminate content and object, psychology, whose object is always immanent, may dispense with the distinction.[88] But Witasek (1908) draws a less simple picture. Every elementary psychical phenomenon is now taken as twofold or two-sided, as at once act and content. There can be no act without content, and no content without act; the distinction is no more partitive than that of the colour and spread of a surface or the velocity and direction of a movement. Logically, however, the separation may be made, and psychologically—act and content are equally 'psy-

---

[87] A. Meinong, "Ueber Gegenstände höherer Ordnung und deren Verhältniss zur inneren Wahrnehmung," *Zeits. f. Psychol. u. Physiol. d. Sinnesorg.*, xxi, 1899, 185 ff.; E. Husserl, *Logische Untersuchungen*, ii, 1901, 344 ff. (esp. 353), 396 ff., 694 ff. A little later comes T. Lipps, *Leitfaden der Psychologie*, 1903, 53 ff., 139 (1906, 5 ff.; 1909, 8 ff.): cf. also "Bewusstsein und Gegenstände," *Psychol. Untersuchungen*, 1905, 1 ff., and "Inhalt und Gegenstand: Psychologie und Logik," *Sitzungsber. d. kgl. bayer. Akad. d. Wiss.*, 1905, 511 ff. The general statement of the text applies more closely to Husserl than to Meinong, who still speaks of immanent objects. Husserl, of course, recognizes the limiting case in which object and content coincide (333, 337 f., 352, 363, 376, etc.). But it is not my purpose at this point to enter into details. Nor have I thought it worth while to try to carry the distinction of content and object further back. Höfler's claim ("Sind wir Psychologisten?" in *Atti del V. Congresso Internazionale di Psicologia*, 1905, 327) will hardly hold water, in view of his own statements in the *Logik* (1890, 7) and the *Psychologie* (1897, 3): cf. Husserl, 470.

[88] A. Höfler, *Psychologie, loc. cit.*

chical'—separate treatment is, within limits, convenient.[89]

The 'content' of a psychical phenomenon is the 'part' whereby it brings a determinate object to consciousness, and the 'act' is the 'part' which makes the object an object of perception or imagination or judgment. The essential character of the psychical, the character that marks it off from the physical, is accordingly this reference to a transsubjective object, a transeunt reference to something beyond itself. In Witasek's own words:

"My ideating, my thinking, my feeling and my willing are always in their own peculiar way 'aimed' at something. I ideate *something,* a something that is not the ideating, perhaps a book; my thinking grasps things that are not themselves thinkings, indeed, that do not belong to the mind at all; it grasps them, without in any way drawing them into itself; there is, and there can be, no suggestion of a spatial relation; and yet my thinking 'seizes' those things. The same thing holds of feeling and of willing. A relation, truly, that would be mysterious, nay, inconceivable, if we were not so familiar with it from our inner experience! But it is altogether confined to the psychical. Examine the physical, search the world of material things, as carefully as you may, and you will find not a trace of it. You will find relations of space (inside, outside, alongside), you will find movement to and from, you will come upon all manner of relations: but this—this intrinsic reference to, direction upon, pointing toward something else—has no place among them. . . . Here, we may believe, is the most tangible, most characteristic difference between the two spheres." [90]

---

[89] S. Witasek, *Grundlinien der Psychologie,* 1908, 73 ff., 280 ff., 318 f.
[90] *Ibid.,* 3 f., 74.

Psychical phenomena still form a class of their own, separate and distinct from physical phenomena. But for Brentano the psychical phenomenon is an act, in which a content or object (which is primarily physical) is intentionally contained. For Witasek the psychical phenomenon is an act-and-content, whose nature it is to point to some object (very often a physical object) that lies beyond it.[91]

The elementary phenomena of Witasek's system are, on the 'intellectual' side of mind, ideas and thoughts, and on the 'affective' side, feelings and desires.[92] Brentano's loving-hating has thus been subdivided.

§ 11. At the same time that Meinong and Husserl criticise Brentano's definition of act, Münsterberg (1900) objects that the specified acts are not logically coördinate. Brentano, as we saw, gives priority to the act of ideation: "[all psychical phenomena] either are ideations or . . . rest upon ideations as their basis." [93] Münsterberg argues that this ideation is not an act at all. An act is an attitude of the subject, an attitude in which we say Yes or No to a present object or con-

---

[91] I am not quite sure of this interpretation. Witasek seems to say expressly (75) that the reference of the psychical phenomenon is an affair of act, and therefore not of content, and all the terms employed in the quotation just given are, as my rendering shows, names of act, and not of total psychical phenomenon. Yet the content is psychical (5, 74). —For the physical object, cf. ibid., 6, 12, 73 f.

[92] Ibid., 81. Witasek's doctrine of processes and dispositions does not here concern us.

[93] PES, 111; cf. Höfler, op. cit., 3 f.; Witasek, op. cit., 97. Husserl's discussion (op. cit., 399-463) will engage our attention later.

tent.[94] Judgment, for example, covers the paired opposites of acceptance and rejection, affirmation and negation, and interest the paired opposites of loving and hating. But where is the activity, the Yea-saying or the Nay-saying, in the case of ideation? "We speak of an Ideating," declared Brentano, "whenever something appears to us (*wo immer uns etwas erscheint*)." [95] The implication is that we are brought indifferently, apathetically, into the ideational state, and in that event there can be no question of an 'act.'

Münsterberg would, undoubtedly, have urged the same objection against Witasek's system. For here, also, we find a recognition of the Yes-No attitude in all the elementary phenomena except ideation: in thought (affirmation and negation), in feeling (pleasantness and unpleasantness) and in desire (wanting and spurning.) [96] Witasek declines to give a formal definition of ideation, and contents himself with examples. He sums up his discussion, however, in the remark that ideas, the wholes of act-and-content, are "so to say the psychical copies (*Bilder*) of the objects with which our consciousness is occupied." [97] We need not press the language, but we get, again, the suggestion of indifference on the part of the subject. Moreover, Witasek asserts categorically that "the antithesis of Yes and No is altogether incommensurable with ideation." [98] In

---

[94] H. Münsterberg, *Grundzüge der Psychologie*, i, 1900, 19 f.

[95] *PES*, 261; cf. 106.

[96] *Op. cit.*, 80, 280, 353.

[97] *Ibid.*, 97 f.

[98] *Ibid.*, 308; cf. *PES*, 291. This statement of Witasek's forbids us to read anything like selective attention into the phrases whereby he char-

what sense, then—so Münsterberg might have asked —is ideation an 'act'?

The criticism is telling: but it hinges, of course, upon the definition of act. That is a matter to which we shall presently return. Meantime, it is interesting to note that the objection has been turned by a writer who could not admit its validity. It is turned by Stumpf, in his doctrine of 'psychical functions.'

§ 12. Stumpf finds that the 'immediately given' comprises three irreducibles: phenomena, by which name he denotes sensory and imaginal contents; psychical functions, which include such activities as perceiving, grouping, conceiving, desiring, willing; and the immanent relations between and among functions and phenomena.[99] All functions (with the exception of the primitive function of perceiving) have, further, their specific correlates or contents—forms, concepts, objectives, values—which Stumpf calls collectively formations.[100] Phenomena, relations and formations, as objects of thought, give rise to the three neutral sciences of phenomenology, logology and eidology. These *Vorwissenschaften* taken together may, if we

---

acterises ideation: "[das] sich Präsentieren eines neuen Inhalts" (78), "[die] Vergegenwärtigung eines Gegenstandes" (98), etc. Attention, in fact, is treated both by Höfler (*op. cit.*, 263 ff.) and by Witasek (297 ff.) in the section devoted to Judgment. Stumpf originally followed the alternative road left open by Brentano and made attention a Feeling (*Tonpsychol.*, i, 1883, 68; ii, 1890, 279). Brentano himself would apparently (*PES*, 263) have taken a like course.

[99] C. Stumpf, *Erscheinungen und psychische Funktionen*, 1907, 6 f.; *Zur Einteilung der Wissenschaften*, 1907, 5.

[100] *Gebilde psychischer Funktionen*: cf. *Erscheinungen*, 28 ff.; *Zur Einteilung*, 6 ff., 32 ff.

care so to apply the term, be named theory of knowledge.[101]

We have passed over the psychical functions, which come to their rights in another way. Since relations are common both to functions and to phenomena, the 'immediately given' shows an intrinsic duality.[102] We are led by it, though not directly, to the distinction of psychology and natural science. Phenomena form the starting-point for both—the logically necessary starting-point for natural science, the empirically necessary for psychology.[103] The proper subject-matter of psychology is, however, to be sought in the psychical functions.[104] Throughout our actual experience, these are continually and closely connected with phenomena.[105] Stumpf insists, nevertheless, that the connection is not logically necessary. Though every function must have a content, the content need not be phenomenal. Moreover, even as empirically conjoined, functions and phenomena are independent variables. Their assignment to different sciences is further justified by their radical difference; they have no single character in common, unless it be the character of time.[106]

Psychical functions are also called acts, states, experiences.[107] Stumpf distinguishes, with Meinong and

---

[101] *Zur Einteilung,* 26, 32, 38, 40.

[102] *Ibid.,* 6, 10.

[103] So I interpret Stumpf. Cf. the definition of natural science, *ibid.,* 16, and the *notwendig, ibid.,* 6.

[104] *Ibid.,* 20; *Erscheinungen,* 6, 39.

[105] *Erscheinungen,* 7, 27, 38 f.

[106] *Ibid.,* 11 f., 15.

[107] *Ibid.,* 4 f.

Husserl, between the content and the object of an act, but his distinction is differently worked out. An object is a conceptual formation. Hence an act that stands below the level of conception cannot have an object. In bare perceiving, for instance, we have phenomenal or relational contents, but no object. Conversely, when our thought is directed upon the universal as such, upon concept or law, content and object coincide; the content is, by its very nature, object. Between these limits stand all the cases in which we are occupied with a general or invariant (object) on the basis of a particular or variable (content).[108]

What, then, are the psychical functions? Without professing to make out a complete list, Stumpf distinguishes two great classes, the intellectual and the emotive, and names certain functions under both headings.[109] On the intellectual side, the most primitive function is that of perceiving or remarking or taking note of: it includes the two modes of sensing and ideating.[110] Another fundamental function of the intellectual life is comprehension or grouping (*Zusammenfassen*), whereby "a number of discriminated particular contents, impressions of touch, lines, tones, can be combined into a whole, a figure, a rhythm, a melody." [111] Next follows conception (*das begriffliche Denken, die Bildung von Allgemeinbegriffen*), and last

---

[108] *Zur Einteilung,* 6 ff. I hope that I here express correctly the relation of *das Zentrale, die Invariante* of the conceptual formation to its casual accompaniments. Cf. also *Erscheinungen,* 16 ff.

[109] *Erscheinungen,* 5, 7.

[110] *Ibid.,* 16.

[111] *Ibid.,* 23.

in order stands judgment.[112] On the affective side we have such paired opposites as joy and sorrow, search and avoidance, willing and rejecting.[113]

Here, where we have Münsterberg's objection in mind, we are especially interested in the primitive intellectual function of perceiving, which replaces the 'simple ideation' of Brentano's system. Perceiving or remarking is an intrinsically analytic, as comprehension is an intrinsically synthetic function.[114] From the standpoint of classification it would therefore be simplest to bracket these two functions together, and allow the opposition of analysis and synthesis to replace, in the ideational sphere, the Yes and No of the other functions. Stumpf himself seems to recognize such an opposition in the instance of conception.[115] Yet we are told that perceiving is 'most primitive,' so that it takes precedence of comprehension. Moreover, it is clear that the function has, by its nature as analytic, a negative as well as a positive implication of its own. While we are taking note of a part or attribute, while there is "an accumulation of consciousness over against" [116] this part or attribute, we are necessarily failing to take note of all the rest of the presented whole, from which consciousness to the same degree recedes or is withdrawn. "The barest act of attending or heeding," says

---

[112] Ibid., 24 f.

[113] Ibid., 26 f.

[114] Ibid., 16 ff., 23.

[115] Ibid., 25. Yet it is noteworthy that the illustrative list (7) runs: "Zergliedern, Zusammenfassen, Bejahen und Verneinen, Begehren und Ablehnen," without a connecting und between the first two terms.

[116] Ibid., 17.

Münsterberg, "is of itself an act of subjective evaluation, near akin to emotion, and fundamentally different
from mere ideation." [117]

We may, then, read into Stumpf's view of the intellectual functions either a primitive antithesis of
preference and neglect, or a prejudgmental antithesis
of combining and dividing. There still remains a difference between these and the remaining acts: since
on the one hand the neglect implied in perceiving is,
precisely, implied and not overt, and since on the other
hand both combining and dividing are, so to say, positive activities. In so far, however, as 'ideation' has
ceased to be the purely indifferent entertainment of a
content or object, in so far Münsterberg's objection has
been turned. And it is difficult to believe that the turning is a mere matter of chance.

Yet we must insist that Stumpf could not admit the
validity of Münsterberg's criticism. For, in the first
place, he attributes a duality like that which Münsterberg reserves for acts to certain classes of phenomena,
namely to the affective sense (Gefühlssinn) and the
sense of temperature. He speaks of the 'two-sidedness'
of these senses—pleasure and pain, warmth and
cold.[118] But if the 'two-sidedness' here is an accident
of biological organization, so might it also appear
accidentally and sporadically among the functions. A
second consideration is, however, more important.
Stumpf, we remember, finds the psychical functions

---

[117] Op. cit., 20.
[118] C. Stumpf, "Ueber Gefühlsempfindungen," Zeits. f. Psychol., xliv,
1907, 22; "Apologie der Gefühlsempfindungen," ibid., lxxv, 1916, 3, 32.

in the 'immediately given.' He does not find a 'subject' along with the functions, and he formally declines to base his psychology upon the *Ichbewusstsein*.[119] But if the acts are by logical necessity two-faced, the necessity arises from their being acts of a subject.

§ 13. Let us see, then, if Münsterberg's requirement is met by a system which affirms the compresence of the subject, the 'I of consciousness,' in every conscious experience. Such a system is that of Lipps,[120] which we proceed, briefly and partially,[121] to analyse.

Psychology, Lipps tells us, is the science of consciousness and of the experiences of consciousness (*Bewusstseinserlebnisse*).[122] The peculiar function of con-

---

[119] *Erscheinungen*, 8 f.

[120] Lipps' *Leitfaden* appeared in three editions (1903, 1906, 1909). The second edition, which is the most systematic of the three, is largely different from the first; and the third, which I here follow, differs in certain important respects from the second. Concurrently with these editions Lipps published memoirs and articles—expository, constructive, polemical—in which various phases of his system are worked out in greater detail (cf. the selected bibliography by G. Anschütz, *Arch. f. d. ges. Psych.*, xxxiv, 1915, 13). He was, indeed, continually revising and correcting, expanding and explicating, so that a later work is not only an improvement upon an earlier, but is also itself the starting-point of new insights and arguments. For this reason his psychology, as we shall see, never attained to systematic completion.

[121] In particular, we are not here concerned with Lipps' views of explanatory psychology.

[122] T. Lipps, *Leitfaden der Psychologie*, 1909, 1. The term *Bewusstseinserlebnis* has not settled down to its final definition. (a) An *Inhalt* is not an *Erlebnis*, but an *Erlebtes* (3). But in 1906 (3, 355) *Inhälte* were *Erlebnisse*. So in the index of 1909 (391) they still figure as *eigenartige Bewusstseinserlebnisse*. (b) In 1906 (8, 27) acts were *Erlebnisse*. In 1909 (21, 23) acts of thought are *Erlebnisse* only when their imaginal contents are adequate to the objects of thought, and acts of conation are never *Erlebnisse*, since we do not experience the objects

sciousness is to reach out, beyond itself, into a world transcendent to it; this "jumping over its own shadow," as Lipps put it, is the very essence of consciousness.[123] The experiences are of various kinds.

Lipps begins by differentiating sensations, as 'objective,' from all other conscious experiences, which are 'subjective' or experiences 'of me.' Sensation is the mere 'having' of a sensory 'content.' This 'having' is a 'running against' or 'happening upon' (*Widerfahrnis*); the sensation is a 'receptive experience'; the content of sensation is given only to the 'eye of sense.' [124]

If now I turn my 'mind's eye' upon a content, I pass from receptive experience to an experience of 'activity.' [125] The term is technical: the experience of activity is a line or stretch of consciousness, which begins and ends with punctiform 'acts.' [126] In turning my mind's eye upon the content I start, so to say, with an act of 'hello!'; this act is drawn out into an activity of attention or apprehension (*Auffassung*); and the activity comes to an end, 'snaps to,' with an act which Lipps names the 'simple act of thought' (*den schlicht-*

---

upon which they bear. Yet the older mode of speech is sometimes retained (*e.g.,* 40). One does not see why acts (quite apart from the I-experience involved) should not be *Tunerlebnisse* (cf. "Das Ich und die Gefühle," *Psychol. Untersuchungen,* i , 1907, 693): but Lipps was apparently on the track of a new distinction which he had not thoroughly worked out. Meantime we must accept contents, acts and experiences as in strictness irreducible.

[123] *Ibid.,* 12.
[124] *Ibid.,* 7, 16, 20, 23, 27.
[125] *Ibid.,* 26.
[126] *Ibid.,* 22.

en Denkakt), whereby I disengage an object 'for me'
or 'over against me' from the original content 'in
me.' [127]

With the appearance of objects, consciousness becomes more complex. Not the 'eye of sense,' and not
the 'mind's eye,' but the 'eye of intellect' (*das geistige Auge*) is henceforth in function.[128] I start with
the simple act of thought, which is drawn out into the
activity of 'apperception.' [129] But apperception is of
two kinds: classifying and questioning. If it is of the
classifying kind, I end it either by a simple act of 'fixation' of the intellectual eye, an act which constitutes
my object a single, determinate, particular object; or
else, passing beyond these acts of bare fixation, I bring
it to a close by some act of comprehension, relation,
abstraction.[130] If apperception is of the questioning
kind, a further complication arises. The objects which
I question reply to me; they have their own status and
their own laws, in virtue of which they lay their pre-
tensions or claims before me. And I may just 'listen
to' and experience these claims, or I may acknowledge
them. If I acknowledge them, the activity terminates
in an act of judgment. In this case there is a direct
parallel between apprehension, with its terminal act
of thought, and apperception, with its terminal act of
acknowledgment.[131] If, on the other hand, I only listen

---

[127] *Ibid.*, 23; 14 f., 22, 25 f., 141 ff.; 13, 25; 9, 12, 13, 25 f.

[128] *Ibid.*, 8, 13, 25.

[129] *Ibid.*, 22, 25 f., 144 ff.

[130] *Ibid.*, 26, 149 ff.

[131] *Ibid.*, 26 f., 30; 11, 31; 32 f., 189 ff.

to them, I have what Lipps calls an 'experience of claim' (*Forderungserlebnis*). This is a receptive experience, and therefore akin to the 'having' of a sensory content. It is a feeling of dispositional tendency, of compulsion or constraint.[132]

The experience of claim plays a large part in Lipps' system. For the moment, however, we leave it aside, in order to characterize the 'acts.' These are punctiform 'doings' of the conscious I, and may occur either independently, as 'empty or naked' acts, or in connection, as the initial and final points of an activity. Lipps distinguishes various sorts of acts. There are acts of ideation (that is, of productive imagination), of thought, of conation, of judgment. 'Wishing,' for instance, is a naked act of conation. But since conation, whenever circumstances permit, extends from act to activity, we have acts which institute or inaugurate this activity, acts of impulsion, incitement, urge, and acts which round off the activity, acts of arriving, completing, succeeding.[133]

The mention of conation brings us back to the *Forderungserlebnis*. Consciousness or the conscious I, whose essential nature we have seen to consist in self-transcendence, is also identified by Lipps with activity;[134] and activity is always an act of conation (*Streben*) expanded into a conscious stretch.[135] But conation is itself the 'subjectified experience of claim':

[132] *Ibid.*, 31, 33, 34.
[133] *Ibid.*, 21 f., 33; 22; 21, 22, 23, 32, 42, 263, 296.
[134] *Ibid.*, 6, 39.
[135] *Ibid.*, 23.

it is, so to say, the resultant of two sets of tendencies, the tendencies imposed on the 'I' by objects, and the tendencies, directions, pressures, needs, resident at the time in the 'I,' or it is a claim's 'effective resonance' within me. If the tendencies are in accord, the experience is that of active conation; if the imposed tendencies run counter to the resident, it is that of passive conation. In any case, conation and activity are definable as the interrelation or coöperation of an object, with its claim, and the individual consciousness.[136]

If, however, consciousness is activity, what becomes of the 'receptive' experiences, and more especially of the 'having' of a sensory content? Lipps meets the difficulty by his doctrine of 'potential' activity. To 'have' a sensory content is to have it 'in my power.' I feel that I 'can,' if I so desire, turn toward it, direct upon it my activity of apprehension: or rather, since activity presupposes an object, that I can direct my apprehension upon the object implicitly or potentially contained in it. This distinction of actual and potential activity, though it is psychologically irreducible, is still a distinction within the general experience of activity, and thus guarantees the essential likeness of receptive and active experiences.[137]

To round out this summary account, we must say a word of two further classes of conscious experience. The one of these comprises the feelings proper, the

---

[136] *Ibid.,* 34 ff., 261 ff. Similarly in the acts of thought there is a "peculiar interrelation between the I and the objects," which makes the acts at once creative and receptive (21 f.).

[137] *Ibid.,* 14, 28 ff., 39.

affective feelings, which are 'states (*Zuständlich-keiten*) of the I,' 'colorings' of the activity that is consciousness.[138] The other includes the experienced relations. The resolution of consciousness into a series of acts and activities does not destroy its unity and continuity. For the acts and activities bring with them experiences of conditioning and being conditioned, of dependence, of procession or issuance; in experiencing them, we also and at the same time have experiences of 'motivation,' that is, of their relation to other conscious experiences.[139]

Not everything in this account rhymes or, as Lipps might say, 'snaps to'; the thought is not of the kind that can properly be reduced to tabular form. We have, however, gained a basis for our special question: are the acts and activities two-faced, positive and negative? The answer seems, without a doubt, to run in the affirmative, though there is no evidence that Lipps offers it as the formal answer to a question of doctrine.

Conation, he says—and we remember that conation is fundamental—conation is "positive and negative, endeavour and resistance, wishing and wishing-not, willing and willing-not. The relation between the two is analogous to that between the consciousness of validity

---

[138] *Ibid.,* 37 ff., 40, 314 ff.

[139] *Ibid.,* 40 ff. In 1906 Lipps affirms that "just as conation and activity are an echo or a reflection of the claims [of objects] in the individual consciousness, so is the interconnection of conations and activities by motivation a reflection of the interconnection of claims" (29). This doctrine, and with it the reference to *Zusammenhang der Forderungen* in the index, have disappeared in 1909. Yet 1909, 300, repeats 1906, 266.

and the consciousness of invalidity, or between the positive and the negative judgment." [140] This passage recognizes the two-sidedness of activities (of activity or conation in general and of the activity of willing in particular),[141] of acts (wish and acknowledgment),[142] and of potential activities. For the consciousness of validity and invalidity belongs to the experience of claim, which is a receptive experience, like the having of a sensory content,[143] and this 'having' itself is a 'having in my power' to turn toward or to turn away from.[144] We may add that feeling, the 'tingeing' of our activity, shows the same dual nature; we find the antithesis of pleasant and unpleasant, large and small, familiar and strange, and so forth.[145]

Everything, therefore, except the contents [146] and the experiences of motivation, has the Yes-No character which Münsterberg demands.

---

[140] *Ibid.*, 260 (1906, 230; 1903, 203 f.). Lipps might have added to the negative judgment the negative perception and the negative recollection (201 ff., 212 ff.).

[141] *Ibid.*, 301 ff.

[142] *Ibid.*, 36: Lipps speaks of a feeling "des Anerkennens oder Abweisens, des Fürwahr- oder Fürfalschhaltens."

[143] *Ibid.*, 31.

[144] *Ibid.*, 13 f.

[145] *Ibid.*, 37 f., 314, 329, 332, etc.

[146] Lipps was not writing with Münsterberg in mind. For he compares the antithesis of pleasant-unpleasant with that of light-dark in the domain of colour-contents (*ibid.*, 37, 314). The parallel is only casually drawn, but Lipps found it possible. In the account of the sensory contents (69 ff.) there is, of course, no hint of any *Gegensatz*.

§ 14. We began this discussion with the pioneer work of Brentano, and we have used the criticisms of Meinong and Husserl and of Münsterberg as pegs upon which to hang an account of certain act-systems. We have thus been able to set forth, so far as is necessary for future comment and comparison, the systems of Witasek (as representative of Meinong's school), of Stumpf and of Lipps. The central point upon which these psychologists agree is that consciousness is by its very nature intentional, that it transcends itself and refers to objects beyond it.[147] The word 'intentional,' however, reminds us that our survey is not yet complete. By the side of Meinong, Stumpf, and Lipps we must place a fourth writer—one who is not a psychologist, one indeed who believes that there is a great gulf fixed between his own science and psychology,[148]

---

[147] This statement must be judged in its context; were the present book a history of contemporary psychology there would be much more to say. In a certain sense, for instance, Lipps is the direct antithesis of Brentano. At first, under the influence of Hume and Herbart, Lipps represented that 'psychologism' which Husserl attacks in the first part of his *Logische Untersuchungen*. Later he became a 'logicist,' but a logicist of the dialectic stripe, connected through Herbart and Fichte with Plato. Brentano was never anything but Aristotelian — Meinong, Stumpf and Husserl are all directly related to Brentano. But they, too, have made their changes. It is a far cry from the Husserl of the *Philosophie der Arithmetik* (1891) to the Husserl of the *reine Logik*.

[148] E. Husserl, "Ideen zu einer reinen Phänomenologie und phänomenologischen Philosophie," *Jahrbuch f. Philos. und phänomen. Forschung*, i, 1913, 184: phenomenology is "von aller Psychologie durch Abgründe getrennt." Ten years before, the "rein deskriptive Analyse der Denkerlebnisse" which in psychology should precede explanatory or genetic endeavour is identified with phenomenological analysis ("Bericht über deutsche Schriften zur Logik," *Arch. f. system. Philos.*, ix, 1903, 114); and even in the *Ideen* (143, 159) a bridge is thrown across the abyss in the shape of an *eidetische*

but one who has, nevertheless, exerted a profound influence upon current psychological thought.

Stumpf reserves the term 'phenomenology' for the science that deals with sensory contents and the corresponding images. Husserl's phenomenology is neither this phenomenology of Stumpf's nor is it identical with what is sometimes called 'pure' psychology: it is something wider and deeper than either.[149] All psychology, on Husserl's view—and psychology includes for him the Stumpfian phenomenology—presupposes the attitude of natural science; it is a science of fact, a psychophysics.[150] There is, on the other hand, a science of 'pure' consciousness in the sense of consciousness freed from bodily entanglement and naturalistic presupposition:[151] a science that has to do, not with fact, but with 'essence' (*Wesen*).[152] This science, with its method of 'immanent inspection' or 'contemplation of essence' is phenomenology.[153] To enter upon it, we exchange the naïve and dogmatic attitude of every day life and of natural science for a 'philosophical' atti-

---

Psychologie. Messer ("Husserl's Phänomenologie in ihrem Verhältnis zur Psychologie," *Arch. f. d. ges. Psychol.,* xxii, 1912, 117 ff.; xxxii, 1914, 52 ff.) has done his best to placate the implacable.

[149] E. Husserl, "Philosophie als strenge Wissenschaft," *Logos,* i, 1910, 315; *Ideen,* 5, 121, 290.

[150] *Bericht,* 398, 400, 524 f.; *Philosophie,* 298 f., 302, 315; *Ideen,* 3 f., 8, 69 f. Cf. O. Külpe, *Vorlesungen über Psychologie,* 1920, 22.

[151] *Philosophie,* 302, 315; *Ideen,* 57 ff., 94, 121 f.

[152] *Log. Untersuchungen,* ii, 18 f.; *Philosophie,* 314 ff.; *Ideen,* 4, 7 ff., 114.

[153] "Immanentes Schauen," *Philosophie,* 303, 313; "Wesenserschauung," *Ideen,* 11, 43; "Wesensschauung," *Philosophie,* 315 f. Cf. *Ideen,* 113.

tude, which leaves visible only 'pure' consciousness in
its 'absolute intrinsicality.' [154] And if we should rashly
venture to transfer to the domain of descriptive psy
chology some result of the phenomenological scrutiny
of essence, the responsibility is ours alone; Husserl
washes his hands of us.[155]

Psychology, then, is the empirical science of mental
facts as physics is the empirical science of material
facts.[156] Psychology is concerned with 'experiences,'
physical science with the 'non-experiences' to which
experiences refer, with the 'intended objects' of acts.[157]
And since natural science recognizes the individuation
of organic life, these experiences are the experiences
of an 'I.' [158] Consciousness, in the wide sense, therefore embraces the entire phenomenological make-up
of the mental 'I,' or consciousness is the phenomenological 'I' as 'bundle' or complication of psychical experiences.[159] In a narrower and 'pregnant' sense, con-

---

[154] *Philosophie,* 302, 315; *Ideen,* 3, 46 ff., 48 ff., 94, 120 ff., 182 f.

[155] The thing can be done (*Bericht,* 400; *Philosophie,* 315; *Ideen,*
143), and on Husserl's own showing the psychologist has no choice but
to make the attempt. It seems, however, that every psychologist who
has so far ventured (even the well-intentioned Messer) has flatly
failed. Happily for us, such failure does not greatly matter. We are
interested in Husserl, less for his own sake, than for the way in which
psychologists have understood him.

[156] *Bericht,* 398.

[157] *Log. Untersuchungen,* ii , 338 f.

[158] *Ibid.,* 336; *Bericht,* 399 f., 524 f.; *Philosophie,* 298, 312 f.; *Ideen,*
104.

[159] *Log. Untersuchungen,* ii , 325 ff., 350, 354 f.; *Ideen,* 65, 168 ff.
(esp. 172). Stumpf's phenomenology, which we have accounted a part
of Husserl's psychology, has its phenomenological counterpart in a
phenomenological hyletics; and this, directly, translated into psychological terms, becomes a chapter of eidetic psychology (*Ideen,* 178 f.).

sciousness is the inclusive name for intentional experiences or acts.[160]

The 'act,' it will be noted, is here identified with the complete intentional experience,[161] which includes both the 'content' (upon which the 'object' is based) and the 'intention' or 'act-character.'[162] Since, however, contents (in this narrower sense) are themselves nonintentional experiences, we may use the term 'act' in contradistinction to content for the act-character alone.[163] Acts, in this specialized meaning, lack intensity, but show differences of quality and material. These moments, though inseparable, are independently variable.[164] Quality is that which marks an act as an act of ideation or judgment or question or doubt or wish.[165] Material is the specific direction of an act

---

But Stumpf is an interactionist, and would hardly rule out psychophysics ("Eröffnungsrede," *Dritter internat. Congress f. Psychol.*, 1897, 7 ff.).

Husserl's emphasis upon inference (*Log. Unt.*, 331, 339) has led Wundt ("Psychologismus und Logizismus," *Kleine Schriften*, i, 1910, 570 ff.) to criticize him from the side of the 'unconscious.' For our immediate purpose this criticism is irrelevant.

[160] *Log. Unt.*, ii, 342, 345, 349; *Ideen*, 168, 174 f. Husserl's terminology has changed in the *Ideen*: for 'act,' see *ibid.*, 170.

[161] So, *e.g.*, *Log. Unt.*, ii, 323, 357, 362, 388; cf. A. Messer, *Empfindung und Denken*, 1908, 43.

[162] For the "primary contents," see *Log. Unt.*, ii, 652 (cf. 330, 345, 349, 360, 364 n., 370 ff., 468, 471); *Ideen*, 172. For the 'basing' of the object, *Log. Unt.*, ii, 353, 361, 362, 363, 370, 393, etc. For 'intention,' *ibid.*, 323, 348, 357 f., 361, etc.

[163] Husserl himself speaks of the intentional content (*Log. Unt.*, ii, 375, 378, 386 ff.) and of the intentional essence of the act (392 ff.). It is, however, hardly possible, in any extended discussion, to avoid the narrower use of the term: cf. Messer, *Empfindung und Denken*, 45, 47, 74.

[164] *Log. Unt.*, ii, 374, 386 ff., 391. Cf. 566.

[165] *Ibid.*, 386 f.

upon its object. Thus I may apprehend a given geo-
metrical figure now as an equilateral and now as an
equiangular triangle. Here the objects are the same;
the contents are the same; the act-qualities are the
same; but the act-materials are different. That is to
say, the material of an act determines not only what
object is apprehended, but also as what (with what
attributes, forms, relations) the apprehended object
is taken.[166]

Within this analytical framework Husserl seeks specifically to test the validity of Brentano's law—the
law to which we have found Münsterberg raising formal objection: namely, that all psychical phenomena
either are ideations or rest upon ideations as their
basis.[167] Husserl is able to show that Brentano's formula involves an equivocation. Translated provisionally into his own terms the law would run: every intentional experience either is an ideation (*i.e.*, a bare
or simple ideation) or has an ideation as its basis; but
here the 'ideation' of the first clause means an act-
quality, and the 'ideation' of the second clause an act-
material.[168] Husserl accordingly enters upon an elaborate analysis of the term 'ideation,' which he equates,
in its very widest sense, with the term 'act of objecti-

---

[166] *Ibid.*, 389 f.; for a broader definition, cf. 462. In the *Ideen* the
terminology has again changed: see esp. 267 f. Here and in *Bericht*,
244, the distinction of quality and material is ascribed to Brentano: I
suppose the reference is to the distinction of quality (affirmation,
negation) and *Sinn* in Brentano's doctrine of the judgment (*PES*,
283, 303).

[167] See above, note 93.

[168] *Log. Unt.*, ii, 428 f.

fication.' [169]   The new genus may be differentiated, qualitatively, into thetical and athetical acts of objectification: the former being the acts of 'belief' in the sense of J. S. Mill or of 'judgment' in the sense of Brentano, and the latter being the corresponding acts of 'simple ideation'; and, materially, into propositional and nominal acts ("Columbus discovered America," "Columbus, the discoverer of America").[170] Brentano's law may now be rewritten in the form: every intentional experience either is an act of objectification or has such an act as its basis; so phrased, the formula is valid.[171] The important thing for Husserl is, no doubt, that he has thus thought himself clear. The important things for us are that, by keeping his discussion at the phenomenological level, he has avoided all reference to the attitude of an 'I,' whether empirical or pure,[172] and that with 'act of objectification' he has introduced a term which seems destined to play a large part in empirical psychology.[173]

---

[169] *Ibid.,* 447: cf. 449, 458 ff.

[170] *Ibid.,* 449 f. In the *Ideen* (235) the terms 'thetical' and 'athetical' are replaced by the broader terms 'positional' and 'neutral,' with consequences that do not immediately concern us.

[171] *Log. Unt.,* ii , 458. The second clause may also be paraphrased: "or necessarily includes as constituent an act of objectification whose total material is at the same time, and in the sense of individual identity, *its* total material."

[172] In the *Log. Unt.* (340 f.) the 'pure I' is phenomenologically discredited. In the *Ideen* (109 f.) it comes back, but the consequences again do not immediately concern us. Only, the cutting of Münsterberg's difficulty, in the *Log. Unt.,* would appear to have been premature.

[173] As in Dürr's edition of Ebbinghaus' *Psychologie,* 1911-13.

§ 15. Husserl's influence may, indeed, be traced all through the later and more characteristic work of the Würzburg school. How deeply it had affected the psychology of Külpe himself, we shall probably never know. We have, however, a *Psychologie* from the hand of Messer, a member of the school, whose thinking has been largely shaped by Erdmann, Husserl and Külpe.[174] This book, in default of the promised recasting of Külpe's *Grundriss,* must now engage our attention.

Messer offers three characterisations of the conscious or psychical. He accepts from Münsterberg the formula that physical is shareable, psychical unshareable experience; he accepts from Lipps the view that the psychical always is, while the physical is not, in some sense 'mine'; and he accepts from Husserl the distinction of the psychical as immanent from the physical as transcendent.[175] We may pass over Münster-

---

[174] Messer published in 1908 a little book entitled *Empfindung und Denken,* which bears Husserl's impress on nearly every page. Its main effect upon the reader's mind is a sheer wonder that two things so incompatible as sensation and thinking can lie down together between the same covers. The *Psychologie* of 1914 has the more empirical flavour of the Würzburg school.

Külpe's posthumous work, *Vorlesungen über Psychologie* (ed. K. Bühler, 1920) is utterly inadequate on the side of its author's system. It does not either show Külpe at his best; much of the writing is the work of a jaded and driven man. In any case, Külpe may have been less nearly ready than we supposed. Bühler's preface ends with the (to me surprising) statement: "Ueber den Willen und das Denken hat Külpe nicht gelesen und leider auch keinerlei Aufzeichungen hintergelassen."

[175] A. Messer, *Psychologie,* 1914, 27 f., 32 f.; cf. 55, 73, 127 f., 138, 146. Messer is here speaking of *das bewusst Psychische.* Whether there are also *unbewusst psychische Vorgänge* is a question that he leaves open, though he inclines to answer it affirmatively: 35 ff., 251 ff., 365 f.

berg and Lipps,[176] and come at once to Messer's interpretation of Husserl. Since the transcendence which
characterizes the physical is a transcendence of consciousness, it follows of necessity that some psychical
must, for Messer, take the form of 'consciousness of.'
As a matter of fact, Messer declares roundly that all
consciousness is consciousness-of, *Gegenstandsbewusst-
sein,* though certain elements of consciousness, taken in
isolation from their regular setting, lack intentionality.[177]

---

[176] For Münsterberg's position, see *Grundzüge, i,* 1900, 72. The
Lippsian 'mine' does not mean for Messer the constant and overt
presence in consciousness of 'my I itself'; the I-character or relation
of 'mine' is often represented solely by the unitariness and blended-
ness of experiences: *Psychol.,* 27.

[177] *Ibid.,* 66, 53. The sweeping statement, as always, brings its difficulties. Messer admits, *e. g.,* that conscious complexes (fusions of
pleasant feeling with sexual sensations, fusions of unpleasant feeling with sensation of pain) may occur without reference to an object
(307). Such complexes are obviously far removed from the status
of conscious elements; and pain, at any rate, may be so overwhelm-
ingly itself as to drive away all competitors of the referential kind.
There is difficulty, moreover, in connection with Messer's whole
doctrine of emotion (*Affekt*). In *Psychol.,* 52, feelings and emotions
(apparently, all feelings and all emotions) are intentional. But the
simple feelings of pleasantness and unpleasantness are positively not
intentional (302), and emotions are only strong and sudden feelings
(293). I find, indeed, no reference to affective intentionality in the
pages that deal in detail with emotion and its classification. A feeling
may, however, carry intentional reference in its own right—in which
case it is no longer a bare pleasantness or unpleasantness, but a
Wertgefühl or affective evaluation (303). Hence in a later list we
find no mention of "feelings, emotions," but only of "experiences of
evaluation and will," as intrinsically intentional (374; cf. 52). In
general it seems that Messer recognises three levels of emotive
process: (1) a fusion of feeling with sensations, wholly without objective reference; (2) a fusion of feeling with acts of the consciousness of objects (in the narrower sense), *i.e.,* a complex in which the
feeling is not intentional but the basal ideation carries objective

The experiences (*Erlebnisse*) which make up the subject-matter of psychology may be divided into those of knowing, feeling and willing.[178] We may also speak of consciousness of object (in a narrower sense), consciousness of state, and consciousness of cause.[179] The elements of these experiences are classified as palpable or impalpable, according as they stand up under observation or as they refuse to be observed and must accordingly be recovered through reflection.[180] Of the palpable elements, sensations belong to all three types of consciousness.[181] Knowing, or the consciousness of objects, includes further, as palpable elements, the images which correspond with sensations, temporal and spatial contents, and the impressions (of 'same,' 'like,' 'different,' etc.) which lie at the basis of general concepts.[182] Whether consciousness of state and conscious-

---

reference; and (3) a fusion of affective evaluation with ideation, a complex in which both principal factors carry reference (cf. 66). How these types are to be fitted to his definition of consciousness is not easy to see.

[178] *Ibid.*, 65.

[179] *Ibid.*, 66. This classification is borrowed from J. Rehmke, *Lehrbuch der allgemeinen Psychologie*, 1894, 148 f.

[180] *Ibid.*, 48, 74, 202; *Empfindung und Denken*, 78 f. I suggest 'palpable' and 'impalpable' as the English equivalents of *anschaulich* and *unanschaulich*: cf. "Macbeth," II, i , 40.

[181] *Psychol.*, 66, 74 f.

[182] Messer recognises peripherally excited and centrally excited (or reproduced) sensations in primary and secondary (synaesthetic) form: *Psychol.*, 127 ff. For space and time as contents, see *ibid.*, 149, 155, 175 f., 202. It is expressly said that space is not an attribute of sensation, like quality and intensity (149) ; and time is so far from being an attribute of anything that it may, in Messer's opinion, be experienced for itself, as empty time (176). Yet we are told later that feelings share with sensations the attributes of intensity, quality, and the "extensives Merkmal" of temporal duration, while they lack the

ness of cause embrace palpable elements of a specific (non-sensational) sort is difficult to say: Messer's statements are conflicting. It seems that the simple feelings are, as a class, impalpable, though in exceptional cases they will bear scrutiny.[183] Conation, too, while it is intentional and should therefore by rights be impalpable, may, on occasion—if it is aroused involuntarily, and especially if it is directed upon objects of sense-perception—be observed during its course.[184]

The term 'act' is used by Messer in two senses: first, for the whole of an intentional experience, and secondly, for the act-side or act-character of such an experience.[185] In the first sense, acts are called palpable or impalpable according as their intended object is or is not represented by sensations and images.[186] In the second sense, in which the acts are conscious elements

---

"räumliches Charakter" that attaches to all sensations (280)! For the palpable impressions underlying concepts, see *ibid.*, 180 ff.

[183] *Ibid.*, 48: feelings that are closely connected with sensations and that possess a 'peripheral' character are palpable. But sensations are defined differentially as palpable (74); and feelings are impalpable (278 f., 346). Husserl (*Log. Unt.*, ii, 369 ff.) and Stumpf recognize a class of affective sensations, and thus meet the difficulty. In *Empf. und Denken*, 23, Messer takes the same view: cf. Psychol., 276.

[184] *Ibid.*, 48. But all *Streben* is involuntary (312). Moreover, the later distinction seems to be, not that of peripherally and centrally directed conations, but rather that of less definitely directed conation and more definitely directed desire (312). All conation 'aims at' something (311, 314). Husserl is ready to admit sensations of desire or sensations of impulse (*Begehrungsempfindungen, Triebempfindungen*) as non-intentional elements of will (*Log. Unt.*, ii, 373 f.; *Ideen*, 172).

[185] *Psychol.*, 53, 202.

[186] *Ibid.*, 139, 191, 296, 346.

abstracted from the whole of an intentional experience, they are always (with the exception of peripherally directed conation) impalpable.[187] Messer does not attempt to draw up a list; we must therefore make it up for ourselves as best we can.

Under the head of consciousness of object, we have, first, the acts of ideation in the wider sense: acts of perception, of memory and of imagination.[188] Then follow the acts of conception or thinking or knowing (*Wissen*).[189] Here we find, to begin with, the experience of concept or meaning.[190] Messer further names the acts of relating, of comparing, of judging, and of knowing in the pregnant sense (*Erkenntnis*).[191] Judgment is a synthetic act of relating, comprising at least two members, which is accompanied by the strictly elementary act of affirmation or negation.[192] Since every synthetic act may be translated into a simple act, the

---

[187] *Ibid.*, 202 f. These acts are not characterized attributively, as they are by Husserl and by Messer himself in *Empf. u. Denken* (50 ff.). We get a hint of quality and material, however, in such passages as *Psychol.*, 138 f., 204, 208.

[188] *Ibid.*, 139, 191 f. Messer does not seem to be quite as certain as Husserl (*Log. Unt.*, ii , 364; *Ideen*, 224 ff.) of the specific act-character of imagination. He says, indeed though in the context of explanatory psychology—that the distinction of memory and imagination springs rather from practical and epistemological than from psychological needs (*Psychol.*, 346).—It is to be noted that the total acts (intentional experiences) of memory and imagination may be either palpable or impalpable: 221, 346.
  Whether the *Bildbewusstsein* of *Psychol.*, 138, is elementary, we are not told. According to *Empf. u. Denken*, 60 f., it is not.

[189] *Psychol.*, 139, 202.

[190] *Ibid.*, 207.

[191] *E.g.*, *ibid.*, 214, 212, 209, 216.

[192] *Ibid.*, 207, 211, 212 f.

propositional act of judgment has a nominal act as its parallel.[193] Since, moreover, judgments may be passed with all degrees of subjective assurance, we have attendant acts ranging from conviction to conjecture.[194] Finally, over against judgment stand supposal, which bears the same relation to judgment as imagination to perception and memory, and the bare entertainment of a thought, shorn of all reference whether to validity or to invalidity.[195]

Later in the book we come upon the acts of intellectual evaluation and intellectual preference. The former, as judgments of value, may be subsumed to the general category of judgment. It is not clear that the acts of preference may be subsumed, in like manner, to the general category of comparison.[196]

Under the head of consciousness of state, we have as impalpable elements, first, the non-intentional simple feelings (or the great majority of them), and secondly, the objectively directed feelings (affective evaluations, feelings of value) and the corresponding acts of affective preference.[197] Lastly, the consciousness of cause includes conations, or at least those definitely directed conations which merit the name of appetition or desire, and acts of will. Messer insists that conations and acts of will belong to distinct classes of elementary experiences.[198]

---

[193] *Ibid.*, 208.

[194] *Ibid.*, 219.   [195] *Ibid.*, 220.

[196] *Ibid.*, 303 f., 305. In the latter passage, *Vergleichung* and *Vorziehen* are distinguished.

[197] *Ibid.*, 276, 303, 305. For emotions, see note 177 above.

[198] *Ibid.*, 311.

There remains the phenomenon of attention. Descriptively regarded, attention is not an act; it is rather that attitude (*Verhalten*) of the I in which our consciousness of objects (the phrase is used, at first, in the narrower sense) is formed or constituted: "objects exist for us only in so far as we are attentive to them." [199] Attention thus stands in intimate relation to the consciousness of objects; indeed, we need not scruple to use this phrase in its wider sense, seeing that the objects of affective evaluation, of affective preference and of will are also objects of attention.[200] While, however, the mere fact that an object is given us guarantees the presence of attention, the increase of the clearness and distinctness of the object with increasing concentration of attention is sufficiently regular to serve as a descriptive character.[201]

§ 16. The systems which, in their phenomenological or descriptive aspects, we have now briefly reviewed may fairly be considered as typical of the whole psychology of act. Our purpose is critically to survey this psychology, and in particular to decide whether it has been more successful than functional psychology in its

---

[199] *Ibid.*, 254.

[200] *Ibid.*, 256.

[201] *Ibid.*, 256, 267; cf. 50 f. Messer seems to have forgotten that the object is ordinarily transcendent, so that its clearness and distinctness cannot serve as a psychological character of attention (137 f.). It is true that his instance, of sensitivity and sensible discrimination, implies theoretically an immanent object; but he has told us (140 f.), in regard to this very matter, that in point of fact the observer usually adopts the 'natural,' 'objective' attitude. Surely, then, it is clearness and distinctness of the 'content' or 'sense' of the act (the material, in Husserl's wider sense) that must characterize the attentive experience. See, however, *Empf. u. Denken*, 120, note 3.

attempt to establish a special class of 'psychical' phenomena as the given subject-matter of psychological
investigation. There are, however, among the authors
to whom we have referred, two—Witasek and Messer—who, as experimentalists, make appeal to our
own interest, and who, as writers of text-books, seem
directly to challenge comparison. Witasek, as we have
said, belongs to the school of Meinong, and Messer to
the schools of Husserl and Külpe. Let us see, then, as
a preliminary to our main task, in how far these
psychologists agree in their teaching.

The question that naturally stands first, the question
of the classification of psychical phenomena, we shall
discuss later. Passing this by, we take up in their order
the principal points of the two systems.

(1) Both Witasek and Messer recognize the distinction of
act and content. But Witasek regards these moments as inseparable; there is no act without content, and no content without act; whereas Messer affirms that acts (the act-characters of
intentional experiences) may stand alone, as fully constitutive
of consciousness, and that sensory contents may appear in the
background of consciousness unaccompanied by acts.[202]

---

[202] Witasek, *Grundlinien d. Psychol.* (cited henceforth in this § as
W), 1908, 75; Messer, *Psychol.* (cited henceforth in this § as *M*), 1914,
203, 255. In *Empf. u. Denken,* 1908, Messer grants that sensations may
appear, without acts, in the background of consciousness (40), but
leaves the separate occurrence of contentless acts an open question
(100 ff.). Husserl, in *Log. Unt.,* ii, seems to accept the actless content
(372, 427), but denies that the act-character, the complex of quality
and material, can stand absolutely alone (560 ff.; cf. 68 ff.). In *Ideen*
(172) he leaves both questions unanswered. Lipps (*Leitfaden d.
Psychol.,* 1909, 15) asserts that all contents or images are, implicitly
or explicitly, representative, images of objects; whether there is a
strictly 'imageless thinking' he will not decide. Stumpf believes that
sensations may be present and may undergo change without our

(2) Witasek accepts Brentano's law without reservation; there is no judgment, feeling or desire that is not based upon ideation. Messer, on the contrary, regards all consciousness as consciousness-of: a pleasant or unpleasant feeling may, by its intrinsic nature, be objectively directed; and an object "may just as originally be desired or willed as ideated and thought." Yet it cannot be said that Messer rejects the law: his statements are always qualified.[203]

(3) Witasek defines sensations as "perceptive ideations of the simplest possible contents." There is, therefore, an act of sensation in addition to the sensory content. For Messer there is no act of sensation; the sensory content is "perfused and quickened by the thought-intention" of perception.[204]

'remarking' the fact: but then these sensations are phenomena, not subject-matter of psychology. He inclines toward the acceptance of imageless thinking. but, again, every function must on his view have some sort of correlated content (*Erscheinungen*, 1907, 11, 25, 34).— The experimental data regarding imageless thought do not here concern us.

[203] *W*, 97, 315; *M*, 66, 303, 314. In the first passage from *M*, feeling and will "somehow include or presuppose consciousness of objects [in which sense?]"; it is as if Messer had not yet contemplated the chapter on value. On 303, there is an 'intimate connection' of knowing and feeling: but is the knowing basal? On 314, the reference of conation and willing to objects may be termed "practical ideation," ideation being taken "in the most general meaning of the word." Yet the objective reference has just been declared intrinsic!—In *Empf. u. Denken*, 53 ff., Messer accepts Brentano's law in Husserl's formulation.

[204] *W*, 102, 218, 298 f.; *M*, 75 f., 139; *Empf. u. Denken*, 19 f., 45. So Husserl, *Log. Unt.*, ii, 245, 371, 714; *Ideen* 172. For Stumpf, sensation as a mode of primitive perceiving, is all act (*Ersch.*, 16; cf. Brentano, *PES*, 103, 190, etc.). Lipps spoke in 1903 (*Leitfaden*, 2) of act and content of sensation; the act is the 'my having' of later editions, and the term does not further appear. Indeed, in 1905 Lipps rebukes those who talk of the 'act' of sensation; what they mean, he says, is act of thought! He criticises Husserl on the ground, apparently, that Husserl's athetical act of simple ideation is an act of sensation: but of course it is not. He further criticises those who make sensation a mode of consciousness of objects, and here he undoubtedly has Meinong in mind. See T. Lipps, "Inhalt und Gegenstand: Psychologie and Logik," *Sitzungsber. d. kgl. bayer. Akad. d. Wiss.*, 1905, 516 ff.,

(4) Witasek, after some hesitation, admits the primary data of visual and tactual space-consciousness to the rank of sensations. His position in regard to time is not clear, though he leans toward the acceptance of a true sensation of time-present. Messer, on the other hand, has palpable content-elements of space and time (time-present, time-past, time-future), but no specific acts correlated with these contents.[205]

(5) Messer's palpable impressions of 'same,' 'like,' 'different,' etc., are 'given with' sensory contents and "founded upon" them. They are, psychologically, of the same order as sensations, and have no specific acts. Witasek agrees with respect to concomitance and dependence; but he transforms the 'impressions' into complete ideations of a special kind, namely, 'produced' ideations, or ideations which the subject, under the influence of sensations and by their assistance, produces (so to say) out of himself.[206]

(6) Witasek places, alongside of sensations and produced ideations, the third class of reproduced ideations. He thus brackets together the ideas of memory and of imagination, which Messer keeps apart. It is not clear whether Messer has an act of bare reproduction. He recognizes acts of imagination

---

521; A. Meinong, "Ueber Gegenstände höherer Ordnung," etc., *Zeits. f. Psych.*, xxi, 1899, 187 ff., 198 f.; "Bemerkungen über den Farbenkörper und das Mischungsgesetz," *ibid.*, xxxiii, 1903, 3 ff.; "Ueber Gegenstandstheorie," *Untersuchungen zur Gegenstandstheorie und Psychologie*, 1904, 14; R. Ameseder, "Beiträge zur Grundlegung der Gegenstandstheorie," *ibid.*, 93 ff.—It may be added that Lipps' real process of sensation has its object: *Leitfaden*, 1909, 79 f.

[205] *W*, 171 ff., 201 ff., 215 ff.; *M*, 148 f., 176; *Empf. u. Denken*, 24 ff. Stumpf (*Ersch.*, 4, 23) regards these things as phenomenal. For Lipps, the *Anschauungsformen* of time and space are the qualitatively new products of extensive fusion (of real processes or of conscious contents): *Leitfaden*, 1909, 98 f., 103 ff.

[206] *W*, 225, 232; *M*, 180; *Empf. u. Denken*, 25 f. Stumpf (*Ersch.*, 4, 7, 16, 22 f., 33) has a class of relations distinct both from phenomena and from functions. Lipps ascribes the relations to apperception: they are "modes in which objects are referred to one another in the apperceiving I," though they are "unequivocally determined by the objects" themselves: *Leitfaden*, 1909, 161, 164.

and of memory: the latter (as we shall see) belongs to another part of Witasek's system.[207]

(7) Both Messer and Witasek recognise the specificity of judgment. We note, however, several points of difference. (*a*) For Messer, the act of judgment is always at least bi-membral; the act is, in Meinong's phrase, synthetical. For Witasek, judgment may be either synthetical or merely thetical. (*b*) Witasek finds in the act of judgment two invariable moments, affirmation-negation and belief or conviction, and an occasional moment, evidence (of certainty, of probability). Messer identifies the invariable moments: affirmation-negation, acknowledgment-rejection, taking-as-true (as-untrue) and conviction are, for him, one and the same. Evidence he regards as a condition of affirmation-negation, and judgments experienced evidentially for the first time he marks off as acts of knowledge (*Erkenntnis*). (*c*) Witasek and Messer agree that a judgment may be passed with different degrees of subjective assurance. For Witasek, however, the difference resides in an intensive variation of the act-moment of conviction; for Messer, who does not recognise intensive gradation of act, it consists in the replacement of a taking-as-true by a taking-as-probable or a taking-as-possible. Judgments of possibility, in Witasek's system, are judgments of subsistence, as distinguished from judgments of existence. (*d*) Messer subsumes inference to judgment: it is judgment whose relational members are themselves

---

[207] *W*, 246 ff.; *M*, 192 f. Here the ideas of imagination and recollection are the two principal species of *Vorstellungen*, and recollection is distinguished from the mere 'renewal' of a perception. Yet *M*, 221, hints at an act-difference between perception as such and ideation as such (cf. K. Koffka, *Zur Analyse d. Vorstellungen u. ihrer Gesetze*, 1912, 270 ff.). In general, *M* speaks only of imagination and recollection.— Stumpf (*Ersch.*, 16) includes *Empfinden* and *Vorstellen* under *Wahrnehmen*: it seems that only the phenomena differ. Lipps has a bare *Vorstellen* as receptive experience or *Widerfahrnis*; he has also acts of imagination; and he has acts of (introspective) recollection both at the level of perception and at that of judgment (*Leitfaden*, 1909, 16 ff., 20 f., 336). For Husserl's analysis, see *Log Unt.*, ii, 463 ff., 471 f.

judgment-contents. Witasek looks upon inference as common both to judgment and to supposal.[208]

(8) Messer's perception, as intentional experience, is practically identical with Witasek's produced ideation. Perception proper (as distinct from perceptive ideation) is for Witasek a special case of judgment. Messer, as we have seen, makes all judgment at least bimembral.[209]

(9) Recollection and recognition are also, for Witasek, forms of judgment. Messer does not distinguish between them; and his act of recollection or act of recognition is not a judgment, but a mode of ideation.[210]

(10) Both Messer and Witasek, again, recognise the specificity of supposal. According to Witasek, however, supposal stands to judgment as reproduced ideation (ideas of memory and imagination) stands to perceptive (produced) ideation; according to Messer, it stands to judgment as imagination stands to perception and memory (recollection). Moreover, Witasek's supposal includes what Messer distinguishes as sup-

---

[208] *W*, 279 ff., 295 f., 310; *M*, 206 ff.; *Empf. u. Denken*, 138 ff. The doctrine of judgment (like that of form-quality, which I avoided in a previous note) is too detailed for discussion at this point. For Lipps' view, that judgment is my acknowledgment of an object's claim, see G. Anschütz, "Theodor Lipps' neuere Urteilslehre: eine Darstellung," *Arch. f. d. ges. Psychol.*, xxx , 1914, 240 ff., 329 ff. I further note only that Stumpf (*Ersch.*, 26; cf. Brentano, *PES*, 260 ff.) finds in judgment "a new functional attitude"; that Messer's distinction of one-rayed and many-rayed acts (*M*, 207) derives from Husserl (*Ideen*, 247 f.); and that Meinong discusses thetical and synthetical judgments in *Ueber Annahmen*, 1902, esp. 145.

[209] *W*, 239, 288 ff.; *M*, 162. Stumpf, following Brentano (*Tonpsychol.*, i , 1883, 96; cf. *PES*, 277), at first raised perception to the rank of judgment; he now (*Ersch.*, 16) makes perceiving prejudgmental. Lipps uses *Wahrnehmung* in two senses: for a *Widerfahrnis,* and for the consciousness of reality of the presented object. In either case perception is prejudgmental (*Leitfaden*, 1909, 15 f.; Anschütz, *op. cit.*, 334).

[210] *W*, 290 ff., 292 ff.; *M*, 192 f., 239, 247. Lipps has a feeling of familiarity, over and above the acts ('perceptive' and judgmental) of recollection: *Leitfaden*, 1909, 336.

posal and as the bare entertainment of thoughts. And Witasek's supposal further covers hypothesis, which is for Messer a "more or less probable judgment." [211]

(11) Attention receives markedly different treatment in the two systems. Messer, we remember, places attention outside of his three phenomenological classes. It is neither knowing nor feeling nor willing; it is an attitude of the subject wherein and whereby objects are constituted. Witasek finds the nuclear fact of attention in a thetical act of judgment, an act of apprehension. Attention is thus on all fours with perception, recollection and recognition.[212]

---

[211] *W*, 309, 311; *M*, 220. Lipps agrees with Messer as regards hypothesis, but considers supposals in general to be subjectively conditioned judgments (*Leitfaden*, 1909, 241 ff.). Stumpf also hesitates to accept the specificity of supposals (*Ersch.*, 30). Husserl looks upon supposal as a by-mode of positional consciousness (*eine. . .seitabstehende Modifikation der Glaubenssetzung*), and declares that Meinong's *Annahme* is an equivocal term (*Ideen*, 224, 228). For Meinong himself, supposal is a fundamental psychical fact, to be included along with judgment under the general heading of thought (*Ueber Annahmen*, 1902, 266, 276 ff.). If one is bent upon making it a form of judgment, then it will be a judgment of imagination (*Ueber die Erfahrungsgrundlagen unseres Wissens*, 1906, 60; cf. *Ueber Annahmen*, 285).

[212] *W*, 297; *M*, 254. In *Empf. u. Denken* (120) attention is not constitutive of our consciousness of objects, but is simply "an especially high degree of the consciousness of objects." Husserl, in the *Log. Unt.*, ii, has in fact left things obscure. He is clear that attention covers the whole range "des anschauenden und denkenden Meinens" (162 ff.); and he is clear that "acts must be there" if we are to live ourselves into them, *i.e.*, to attend to their objects (385). But he does not decide whether this attending is itself an act (386). In the *Ideen* attention is, definitely, not an act (65). It is rather a ray, issuing from the pure I and terminating on the object; it is therefore immanent in all acts which are attitudes or acts of the I itself; it shows itself phenomenologically in noetic and correlated noematic modifications which have a peculiarly subjective character (192). Messer in *M* professes to follow Lipps: but he is taking Lipps very loosely (*Leitfaden*, 1909, 79, 142). Objects are constituted, for Lipps, by the terminal act of the conscious activity of apprehension. Stumpf, who (as we saw above, note 20) at first made attention a feeling, now ascribes to the function of remarking a specific attribute (*Merkmal*) of distinct-

(12) In the psychology of feeling, we expect differences. It is noteworthy, nevertheless, that for Witasek feeling is all act, while for Messer it is (save in the case of feelings of value) all content. It is curious, too, that the distinction between sense-feeling and aesthetic feeling is drawn on diametrically opposite lines. According to Witasek, the aesthetic feelings are directed wholly upon ideational content: change of act (as from sensation to reproduction) leaves them unaffected. Sense-feelings, on the other hand, are essentially bound up with ideational act: pain felt and pain remembered are radically different things. According to Messer, the sense-feelings are feelings which attach directly to sensory contents, and the aesthetic feelings are feelings based upon "acts of the consciousness of objects." The difference which we expected could hardly be more extreme.[213]

(13) Messer devotes a chapter of his book to the consciousness of value. The primitive form of this consciousness is the affective, which at its simplest is an act of feeling, i. e., an objectively directed pleasantness or unpleasantness. In Witasek's system its position is very different. Just as there are feelings based upon acts and other feelings based upon contents of sensation, so it is with judgment: the logical feelings or feelings of knowledge are based upon acts of judgment, the feelings of value or ethical feelings upon judgment contents. The difficulty which we feel in Messer's account—how a simple feeling, any more than a simple sensation, can of itself assume or acquire intentionality—is thus avoided. Moreover, Witasek is able to proceed from judgment to supposal. There is no feeling based on the act of supposal; but there are feelings—play-feelings, in contradistinction to real or serious feelings—based upon its contents. Of these Messer says nothing.[214]

---

ness which he characterises figuratively as a greater or lesser "accumulation of consciousness" (*Ersch,* 11, 17).

[213] *W,* 324 f.; *M,* 295 f.

[214] *W,* 328, 330 f.; *M,* 303. For Lipps and Stumpf, feelings of value always imply judgments (*Leitfaden,* 1909, 341 f.; *Ersch.,* 27, 30). Husserl sets the problem in his own terms in *Ideen,* 239 ff.

(14) In the psychology of volition, too, we expect differences; and again, we are not disappointed. The act of will which for Messer is elementary, and which is to be distinguished from the equally elementary conation or desire, is for Witasek the highest development of that same elementary desire. According to Messer, an object may be desired or willed as directly as it may be ideated or thought; according to Witasek, no object, but only an objective, may be desired or willed; desire rests always upon some supposal. And so the differences continue. It may be remarked, as a curiosity of system-making, that in Witasek's chapter the simple reaction figures, in Külpe's sense, as the primary means "of an exact experimental investigation of volition, indeed, of conation at large," while Messer, a member of Külpe's school, disposes of it in his chapter on attention.[215]

These fourteen points may suffice to show the likenesses and differences of the two systems. There is resemblance. We saw that there was a likeness between Wundt and Brentano as long ago as 1874,[216] and it would be strange if there were none between two experimental systems of forty years later. The resemblance, too, is more than general; it is a family likeness; the systems are of the same type. Yet the differences are many, so many that every chapter invites us to a choice between alternatives.

To trace the sources of such difference is not an easy matter. It is plain on the surface that Messer's system is syncretistic and that Witasek's is logically compact;

---

[215] *W*, 349, 351; *M*, 311, 314: for reaction, *W*, 363, *M*, 265, 273. Lipps derives will from conation (*Leitfaden*, 1909, 258, 301 ff.). Stumpf (*Ersch.*, 26 f., 30) seems to include will under the emotive functions.

[216] Cf. above pp. 2 f.

several influences have been at work on the one, and a single predominant influence has moulded the other. If, however, we consider the systems as wholes, we may perhaps formulate a chief ground of difference as follows. Messer is bent upon bridging the gulf between the palpable and the impalpable factors of consciousness, or (in Humean terms) upon linking up 'ideas' to 'impressions.' Hence, in spite of his aversion from 'sensationalism,' he devotes a great deal of space to the palpable, and even coquets with the notion of a 'functional indefiniteness' of palpable contents.[217] Witasek, on the contrary, carries the distinction of act and content back to the very lowest terms of conscious experience. But Witasek, in his turn, has all Brentano's affection for the judgment—to which he adds Meinong's affection for the supposal: and so we find these things looming large throughout the second part of his system, where Messer deals upon a more independent basis with feeling and will.[218] Here is a real

---

[217] *M*, 180: the idea recurs in *Arch. f. d. ges. Psych.*, xxxii, 1914, 54. The notion of functional indefiniteness (*M*, 195) is, on Messer's own showing, altogether out of place in the context of content: cf. the distinction of descriptive and functional concepts in "Ueber den Begriff des 'Aktes,'" *Arch. f. d. ges. Psych.*, xxiv, 1912, 250, etc. For the notion itself, see G. E. Müller, *Zur Analyse d. Gedächtnistätigkeit u. d. Vorstellungsverlaufes*, iii, 1913, 545 ff.

[218] Witasek's enthusiasm leads him to remark that "the transcending which is peculiar to our mind, the direction upon objects, is in strictness a function only of judgment or supposal" (*W*, 310). At least an incautious statement! For if direction-upon is the earmark of the psychical, and if the direction of an ideation is due to the 'coöperation' of a judgment or a supposal, it follows that the ideation as such is not psychical: in which case Brentano's law implies the commingling of psychical and non-psychical at the very centre of the psychical realm.

cause of systematic divergence. There are others, still upon our phenomenological level; and there are others, again, at the levels which we have not touched. While, then, a detached view brings out the family resemblance of which we have spoken, the nearer and more limited view of a disciple can hardly fail to lead to partisanship. To the student of Messer, Witasek will appear heretical; and the student of Witasek must sharply question the orthodoxy of Messer.

§ 17. From this digression we turn to our main task: the appreciation of the psychology of act taken as a whole. It would of course be easy, if our aim were simply polemical, to dismiss the matter with the simple statement that, 'as a whole,' there is no psychology of act. And it is true that, in the concrete, we have had to do with psychologies rather than psychology, with differentiation rather than consolidation. From the common starting-point of intentionalism our authors have taken widely divergent paths. The question remains, however, how deep the sources of divergence lie —whether they are only superficial and accidental, or whether they are fundamental. Until this question is faced and answered, we cannot either affirm or deny that psychology may be wrought out in terms of a peculiar class of intentional facts.

We shall put the act-systems, first, to a triple test, by considering their attitude in regard to classification, and to the special topics of sensation and attention.

(1) We begin with the classification of psychical phenomena. Here, again, it would be easy to show that the systems differ. Indeed, they differ so radically that

one, two, three or four ultimates may be recognised.[219] We must remember, however, that classification is, primarily, a matter of convenience, and that the functional and experimental schools have also been unable to supply a classification that should be generally accepted. All that the differences prove, therefore, is that intentionalism is no unerring or unequivocal guide to arrangement. That is worth noting: but we shall get more light if we consider the classifications adopted by an individual psychologist at different stages of his systematic thinking. We have, fortunately, two examples of the kind required, in the works of Stout and Lipps.

The classification put forward in the first edition of Stout's *Manual* (1899) is very simple. It may be represented as follows:

I. Ultimate modes of being conscious of an object
   a. The cognitive attitude or cognition or knowing
   b. The feeling attitude or feeling [always dependent upon cognition]

---

[219] The single ultimate, of which we have so far had no example, is characteristic of the conational system of S. Alexander: "there is but one ultimate mental process [a continuous tissue of acts, or awarenesses, or enjoyments], namely conation" ("Foundations and Sketchplan of a Conational Psychology," *Brit. Journ. Psych.,* iv , 1911, 243; cf. H. A. Reyburn, "Mental Process," *Mind,* N. S. xxviii , 1919, 19 ff.). Something of the same sort appears in the psychology of P. Natorp. Consciousness has three moments, which may be distinguished by abstraction: the I, the content, and the relation between them. Since the I is presupposed by psychology, and since the relation to the I is an irreducible and indescribable ultimate which, like the I, is a precondition of psychology, it follows that psychology has to do only with content (*Allgemeine Psychologie,* i , 1912, 24, 33.).

    c. The conative attitude or striving [coördinate with cognition]
II. Experience not at the moment contributing to the cognitive function of consciousness
    d. Sentience or sub-consciousness

There can be no doubt that Stout is here trying to cover the whole field of consciousness by way of objective reference. Sentience, the outlying category, is after all nothing more than cognition at rest: modifications of consciousness that may and will present objects happen, at some given time, not to be discharging this presentational function, and must accordingly be distinguished from their active kindred. They are, nevertheless, as the term sub consciousness attests, only at a lower level of the development which culminates in presentation.[220]

The classification of the third edition (1913) is less simple. It may perhaps be represented as follows:[221]

MODES OF CONSCIOUSNESS

  I. Immediate experiences which are primarily objective (are themselves primarily objects), or presentations
    a. Sensations
    b. Images
    c. Imageless or amorphous presentations

---

[220] G. F. Stout, *A Manual of Psychology*, 1899, 56 ff., 68 ff. That all was not well with the concept of 'sentience' I pointed out in *Thought-processes*, 1909, 224 ff.

[221] I say 'perhaps' only because I am taking the three forms of simple apprehension from the chapter on Attention, and attention is conation (*ibid.*, 1913, 125).

II. Immediate experiences which are primarily subjective, or ultimate modes of the relation of the
conscious subject to its objects
　　a. Simple apprehension [precondition of *b*
　　　and *c*]
　　　　1. Implicit apprehension or sub-con-
　　　　　sciousness
　　　　2. Marginal awareness
　　　　3. Explicit apprehension
　　b. The cognitive attitude
　　c. The attitude of interest
　　　　1. Passive: the feeling attitude
　　　　2. Active: the conative attitude

Both tables have two main divisions; but we note
at once that the divisions do not tally; in the second
table Stout has given up the attempt to classify by
way of objective reference alone. The presentations of
1899 were, in the language of 1913, 'subjective' experiences, modes of cognition; and if sentience is not presentation, it is at any rate something that was presentation a moment ago and will be presentation a
moment hence. Now, however, this sentience has been
marked off from its alternative sub-consciousness, and
has expanded into a new category of objective presentation, altogether distinct from cognition; while
sub-consciousness, remaining 'subjective,' finds its place
within a new—and fundamental—differentiation of
objective reference. The whole perspective of the system has changed.[222]

Lipps' original classification (1903) is also very
simple. There are four ultimate classes of the "con-

---

[222] *Ibid.,* 1913, 3 f., 5 ff., 11, 102 ff., 129, 140, 176, 532.

scious contents or conscious experiences" which form the subject-matter of psychology:

I. "The directly experienced I with its determinations, the feelings" (absolutely subjective contents);

II. "The contents of sensation and sense-perception, *i. e.,* the simple sensory contents, the complexes of sensory contents, and the spatial and temporal forms and modes of their arrangement" (absolutely objective contents);

III. "The directly experienced relations of the I to what is objective, and the relations of the I in general" (intermediate contents); and

IV. "The ideational contents corresponding with all these conscious contents" (secondarily objective contents).

This table is exhaustive; it names all the genera of contents of consciousness; "there are no other conscious experiences." [223] And when the reader has assured himself that the "phenomenal acts" belong to the class of relations, or contents intermediate between the I and its objects, the complete outline of Lipps' system lies before him.

In 1909, however, Lipps has given up the idea of an inventory of consciousness. Psychology now has to do with "consciousness and conscious experiences"; and as this subject-matter unfolds, in the introductory sections of the book,[224] we find an intercrossing complexity that cannot by any trick of straitjacketing

---

[223] Lipps, *Leitfaden,* 1903, 16 ff., esp. 20.
[224] *Ibid.,* 1909, 1-43.

be reduced to a single table. The following summary shows some of the complications with which the beginning student must contend.

(1) Lipps speaks of experiences, contents, acts, activities, states and colourings of consciousness.

Contents are not experiences; they are rather the images or impressions experienced in consciousness.

Acts, too, are not intrinsically experiences. In our acts of thought and conation we do not ordinarily experience the objects apprehended and desired. We experience objects "only in so far as we have adequate images of them."

Activities and states (which later are identical with colourings) are experiences.

(2) Experiences are either objective or subjective. The type of objective experience is sensation, the having of a simple sensory content. The term covers also experiences of bare sense-perception, the mere having of a complex of sensory contents in spatial and temporal arrangement; and the bare ideation in which we have, as imaginal content, the image of some object in the outside world. All other experiences are subjective. Their type is the feeling.

The acts of thought, again, although (as we have seen) they are not intrinsically experiences, are either subjective or objective, according to the nature of their object.

(3) It is to be noted that 'experience' by no means implies completeness or independence of the conscious datum so named. In sensation, for example, I have as objective experience the having of a sensory content, and as subjective experience the experience of myself as sensing. Every objective experience thus includes or incorporates a subjective experience. In the same way my acts, though not in themselves experiences, are subjective experiences in the sense that in and with them I experience myself as thinking, desiring, etc.

(4) Lipps distinguishes receptive experiences, acts and states. The receptive experiences are those that we 'run up against':

sensations, the experience of claim. At the opposite pole from them stand the acts of conation, in which we aim at some object. The affective states differ from both.

(5) Sensations are differentiated as sight, hearing, etc.

States are all included within the opposition pleasantness-unpleasantness, or move in that dimension. Since, however, many states are named, it appears that a further differentiation must be made.

Acts are specified in some detail. Thus we have acts of production (evocation of images of imagination), acts of mixed reception and production (thought), acts of aiming (conation), acts of 'bracing up to' and 'putting the final touch on' (starting and stopping points of conative activity), acts of acknowledgment (judgment). The relations are not quite clear. Perhaps there are two genera of acts: the one including as species the acts of imagination, thought and judgment, the other those of conation and conative activity.

(6) Conation and activity may be either active or passive.

Conation and activity may, further, be either inner or outer, according to the nature of the object on which they are directed. Inner activity is activity of apprehension, activity of imagination, activity of apperception (which latter is, again, variously specified). Outer activity is bodily activity.

It appears that we have in the experiences of conation (subjectified experience of claim) and of conative activity (feelings of actual and potential activity) a foundation or undercurrent of subjective experience distinguishable from the specific feelings which colour it: but the point is not clear.

(7) Along with acts and activities are given subjective experiences of their relation: experiences of conditioning, of issuance, of dependence, which Lipps groups together as experiences of motivation.

(8) Every conscious experience and everything experienced in consciousness may later recur in the form of a reproductive image or image of ideation.

(9) Consciousness is intentional, but it is intentional in varying manner and degree. Sensations contain an object only

potentially or implicitly. Acts of thought explicate these objects, in such wise that consciousness may thereafter busy itself with them; there is in thought "a peculiar interaction between the I and the objects." Conation and conative activity are, on the other hand, always 'aimed at' something; they 'are' the interrelation or the coöperation between the object with its claim and the individual consciousness. And since all feelings are colourings of this conative activity, I cannot feel without feeling myself somehow related to an object; I am cheerful or depressed, confident or in despair, 'about' something. Finally the experiences of motivation appear to be intentional in the same way as experiences of conation in general.

There is little here to suggest the tabular statement of 1903. No doubt, all the four classes of the earlier edition may be traced in the later; but our efforts at precise arrangements are baffled, and we wonder whether, after all, the simplicity of Lipps' first exposition was not itself rather apparent than real. At any rate, no clue to the psychological labyrinth is now to be found among the conscious experiences. If we wish to set things in order we must go below and behind consciousness to the unconscious real.

Summaries are tedious to make and tedious to read. We have undertaken them, in these two instances, for the light that they and the comparisons resulting from them may throw upon the act-systems in general. And we note, first, that they raise, pretty definitely, the doubt whether intentionalism is adequate to the whole subject-matter of psychology. That, to be sure, is a large question, which we could not, in any event, seek to answer at this point: we note only that it is raised, and raised at the very outset, by the act-systems themselves. Stout appears to have transgressed the boundaries which he originally accepted, and Lipps saves the principle only by adding an implicit to his explicit intentionality. In another way, however, the summaries afford us positive light—light upon the attitude and interest of the authors of these systems. It is clear that the interest lies in argument and discussion and explication and distinction, in the logic of system, rather than in the facts of observation.

It is, indeed, nothing less than illuminating to read Stout's editions with an eye to facts. The third edition has sought to bring its references down to date, so that Sherrington replaces Foster, and Myers replaces Ebbinghaus. But the writer's factual equipment has increased hardly at all. 'Views' are what Stout is concerned with, the critical discussion of other men's views and the exposition of his own. The whole vast field of experiment, with its perplexing entanglements of dependence on conditions and theoretical bias and degree of training of observers and all the rest—this whole bulk of raw material for the science of psychology is passed indifferently by, for what Locke and Hume and Lotze, and Ward and James and Ladd and Marshall and Stout himself, 'think' about psychology. Even where, as in the instance of experiments upon the lower animals, Stout refers to monographic sources, even here his attitude is not primarily that of the man of science, careful of method and wary of generalisation; he is interested rather in the inferences that have been drawn from observation, in the systematic setting of the facts, in their interpretation and explanation. And as to Lipps! the student of Lipps will hardly realise that there may be, within the compass of psychology, facts of the same existential order that he has met in his study of physics and biology. He reads of unutterables, indescribables, indefinables, uniques, which he is required to 'experience'; and he reads through a serried array of imperatively dogmatic statements regarding these ultimates, which he is required to accept. Should he wish to go further, he is referred to other works by Lipps himself.[225]

We may grant that Lipps' opinions, and Stout's too, are heartily worth knowing; we may grant also—nay more, we shall insist—that logical construction has its necessary place, is (so to say) the full half of a scientific system. Only we cannot forget that the half here is less than the whole. Moreover, we see from our summaries that the statements originally made, whether dogmatic or argumentative, are sadly instable. Ward once remarked that systematic psychology "is not liable to change every half-dozen years." [226] What is it then, in this psychology of act, that does change? Something changes: simple apprehension is superadded upon cognition, the pure I is ruled out and invited in, perception drops from the judgmental to the prejudgmental level, contents are and are not experiences, sensation has and has not an act of its own, and so forth. Here, surely, are systematic changes! Nor would they be open to criticism if they reflected and

---

[225] The third edition of the *Leitfaden* refers the reader to three books written by other authors: for sensation and fusion to Wundt's *Physiol. Psych.*, for tonal fusion to Stumpf's *Tonpsych.*, and for memory to M. Offner's *Das Gedächtnis,* a work which appeared while the new edition of the *Leitfaden* was in preparation.

[226] *Mind,* N. S. iii , 1894, 143.

kept pace with the growing store of facts, and if the facts were set out at large as ground and warrant of the changes. In the absence of grounding facts, and in view of the general trend and tenor of their work, we must conclude that the psychologising of Stout and Lipps is, essentially, a matter of applied logic. They begin with certain empirical concepts—the objective reference of consciousness, the conscious I; they proceed to explicate these concepts as thoroughly and minutely as they can; and the longer and more earnestly they meditate, the greater is the wealth of discoverable meaning, the greater the number of its discriminable aspects. This, then, is the positive light that our summaries throw upon the act-systems.[227]

(2) The mention of act and content of sensation brings us to a second point. There can be no possible question that sensation—however it is to be defined, and we need not, for a long time to come, enquire too curiously about its definition—has been, from the beginning, a source of real difficulty to the act-systems. The story is roughly told in the following table:

Sensation	Act	Content
Brentano, Höfler, Alexander	Psychical	Physical
Witasek, Geyser	Psychical	Psychical
Stumpf	Psychical	Phenomenological
Lipps, Husserl, Messer	None	Psychical

---

[227] It may be added, in the sense of our previous discussions, that the scientific psychologist, whose addiction to fact may leave him neglectful of his logic, has a good deal to learn from this explication of concepts. I have sometimes been staggered to read what my own 'sensationalism' logically 'implied,' when I neither admitted the sensationalism nor acknowledged the implications. All the same, such logical criticism is salutary.

The table, as a mere outline, obscures many differences. Brentano identifies content with object; Höfler has an analogue to sensation proper in the ideation of a simple psychical, a psychological element; Alexander regards all psychical acts as acts of conation; and so on. The table takes account, too, only of certain systems in which the term 'act' is systematically employed. It omits Münsterberg's 'noetic relation,' and Stout's 'presentative function,' and so on. It shows, nevertheless, how real the difficulty is. The one thing certain is that, somewhere in the world, we come upon sensory contents; and then we must decide for ourselves whether they are physical or psychical or neither physical nor psychical. And we have not even so much of assurance as regards the sensory act.[228]

The doubt raised by our summaries, whether intentionalism is adequate to the subject-matter of psychology, seems therefore to be well founded. For if one starts out with intentionalism one can hardly find anything simpler than the perception of external objects. But then one is reminded, whether historically or empirically, that there is something logically prior [229] to perception, namely, sensation; and yet sensation is not obviously intentional. What, then, is to be done? Well, one may speak of intentional consciousness as 'consciousness in the pregnant sense'—whatever that

---

[228] A. Höfler, *Psychologie*, 1907, 210; S. Alexander, "On Sensations and Images," *Proc. of the Aristot. Soc.*, N. S. x, 1910, 1 ff.; J. Geyser, *Lehrbuch d. allg. Psych.*, 1912, 49, 224, 306; H. Münsterberg, *Grundzüge d. Psych.*, i, 1900, 309; Stout, *Manual*, 1913, 210.

[229] Or, perhaps, chronologically prior; sensation, in certain systems, still has a genetic flavour. Cf. H. Hofmann, "Untersuchungen über den Empfindungsbegriff," *Arch. f. d. ges. Psych.*, xxvi, 1913, 1 ff.

may mean; one may draw a distinction between matter and form of consciousness—as if form were in some way a guarantee of intention; one may oppose 'potential' to 'actual' intention—whatever, again, that may mean. Or one may throw the sensory content overboard, and keep the sensory act as a mode of perception or ideation or conation. Or one may hold fast to the letter of intentionalism, and make the sensation, act and content together, an humbler understudy of perception. It is a matter of taste which course one adopts, and it is a matter of skill how well the resulting system holds together. Whence of course it follows that no degree of subjective assurance and no refinement of critical acumen on one's own part can prevent a like assurance and a countering criticism on the part of others. But a house divided against itself shall not stand.

(3) After all, though, it may be said, we have not proved that the 'house' is divided. Sensations lie on the outskirts of psychology, form the ragged edge of the psychological system; we meet them at the outset, but we have very little to do with them thereafter. Besides, the difficulty, such as it is, may readily be cut; it has been cut cleanly enough by Stumpf, who dismisses all the doubtful elements, all sensory and imaginal contents, to a limbo of their own. Why should we lay so much emphasis upon a merely preliminary difficulty?

The objection forgets that we are talking of system, and that a system must be systematic throughout. It forgets that the diversity of opinion among the psychologists of act is due precisely to their effort toward a consistent systematisation. Their chief interest is here, on the side of applied logic; and a breakdown at the beginning is, logically, as serious as a breakdown later on. We need not rest, however, with this reply. We will go to the heart of the systems, to the doctrine of attention; and we shall find that attention, no less than sensation, is a stumbling-block to the intentionalist school.

We hasten to make an exception of Lipps; but then Lipps' whole system is exceptional. It embodies, so to say, two psychologies, real and phenomenal, unconscious and conscious. Every real psychical process has, according to Lipps, an intrinsic energy, in virtue of which it attracts or appropriates psychical force. Attention, now, is a term which belongs in strictness, not to consciousness, but to the domain of the real mind: it is nothing else than the psychical force which, accruing to a real process, lifts it (under favourable conditions) above the limen of consciousness. We then 'have' a conscious content. If the process appropriates still more force, or if attention turns to it in greater degree, it becomes a process of thought, and we have in consciousness the activity of apprehension which culminates in the simple act of thought. Here is the intellectual limen. If the process is capable of yet further appropriation, it becomes an apperceptive process, and we experience in consciousness the activity of apperception, which results, according to circumstances, in various acts of higher intellectual orders. Attention, throughout, is the psychical force which 'turns to' or 'is appropriated by' the real process of ideation, of thought, of apperception.

No one will deny that this doctrine of attention is

logically constructed. Our objection, if we object at all, can only be that it rests upon a basis of pure invention. That is for Lipps neither an objection nor a difficulty; he insists that invention is necessary, and that his own "substructure of thought" is adequate to the psychological occasion. If, as he admits, we know nothing of process and stage of process, of psychical energy and psychical force, that truly is our misfortune; but we may then be all the more grateful to thought for supplying the deficiencies of knowledge.[230]

Such is the exceptional system, for which attention has no terrors. The rest are less happy. Stumpf, as we know, identifies his primitive function of perceiving with a 'taking note of'; attention thus seems to be present to consciousness from the first. This perceiving has a graded attribute of distinctness (*Deutlichkeit*), which Stumpf nevertheless trusts so little that he is forced to speak figuratively of an 'accumulation of consciousness.' Messer, getting no help from Husserl, turns to Lipps; attention is an attitude of the I, logically prior to our consciousness of objects—and all consciousness is consciousness of objects. Witasek, in flat contradiction to the school of Husserl, makes attention an act, one of the ubiquitous acts of judgment. "To many contemporary psychologists," he adds, "this opinion will appear nothing less than monstrous; all the same it is true; and anyone who has a discerning eye for the psychological specificity of the act of judgment will recognise it without difficulty in the constitution of attention." Geyser, who paraphrases attention in Lippsian

---

[230] *Leitfaden,* 1909, 78-83, 141-148.

terms as our "intellectual occupation" with an object, must transcend consciousness in both directions in order to bring his subject under control. Attention as psycho-physiological energy is responsible for the clearness of certain conscious contents; and attention as the intellectual occupation of the mind with the contents of consciousness (this 'mind' is a matter of supplementary inference, not of observation) is responsible for our reflective fixation of them. So there are two attentions, and neither is psychological. Pfänder, like the Messer of *Empfindung und Denken,* makes attention the higher degree of our consciousness of objects, the denser or more concentrated portion of the cone of light which issues from the I of consciousness and plays upon its immediate objects. Finally, Stout retains in all three editions the statements that "attention is simply identical with conation considered in its cognitive aspect" and that "conation and cognition are different aspects of one and the same process," statements which, in default of some equivocation, would seem to be irreconcilable.[231]

It was plainly a bad day for empiricism when the experimental movement brought attention to the forefront of systematic psychology.[232] Intentionalism can

---

[231] Witasek, *Grundlinien,* 297; Geyser, *Lehrbuch,* 256 ff., 261 ff., 724 f. See esp. 263: "This reflective fixation does not represent the consciousness-of, *i.e.,* is not a mode of awareness, but is a holding fast of the content of which we are conscious, to the end that the mind energise on this content its acts of relating, and thereby extend contentwise its awareness of the content"—Stout, *Manual,* 1899, 247, 581; 1907, 257, 599; 1913, 367, 704; A. Pfänder, *Einführung in d. Psychol.,* 1904, 272 ff., 354 ff.

[232] Cf. my *Feeling and Attention,* 1908, 171 ff.

deal with perception and imagination and memory and
thought and emotion and desire, but hardly with attention. As in sensation it finds too little, so in attention
it finds too much. For what is attention, empirically
taken, if it is not already and of its own nature intentional? It too is a surplusage, and so it suffers a fate
akin to the fate of sensation. Either it is thrown out
of consciousness, not (to be sure) into physics or phenomenology, but into a realm of logical priority; or
else it is identified with some particular intentional
process. And the extremes meet. Perception, which at
its simplest is for Höfler and Witasek sensation, becomes for Stumpf, still in its simplest form, an implicit
attention.

§ 18. It would seem then, that the differences among
the act-systems are in fact fundamental and inevitable,
not superficial and accidental. On the side of subject-
matter, intentionalism cannot cope with sensation and
attention, while it cannot either dispense with them.
Witasek, it is true, takes heroic measures; sensation is
perception, and attention is judgment: the system is
saved. But who, outside of Meinong's school, will accept a salvation offered on such Procrustean terms?
Besides, the interest in systemisation, in applied logic
for the sake of the logic, characterises all the psychologists of act. Psychology appeals, so to say, to their
personal ingenuity in relating and distinguishing and
constructing; and where the appeal is thus individual,
there—as in philosophy or poetry—the outcome will
of necessity reflect the personality of the writer. We
saw that there are many differences between Witasek
and Messer. We may now safely say that these differ-

ences go deep. They are the differences, not of two scientific psychologists, but of two personalities expressing themselves in the terms of systematic psychology. If intentionalism is scientific, then science can no longer be called impersonal.

How indeed shall we account, otherwise than by personality, by training induced upon given temperament, for the varying definitions of the 'act' itself? An act for Lipps is a doing, the deed of the I of consciousness. The picture that rises from his pages is that of a strenuous and resourceful, highly self-conscious 'individual,' acting and reacting in a world of other individuals and of material things. An act for Husserl is something very different, something that by contrast almost suggests passivity: an experience of a certain essential constitution, of intrinsically intentional make-up. Husserl accordingly reminds us of nothing so much as the skilled lexicographer, teasing from the word before him every discriminable shape of meaning, and nicely distinguishing it from the words that everyday use has made us think synonymous. Stumpf's act, lastly, lies between these other two. It is active, in the sense that it is found or given as active; it is by no means the deed of an I. It is an active verb, moving amidst phenomena and relations, and generating its 'correlate'—a sort of caddis-worm that houses itself variously in the sticks and shells and stones of its independently variable surroundings. We need not go further. We have an act which is my doing and is experienced as my doing; we have an act found as active ultimate among inactive ultimates; we have an act which is an embodied intention, the subject-matter of a morphology of knowledge. What, then, for psychology, is 'the act'? We are brought back, after all, to our polemical starting point: there is no psychology of act, there are only psychologies. But we may now add, as at the beginning we could not, that on the basis of intentionalism there will be only psychologies.

Here, however, we remark a notable difference between the psychology of act and the psychology of function. There is no reason to suppose that functional psychology enjoys any long lease of life. It was born of the enthusiasm of the post-Darwinian days, when evolution seemed to answer all the riddles of the universe; it has been nourished on analogies drawn from a loose and popular biology; it will pass as other fashions pass. Even now, indeed, it may be passing. The movement that has labelled itself 'behaviourism'—a 'psychology' not only without a psyche and a psychical, but also without a psychological—appears to get its motivation, at any rate on the negative side, from dissatisfaction with the psychology of function.[233] But be that as it may, there is no seed of life in functionalism

---

[233] Behaviourism has not yet become clear either as to its own working concepts or as to its relations to psychology: see A. Robinson, "Behaviour as a Psychological Concept," *Proc. Arist. Soc.*, N. S. xviii, 1918, 271 ff. A reaction against functionalism is suggested by the biological flavour of behaviouristic writings, and is expressly admitted by J. B. Watson (*Behavior, an Introduction to Comparative Psychology*, 1914, 8 f.). Logically, indeed, a strict behaviourism can have no quarrel with an existential psychology, since there is no point of contact between the two disciplines. The only possible relation is that of correlation, and the extreme behaviourist declines to correlate. Cf. my critique of Watson, "On 'Psychology as the Behaviorist Views It,'" *Proc. Amer. Philos. Soc.*, liii, 1914, no. 213.

compared with the power of perennial self-renewal that inheres in intentionalism. Functional psychology (if we may again change the figure) is a parasite, and the parasite of an organism doomed to extinction, whereas intentionalism is as durable as common-sense. We noted long ago that the empirical psychologist (we may now say, the psychologist of intention) means to take mind as he finds it, and that like all the rest of the world, who are not psychologists, he finds it in use; he finds it actively at work in man's intercourse with nature and with his fellow-man, and in his discourse with himself.[234] That is how 'mind' naturally presents itself to common-sense, to the man of affairs, to the intelligent man of science who lacks psychological training. A great mathematician and physicist, speaking in 1869 of the "phenomena of mind," declared that "science can be expected to do but little to help us here, since the instrument of research is itself the object of investigation," since (that is to say) the mind which we study is the mind by which we study, or the intentional experiences which we seek to know are the intentional experiences whereby we know. And if it is objected that fifty years have allowed a good deal of water to flow under our scientific bridges, we may point out that Stokes' words are repeated by the physicist Tait in 1885 and by the biologist Thomson in 1911.[235] They would be accepted today, without objection or

---

[234] P. 20 above.

[235] G. G. Stokes, Presidential Address, in *Report of the 39th Meeting of the Brit. Assn. for the Advancement of Science,* 1870, cv ; P. G. Tait, *Lectures on some Recent Advances in Physical Science,* 1885, 26; J. A. Thomson, *Introduction to Science,* 1911, 105.

reflection, by the vast majority of scientific men out-side of psychology itself. Small wonder, then, that within psychology too this same common-sense attitude, an attitude natural to us as our mother-tongue, should never fail of representatives! We shall always have psychologists of Brentano's stripe: what we have tried to make clear is that these men will give us psychologies, but not (as Brentano hoped) psychology.

These conclusions may content us. In showing that intentionalism takes the obvious, natural, proximate, common-sense view of psychology, and psychological problems, and that the adoption of this pre-scientific view as scientific puts a premium upon individual dif-ferences, upon personal ingenuity of explication and arrangement, we have probably done as much as by mere counter-argument we are able to do. It would be useless to write out, over against the psychologists of act, the list of those who deny that they find inten-tional experiences in the contents of consciousness, for the affirmative is always in better logical case than the negative. Moreover, the denial itself shifts the uni-verse of discourse, or changes the point of view from which 'consciousness' is regarded. When Ach tells us that an observer reports, from the fore-period of a simple sensory reaction, one knowing (*Wissen*) and three to five awarenesses (*Bewusstheiten*), we may perhaps be surprised by the fullness of the report, and may even go so far as to suspect the influence of sug-gestive questioning; but we do not meet the situation by declaring that "a knowing (*Wissen*) is never given in consciousness"; we have then simply substituted our own definition of psychology for that of Ach.[236] The one complete and positive reply to intentionalism is the existential system, the system that is partially and confusedly set forth (anything like completeness and purity of exposition is not possible to our present knowledge) in the works of Wundt and Külpe and Ebbinghaus.[237] If we can build psychology upon a definition that is scientific as the word 'science' is to be understood in the light of the whole history of human thought; and if we can follow methods and achieve results that are not unique and apart but, on the contrary, of the same order as the methods and results of physics and biology; then, by sheer shock of difference, the act-systems will appear as exercises in applied logic, stamped with the personality of their authors. They will not, on that account, languish and die, because 'mind in use' will always have its fascination, but they will no longer venture to offer themselves as science.[238]

---

[236] N. Ach, *Ueber die Willenstätigkeit und das Denken,* 1905, 40 f.; K. Marbe, *Experimentell-psychologische Untersuchungen über das Urteil, eine Einleitung in die Logik,* 1901, 92; cf. G. E. Müller, *Zur Analyse der Gedächtnistätigkeit und des Vorstellungsverlaufes,* iii, 1913, 542; A. Messer, "Experimentell-psychologische Untersuchungen über das Denken," *Arch. f. d. ges. Psych.,* viii, 1906, 207 *n.* It is needless to say, after the criticism made of Ladd's psychology, that I agree with Marbe; I am here concerned with formal argument.

[237] I am thinking, of course, of the earlier Külpe ("Das Ich und die Aussenwelt," i, *Philos. Studien,* vii, 1892, 405; *Grundriss der Psychol.,* 1893, 27), and of Ebbinghaus before his work was edited by Dürr.

[238] In *Thought-processes,* 60 f., I sought to 'psychologise' Brentano's act as being, existentially, the temporal factor intrinsic to psychological subject-matter. Thereupon a friendly critic remarked: "On peut s'étonner que Titchener . . . ait cru devoir exposer et discuter des théories dont la valeur psychologique est douteuse. Il s'agit plutôt d'analyses verbales, d'idéologie, de subtilités, de distinctions scolastiques" (T. Ribot, *Rev. phil.,* lxix, 1910, 650). My attempt sprang,

§ 19. Negative criticism always needs more words than positive construction. The upshot of the preceding paragraphs may, however, be condensed into a brief statement. The claim has been made that 'conscious' phenomena constitute a special class of objects of experience, immediately and radically distinct from phenomena that are not-conscious, and that the science of psychology has to do with the objects of this given class. The resulting systems are either functional or intentional. We have found that in both cases they are empirical, that is, technological; they begin and end with 'mind in use.' They represent what we may call an art of mental living as distinguished from a science of mental life—a general 'applied psychology' that is logically prior to the special 'applied psychologies' of education, vocation, law, medicine, industry. Functional psychology is through and through teleological, and by biological analogy lays down general norms, either directly or through the intermediation of philosophical theory, for the right conduct of our practical life. Intentional psychology is at once more individual and less naïve than functional. We may perhaps say that its central task is logically to analyse, to explicate, the operations of perception and thought, as these

---

indeed, from a rather desperate desire somehow to bring intentionalism and existentialism together at close quarters, and to transcend the mere calling of names. If the two schools were in any real sense schools of psychology, then—I thought—they must after all be concerned at bottom with the same problems; and I knew that the epithets 'scholastic' and 'sensationalist' were often applied ignorantly and unintelligently. The same year, 1910, gave us, however, Wundt's essay on "Psychologismus und Logizismus" (*Kleine Schriften,* i, 511 ff.), which amply justifies Ribot's reproaches.

terms are understood by the average educated person or are received from philosophical tradition; that it extends this procedure of logical analysis to emotion and will, understood in the same way; and that it seeks finally, with marked individual difference, to base the whole of psychology upon the intentional principle. It is thus, like common-sense, an applied logic, though unlike common-sense its interest lies more in the logic and less in the results of application. Hence it has a natural affiliation to philosophy, and especially to theory of knowledge or pure logic. Since, however, it is not itself pure logic, but rather a logical account of 'psychical phenomena,' it stands also in close relation to the particular technologies of mind, and especially to education.[239]

We see, then, that these 'psychologies of consciousness,' in order ·to maintain a logical continuity with philosophy above and everyday practice below, sever psychology from the other sciences, and redefine 'science' to suit their case. We can understand how philosophy, while wholly unconscious of bias, should look with favour upon such systems and with disfavour or indifference upon a truly scientific psychology. We can understand, too, how it comes about that current philosophy should have much to say concerning psychology, and but little to say of physics and chemistry. We can understand that psychiatrists and educators, eager to turn psychology to practical ends, should appeal to systems that are already technological and should look

---

[239] I am here characterising technology *a potiori* by reference to the pure science upon which it preponderantly draws. In strictness such characterisation is not permissible.

impatiently away from the bare impersonal facts of an existential science.[240] All this we can understand, and understanding takes off the bitter edge of controversy. But we see, on the other hand, that physics and chemistry, and of late years biology also, are going their theoretical way without looking aside either to philosophy or to application. We see that they are achieving results of which philosophy must, in the long run, take account; and we see that these results are at once finding technical application. All this, therefore, is ground of encouragement to the votary of a strictly scientific psychology. And if our negative criticism is valid, then the feeling of encouragement becomes an imperative 'experience of claim.' Psychology fairly challenges us to attempt its systematic exposition on an existential basis.

§ 20. It need hardly be pointed out that the acceptance of this challenge does not commit us, logically, to a definition or characterisation of the subject-matter of psychology. In starting out upon a quest, we do not pledge ourselves to reach the goal. We might proceed

---

[240] The appeal is intelligible in the light of history and of the historically conditioned education that these technologists receive. Yet it is worth remembering that there is no general technology of physics or chemistry or biology to mediate between the sciences and their special technologies, the special branches of engineering and medicine. Remote and aloof from everyday life as the laboratories are, their results are taken up into practice at first hand. It is worth remembering too that, despite all the psychological systems from Aristotle down, it is only since the appearance of experimental psychology and its attainment of impersonal results that the special technologies of mind have sprung into vigorous being. Cf. G. E. Müller, *Zur Analyse der Gedächtnistätigkeit und des Vorstellungsverlaufes*, i, 1911, 147; H. Münsterberg, *Psychology and Social Sanity*, 1914, 291 ff.

with the task before us, and leave the subject-matter to take shape as we proceed: a working definition of the point of view of psychology is fully sufficient. Moreover, since we believe that the subject-matter of the various sciences does, in fact, take shape as the sciences proceed, any definition offered while a science is still in the formative stage must, by hypothesis, be merely tentative and provisional. It would, on the other hand, be contrary to the whole spirit of this enquiry, and it would betray a lack of courage to express conviction, if we were to let the question pass without an attempt at answer. Only, in addressing ourselves to it, we remind the reader that he may reject what follows, or may at any point suspend his judgment, without the least impairment of the positive and negative arguments that have gone before.

The terms whereby we characterise and differentiate the subject-matter of a science may, evidently, be of two kinds, material and formal. A material term expresses the common nature of all items of the subject-matter in question in a substantive, constitutive, we may perhaps say in a qualitative, way. A formal term tells us nothing of nature or constitution; it simply delimits the logical universe within which the subject-matter lies. Formal terms are therefore earlier available than material. Indeed, a science must have reached a fairly high level of development before a material characterisation of its subject-matter is even tentatively permissible.

We begin, now, with physics, which (in the widest sense) we have defined as the science of existential experience regarded as functionally or logically interdependent. It does not seem overbold to say that the subject-matter of physics, materially considered, is energetic and, formally considered, is universal. The first of these adjectives will probably receive general assent. By 'universal' we mean that the phenomenal modes in which the developed subject-matter presents itself are strictly interchangeable and interreducible. If, however, any scruple should arise in this regard, we may be content to put the formal character in negative fashion: it is enough for our purpose to say that all samples of physical subject-matter are inter-reducible within a phenomenal mode, or that the subject-matter of physics is non-individuate. Hence we assume that the adjectives 'energetic' and 'non-individuate' characterise, materially and formally, the subject-matter of the physical sciences.

We defined biology, again, as the science of existential experience regarded as functionally or logically dependent upon a physical (that is, as we may now say, an energetic and non-individuate) environment. There can be no doubt that the corresponding subject-matter is, on the formal side, individuate. Biologists profess, with one accord, to be dealing with organisms and with the phenomena peculiarly characteristic of organisms. When, however, we enquire concerning the material nature of biological phenomena, we find the concept of energy lying directly in our path. To suggest that these phenomena are non-energetic is to breast the tide of current opinion and to arouse all manner of protest and objection. We suggest, then, more modestly, that the view be at any rate seriously considered. Its acceptance would mean, of course, that our first statement regarding the subject-matter of physics is convertible; not only is that subject-matter energetic, but whatever is energetic also falls within the compass of physics. The physicochemistry of the organism would, accordingly, not be individuate; it would be plain physics and plain chemistry. But is it really anything more or less? Is there any sense in which, within the realm of physical fact and law, we can apply the notion of individuation? [241] Again: the acceptance of our view would mean that the environment of which the definition speaks includes the organism itself, in so far as organic phenomena are not individuate but energetic, visible from the physical standpoint. But is there any valid reason why it should not? And finally, the acceptance would bring certain advantages. We should be free of the controversy between mechanism and vital entelechies. We should have no ground of quarrel with those biologists who devote themselves to an exclusively physicochemical rendering of the animal body. We should say to them: You are in logical strictness chemists and physicists, concerned with special modes of the subject-matter of physical science; you are wholly within your right in describing everything, without exception, that enters your field of view; we, on our side, maintain only that there are other phenomena to be described, namely, the individ-

---

[241] We can, of course, devise physicochemical 'systems' which show, within certain limits, processes of equilibrium. Surely, however, it is only by an unwarranted stretch of definition that we can call such systems individuate.—For a discussion of individuation, from the zoological standpoint, see J. S. Huxley, *The Individual in the Animal Kingdom*, 1912.

uate and non-energetic phenomena that become manifest when we regard experience as logically dependent upon environment. It is true, of course, that a flat denial of the existence of peculiarly biological phenomena puts an end to argument, just as the flat denial of psychological phenomena, on the part of an extreme behaviourist, puts an end to argument in the parallel case of psychology. But there is a whole world of difference between denial and proof of the negative— if a negative can at all be proved; and so long as biologists are able to convince one another, so long will the affirmative position be held. On the whole, then, our view is perhaps less fanciful and more illuminating than at first glance it appeared.[242] And it does us here the final service of putting a new and pregnant meaning upon the term whereby we must be content to characterise biological phenomena from the material side —upon the term 'behaviour.' All biological facts, we propose to say, are 'behavioural,' just as all physical facts are energetic. The term has upon it associations that render it far from ideal. It has, nevertheless, a certain appositeness for a biology that has shaken free of physical and technological analogies and has purged itself of teleology.[243]

---

[242] It seems to me (though the author might vigorously repel the suggestion) that the views of C. M. Child may, without great difficulty, be translated into non-energetic terms in accordance with the proposals of the text. See, e.g., "The Regulatory Processes in Organisms," Journ. of Morphol., xxii , 1911, 178, etc.

[243] There need, I hope, be no confusion between 'behavioural' and 'behaviouristic,' though I should have been glad to avoid that possibility. All 'behaviouristic' phenomena are, of course, energetic.—A parallel for the use of the two adjectives is afforded by the terms 'psychological' and 'psychologistic.'

We defined psychology, lastly, as the science of existential experience regarded as logically or functionally dependent upon a nervous system or its biological equivalent. Biology here becomes the term of reference: and the fact is important, because it means that we can no longer characterise subject-matter by formal opposites. The definition of biology already replaces the interdependence of physical phenomena by a special dependence, and the definition of psychology simply carries specificity of dependence one step further. If, therefore, biological phenomena are individuate and non-energetic, so also are the phenomena of psychology; the difference is that the former lie at one remove, the latter at two, from the energetic and universal phenomena of physics. To express this difference, we must change our orientation, and look back upon biology from the standpoint of psychology. We then see that, while the subject-matter of biology is, without qualification, individuate, the subject-matter of psychology, within this formal limit of individuation, is systemic; the one correlates with a total environmental complex, the other with a single organic system. It is symptomatic of the difference that biological phenomena are continuous in time, while psychological phenomena are temporally intermittent. The psychological intermittence carries with it, of course, a temporal lapse of the correlated biological phenomena, but this systemic lapse does not interrupt the continuity of 'life.'

If we ask, further, for a material characterisation of psychological phenomena, we are again baffled by the intervention of the concept of energy. The controversy of parallelism and interactionism does not repeat the controversy of mechanism and vitalism, but in the present connection it has a like inhibiting effect. We come out, at best, with the adjective 'epiphenomenal': and the adjective does not help us, partly because it is formal and not material, and partly because it suggests that the epiphenomenon is something less than a phenomenon. If we turn to current usage, we find the German *Erlebnis* and the English equivalent 'experience' (used in a specific and narrow sense). But these terms too cannot help us: they are vague enough to suit either parallelism or interactionism, to figure either in functional and intentional or in existential contexts. All things considered, it would perhaps be the part of wisdom to put off the material characterisation of psychological subject-matter until such time as the accumulated facts point to their natural adjective.[244] Since, however, the very nature of these facts is in dispute, and the postponement must therefore be altogether indefinite, we venture a leap into the half-dark, and choose the term 'sensory' as the counterpart of 'behavioural.' The word has its traditional rights, and many modern psychologists will be ready to accept it—with the proviso that they be permitted to define it for

---

[244] The difficulty of finding non-committal terms is illustrated by Alexander's recourse to 'enjoyment' and 'contemplation' (*Brit. Journ. Psych.*, iv, 1911, 241). These particular words are of no assistance to us, partly because 'enjoyment' is interpreted as mental act, and partly because the distinction implies a divergence, which we cannot admit, in primary scientific method.

themselves.[245] Our own definition may still wait. We note only that the suggestion of a qualitative homogeneity of subject-matter squares with the like suggestion of the formal character 'systemic.'

In sum, then, we have reached the following characterisations:

SUBJECT-MATTER OF	FORMAL	MATERIAL
Physics	Universal	Energetic
Biology	Individuate	Behavioural
Psychology	Systemic	Sensory

and we repeat that the reader may accept, reject or ignore them, without prejudice to the arguments of preceding paragraphs. If, however, he will accept them, at least as a basis for further discussion, we may proceed to show that they throw a very definite light upon the biological and psychological technologies.

A technology is always concerned to do something, to accomplish some practical end. But the 'doing' of anything implies a recourse to energy. Hence the biological technologist (*e.g.*, the physician) must always work with those environmental energies with which biological phenomena are directly correlated, and the psychological technologist (*e.g.*, the educator, the psychiatrist) must work with the energies most readily available, that is, with the same environmental energies, with which psychological phenomena are corre-

---

[245] See, *e.g.*, H. J. Watt's art. "Psychology," *Encycl. Rel. Eth.*, 426 f. A 'moderate behaviourist' would regard sensory phenomena as a department of behaviour, or perhaps rather as factors in certain modes of behaviour; our table makes them logically posterior to behaviour, and assigns them to a separate genus.

lated indirectly, by way of biology. In practice, this requirement of an energetic foothold or leverage has two natural consequences. On the one hand, it disposes the technologist to read the character of energy into his immediate subject-matter. On the other hand, it disposes him to accept that theoretical view which attributes an energetic subject-matter to the pure science to which he stands in nearest relation. So we have, on the one hand, a tendency to behave, if not to write, as if vital and mental 'causes' produced vital and mental 'effects,' and on the other hand a tendency for the theoretical physician to embrace mechanism or an energetic vitalism, and for the theoretical educator or psychiatrist to embrace interactionism or behaviourism. The practical attitude toward 'cause' and 'effect' is practically justified. So long as we do not possess a fuller knowledge of physicochemistry, so long must we handle the organism by way of vital or mental 'symptom'; and, though mistakes will be made, the actual correlation with the physical of the biological and (through that) of the psychological will also ensure a growing measure of empirical success. The theoretical attitude, on the contrary, is likely to have less justification. The anathemas which current psychiatry hurls against the doctrine of parallelism, for example, are only rarely—what they might be on the lips of a psychologist—the emotional summing-up of a serious and considered examination; more often they express an unreflecting professional reaction, the impatience (of those who want mind to 'do' something) with a view which removes all trace or possibility of 'doing' from the mental sphere. Yet in truth there is no incompatibility between a parallelistic psychology and an energetic psychiatry, and in truth there can be no psychiatry that is anything other than energetic.

The technologist, nevertheless, generalising in all good faith from the necessities of his position, believes himself to be drawing psychology down from the clouds of theory and relating it to the actualities of human life. And it is, we may repeat, a real gain that we understand this belief, see it in perspective, grasp its motives. In point of fact, however, we are taught by our formal differentiation of subject-matters—and the same result issues from our earlier discussions—that technology is advantaged by that very aloofness of science which it is aiming to destroy. For only as we acquire a detailed knowledge of biological and psychological phenomena can we seek intelligently for correlations, the correlations of these phenomena with one another and the correlations of biology with physics; and only when we have acquired a detailed knowledge of the correlations, and so have at our command the phenomena of last resort, the relevant energies of physicochemistry, only then can we bring our technologies, in the domain of biology and psychology, to their utmost pitch of efficiency. Here is plain logic: and the reasoning is, surely, borne out by the cumulative testimony of history.

§ 21. We may now bring this long chapter to its close. And, as a final word, we must warn the reader not to expect too much, by way of practical consequence for systematic psychology, from the foregoing discussions. We have argued that all the sciences have the same primordial subject-matter, which they approach from definitely different points of view, and that their developed subject-matters diverge because and only because these different standpoints afford different readings of existential experience. We have sought to make clear that psychology may be given a place, as science, alongside of the acknowledged sciences, and we have sought to justify this adventure by the proof that psychologies built upon what, in our view, is a non-scientific foundation are contradictory and instable. But we have, of course, no access to any private store of psychological facts, and no short and easy method of adding to the results of observation; all that we can do is to take the available facts, and exhibit them in our scientific setting. We cannot avoid the problems that are historically recognised as psychological, not though we believe that a scientific psychology would of itself never have raised them or must have formulated them in other terms; all that we can do is to analyse these problems, and show what part or phase of them, if any there be, is open to our scientific method. We cannot, any more than can physics or biology, set forth our scientific facts and uniformities otherwise than in a matrix of logic; all that we can do is to keep the logic separate from the facts and uniformities, so that on the one hand the facts are uncoloured by logic and on the other hand the full colour of the facts appears in our logical conclusions.

Here, then, is nothing revolutionary. That adjective, if it can be applied at all in a scientific context, characterises work of a radically different order. We do not even aim at imprinting a new pattern upon the data of psychology, or at setting them into a novel perspective; we hope only to weave them all consistently into a pattern already in part designed, to bring them all consistently into a perspective already in part blocked out. Our whole undertaking is implied in the historical development of psychology and of science; at every step we shall rely upon the work of those who have gone before. If we may claim a vision clearer than these others attained, of the path which a scientific psychology must follow, we claim therefore no more than the right and duty to take advantage of our own later arrival upon the scientific scene. And even so, we are at the very heels of the pioneers. Generations will come and pass before the straight road of psychological endeavour lies, plain and unobstructed, before the eyes of the student.

APPENDIX:

EXPLANATORY NOTES

Introduction, p. 3: "Empirical and Experimental Psychology"

Titchener uses 'empirical' here in the narrow sense. Broadly speaking, both Brentano and Wundt are empirical—they both depend on experience to a greater or lesser degree for their data. *A posteriori* does not necessitate experiment, however. Brentano is empirical in the way that philosophers are. His is an 'arm-chair' psychology, having its sources in the observations and experiences of the philosophers of the past but not in experiment. Wundt, on the other hand, relies heavily (though not entirely) on experimental evidence. There are empirical (in the narrow sense) aspects to Wundt's book, but his psychology is primarily experimental. One objection to this narrow usage of empirical is given by Leonard Carmichael in "What is empirical psychology?" *Amer. Journ. Psych., xxxvii*, 1926, 531 ff. For Titchener's reply, see his "Empirical and experimental psychology," *Journ. Gen. Psych., i*, 1928, 176 f.

Chapter I, p. 32: "bare existences" and "sheer existence"

See the Foreword for a discussion of the existential universe.

Chapter I, p. 37: "common-sense"

Common-sense in the broad usage is the value-system of every-day man. In Titchener's schema there are three representative views of the world of experience—common-sense, technology, and science. They are differentiated by their object, attitude, and aim, as follows:

	SCIENCE	TECHNOLOGY	COMMON-SENSE
Object	Facts	Fact-values	Values
Attitude	Disinterested	Interested	Interested
	(Impersonal)	(Personal)	(Personal)
Aim	Understanding	Utilization	Utilization

In many ways, common-sense is at the opposite pole from science and is the 'normal' view of mankind as a whole. Technology is, then, an extension of common-sense, since it seeks the values in the facts of observation of the existential universe. Technology is narrower than common-sense, since the common-sense man need not have as his basis for judgment facts of experience. He may depend on faith, speculation, or any other such basis. In a more narrow usage, when dealing with the subject of mind, Titchener considered the common-sense view to be a 'watered-down Cartesianism'—a crude dualism or interactionism.

Chapter I, p. 56: "sufficient reason"

Prolegomena, p. 101. Also see William Hamilton, *Lectures on Metaphysics and Logic,* H. L. Mansel and John Veitch, eds. (Blackwood and Sons: London, 1860), i, Lecture V, par. 17, 84 *ff.*

Chapter II, pp. 117 f.: "psychology is the science of experience at large, as dependent variable of the psychophysical brain-centres"

This should not be taken to mean that psychology, in Titchener's view, must be reductionistic. This is a common misreading of Titchener. Met with this interpretation, he once replied, "You attribute to me a definition of the subject-matter of psychology as 'that which . . . (is) dependent on the nervous system.' Not at all! That would be to slip back into the belief in separate objects or genera. I define the subject-matter of psychology as 'all existential experience *regarded as* dependent on the nervous system,' that is, as existential experience ueberhaupt (wholly) taken from the point-of-view of its dependence" (letter to Adolf Meyer, May 4, 1918).

This is description in the context of the dependency of experience on the nervous system. One may seek to 'explain' experience in terms of the nervous system, but it is not clear that Titchener felt this was part of his problem. "I don't *explain* or *causally relate* at all, at all! In science all the 'explanation' that there is for me is the correlation of a dependent with a (logically prior) independent variable. In psychology the logically prior is biology, in biology the logically prior is physics. In physics we set up independent variables for intra-physical methodological purposes, and what figures as dependent in one context figures as independent in another: we have in fact only interdependences. So if I 'explain' psychology by biology, that means very simply that I take the biological as independent variable in any case where correlation is involved. I use the word 'explanation' to students just to show them that there is nothing in science like the 'accounting for,' 'giving a reason for,' which is the meaning of the word in logic. Causality I regard as mythological,—if you mean by it anything more than correlation."

"Parallelism is the historical antecedent of this doctrine of correlation, and as such is preferable to interaction, which skips from one logical universe to another. But the parallelism of objects (neural things and psychical things) I take to be transcended" (letter to Meyer, May 13, 1918).

INDEX

Library of Congress Cataloging in Publication Data
(For library cataloging purposes only)

Titchener, Edward Bradford, 1867–1927.
    Systematic psychology.

    First published in 1929.
    Includes bibliographical references.
    1. Psychology. 2. Science. 3. Psychology
—History. I. Title.
BF64.T5 1972   150'.9   72-38117
ISBN 0-8014-0707-9